A Memory of Vermont

THE JOHNNY APPLESEED BOOKSHOP

MARGARET HARD

A Memory of Vermont

OUR LIFE IN THE

JOHNNY APPLESEED BOOKSHOP

1930–1965

HARCOURT, BRACE & WORLD, INC., NEW YORK

974.3

For those of the original personnel

who have filled my life,

Walter Hard, Ruth Hard Bonner, Walter Hard, Jr.

and for

Alison Rees Mabry

Foreword

*A*NYONE READING this book in the hope of finding a blueprint for acquiring, equipping, and operating a bookshop is doomed to disappointment. Anyone hoping to find a success story is also destined to disillusionment. That is, if he defines success as accomplishment along the usual lines of a success story. But if he conceives of success as something that creates a distinctive, puzzling, delicious output he may decide that, after all, there is something for him between the covers of this book.

Anyone who has known a country kitchen where pastry is rolled out on a floured board or a thin marble slab set on the kitchen-pantry shelf, as is often the case in old Vermont farmhouses, knows that the resulting perfection in flavor and design is frequently accomplished by an unexplainable gift for measuring ingredients casually, and possessing a seemingly careless knack of fluting the edge of the pie crust. Yet here is a pie of which one eagerly accepts a second piece. If that indefinable something typifies a certain kind of satisfying, successful flavor it may, perhaps, be found in this particular book. For it is about a bookshop that has been a *life* rather than an *occupation*. It provided certain assets that never were rung up in the cash register or entered in the weekly ledger.

In the spring of 1965 we made up our minds at long last, after thirty-five years, that we must definitely consider selling our Vermont Johnny Appleseed Bookshop. It was a little like relin-

quishing our daughter in marriage. Bestowal is made in trust and
hope; yet it is a heart-wrenching experience. "Who gives this
bookshop to be married to this man? Will he love her, comfort
her, and hold to her for better, for worse, for richer or poorer, and
cherish her to the end?" This is not irreverent parody. It is exactly
how we felt about our bookshop.

What made the bookshop an absorbing life for us was primarily the people who came into it. All sorts and conditions of men,
women, and children. In the aggregate they told a continuous
story of human attitudes toward life: wise and inconsequential,
humorous and pathetic, joyous and tragic.

Along with all the talk of books, all the business of ordering
and selling them, something else went on. There were sudden
enriching insights into people's thoughts, into their courage and
high-mindedness. Just as there were startling revelations of frustration and futility, pettiness and meanness. There were all the
experiences with children—delightful, heart-warming, and comforting. And sometimes exasperating.

But forever this hidden stream of life flowed in and out of the
bookshop. What we garnered from it is the real story of the
bookshop. It was that constant revealing contact with people and
books that made it a life that became inseparably entwined with
our own and with incidents that accompanied both.

The constant interchange and interrelation between people and
books must be the substance and stamina of any bookshop business that hopes for success. What is the book especially suited to
the need and interest of this man, woman, or child? Or what
man, woman, or child will be especially interested in this book
in my hand, or on our shelves and tables? It is like putting together the pieces of an intricate puzzle. When the piece fits into
the open space and magically completes a portion of the picture,
then the bookshop day goes forward with a leap of pleasure.

People and Books: Yet there is another unique factor that sur-
rounds the Johnny Appleseed Bookshop in Manchester, Vermont. It is the beauty of the village in which it is located and
the extending beauty of the state to which it belongs. Royal
Cortissoz, the distinguished art critic, used to sit on the Equinox

Hotel porch, looking off to the Green Mountains so close across the valley. If we paused in passing he would lure us up to sit beside him. Presently he would talk.

"All this country has a peculiar friendliness of sentiment," he would say. "In some indefinable manner it is always present in the Vermont scene. Those webs of trees veiling the ruggedness of hills, and over hills and valley an incessant enchantment of light and shade."

Through the great glass pane of the old door of the Johnny Appleseed Bookshop one looks out upon exactly that scene. To stand there at any time of day, at any season of the year, is to receive a sense of security and stability. The distant mountains do not change. How many thousands of years have they stood there? Against a troubled background of world turmoil they give reassurance. In the words of our daughter, who started the bookshop in an apple orchard when she was eighteen, "Here is agelessness that restores the heart as fully as the hushed interval of peace which we call twilight."

Contents

A Memory of Vermont

CHAPTER ONE

An Introductory Chapter about a Mountain Township

*T*HE JOHNNY APPLESEED BOOKSHOP began its life in 1930 in the village of Manchester, in the township of Manchester, in Vermont. In 1930 the township had a voting population of about two thousand people; and the township itself was six miles square. This was a matter of history. Ever since 1761 most Vermont townships had been six miles square. But Vermont was not then called Vermont. It was known as "the Hampshire Grants" because Benning Wentworth, the royal governor of New Hampshire, was selling grants there to various named grantees under the authorization of King George the Third of Great Britain.

New Hampshire claimed the rich wilderness territory lying between itself and the royal province of New York, the Connecticut River serving as a boundary line on the east. The fact that the province of New York was also claiming the territory and selling grants did not disturb Benning Wentworth. He knew a good thing when he saw it and he felt he was in a position of peculiar favor with the king. From his beautiful mansion in Portsmouth he continued to make grants of townships.

He always reserved certain desirable sites in the townships he granted. One for himself—in the case of Manchester Township it comprised five hundred acres—and other sites which he designated as follows: one for the Incorporated Society for the Propagation of the Gospel in Foreign Parts, one for a glebe for the

3

Church of England as by law established, one for the first
settled minister of the Gospel, and one for the benefit of a
school in said town. If we consider that the area of each individual township amounted to twenty-three thousand and forty
acres, his retention of five hundred acres for himself seems not
unreasonable.

The original Charter of Manchester Township says, ". . .
as granted by the King's trusty and well beloved Benning Wentworth, Esq., Governor and Commander in Chief of a new
plantation within our said Province." It is, in fact, headed,
"Manchester in the Province of New Hampshire."

By 1791 the township of Manchester had passed through
thirty years of strife and struggle. It had existed in what were
then the Hampshire Grants, which, during the final fourteen
years of that period (between 1777 and 1791), became the Independent Republic of Vermont, thereby presenting an era and
a situation without parallel in American history. Since it had
no fixed capital, Thomas Chittenden, its governor, lived in
Arlington. Ira Allen, its state treasurer, lived in Sunderland,
and Ethan Allen, who had just been released from captivity in
British prisons, was the general of militia. As Carl Chapin says
in his little pamphlet, *Manchester in Vermont History,* "Ethan
was also a sort of Cabinet Minister without portfolio." The
Legislature met in various towns; a number of times in Manchester. First at the Weller tavern and later at the old meeting-
house which stood on the site of the present Congregational
Church. At last, in 1791, Vermont formally entered the Union
as the fourteenth state. The population of the township of Manchester was given as 1,276.

When we move forward to 1930, about one hundred and
forty years later, the increase in permanent population seems
unbelievably slight. A rise of 728 inhabitants in almost a century
and a half makes one wonder. Not until 1910 had it reached
the 2,000 mark. But there was a continuous and surprising
summertime increase in population that could not be listed as
regular residents.

This was explained by the fact that as early as 1801, when

Thomas Jefferson was inaugurated, Manchester celebrated the event by raising a new tavern. By 1850, only fifty years later, the village's outstanding business was that of a summer resort. It had always been a village of taverns and inns. Its scenic beauty, its accessibility for travelers from distant points, and its healthful location brought guests from other states and swelled its population regularly for a third of the year.

All of these factors made it seem reasonable to think of a bookshop in the village in the year before 1930 with the hope that it might thrive. It, too, would, of course, be a summer season operation. When it eventually took shape the next year it began with a personnel of four—the family. Our daughter, Ruth, and myself would be the active daily force in charge. Ruth's father would be the financial and advisory backing. Finally, there would be Walter, Jr., who was thirteen and a student at Burr and Burton, already helping each summer in the drugstore. He now became part of the bookshop's future staff, in the special way he had of becoming part of any family project. He was our "whenever-in-trouble-or-desperation-call-on-me" assistant in a thousand varied emergencies. But it was Ruth who was the actual originator of the bookshop idea, although we had sometimes thought of it.

When she came home from her freshman year at Smith in 1929, aged seventeen, she had already planned her future.

"When I graduate I want to learn the publishing business from A to Z. Any publisher I go to for a job will ask what I know about the business end of books. I won't know a thing about it, no matter how many English Lit courses I may have had, and no matter how many hours of Creative Writing I've had under Mary Ellen Chase. But I've an *idea*. I hope it won't sound crazy to you. I think it might work. It's to have a small bookshop here in Manchester. I'd have three summers of business experience to offer when I went for a job in the fall of 1932, if I could do that."

The idea appealed to all of us. In fact, Walter had seriously speculated as to whether a book business could sustain itself as an individual operation in Manchester. As it was, he had

long had a big table of books in the drugstore. He had unex-
pectedly and reluctantly fallen heir to the drugstore because
of the death of his father when he had been a senior at Williams.
He was bent upon a journalistic career. To find himself confronted with such a change of plans was baffling and painful.
As he later said, ruefully yet with a smile, "I took over the
drugstore *temporarily* and stayed for thirty years." Perhaps the
long table of books and the big bench he built in the corner
near it, where men of political, financial, and literary importance,
summering in the village, sat down to read their morning mail
and eventually to be drawn to him in conversation, were initial
things that tided him over the first years of the difficult adjust-
ment. That, and the writing that he began to do, at first just
for his own relief and pleasure. "Somehow, I could never see
a blank sheet of paper without wanting to fill it with writing."
So the suggestion of his daughter found a receptive ear.

To decide upon the proposition we began realistically to weigh
the actual possibilities of the plan. In the first place, Manchester truly was uniquely located in Vermont and New England. Its long-established resort and tourist business was the
immediate answer to the question of patrons for a bookshop.
The town of Manchester was an artery of travel for Route 7 and
its many adjacent towns. It was the northern terminus of the
highway from Bennington, and into it came roads from east
and west, and the touring public followed from north and south.

To the east the roads connected with the Connecticut River
Valley, to the west with New York State and the Adirondacks.
From the south there was continuous connection with Williamstown and Massachusetts. Northward, the highway was the direct
route to Burlington, and Montreal, Canada. Manchester's railroad connection was with the direct line of the New York Central, and the connecting Rutland, Vermont, lines, eastward to
the Connecticut Valley and Boston.

With Williams and Bennington Colleges to the south of
Manchester, and with Green Mountain Junior College, Castleton
Teachers College, Middlebury College and its Bread Loaf Sum-
mer School at Ripton, plus the University of Vermont in Burling-

ton, Manchester had an advantageous position on a "college high-way." Numerous small lake resorts, as well as those following the shore line of Lake Champlain bordering the western edge of Route 7, provided an extended but continually traveling public that passed through Manchester. The fact that Manchester was a famous center for golfing provided an assured number of summer visitors. But would they like books? That was the question. As well as the further one of the actual location of the shop.

The bookshop was eventually to have three different locations in the village; but the immediate one was the paramount problem to decide. It happened that we owned a still-existing remnant of apple orchard adjacent to the village library. Its location was not ideal but it was adequate. If one stood at the apex formed by the main street, through the heart of the village, and the side street that joined it at an angle so slight that it almost ran parallel with it, one could easily see the bit of orchard. The library was a landmark for directing people about the village. It stood exactly in the point of the apex just mentioned. One could also see a group of houses and a recently established inn surrounding the vicinity of the small persistent piece of orchard. Clearly visible also was the village schoolhouse on this street commonly known as "the West Road." In an earlier day, of my husband's boyhood, it had been dubbed "Pill Alley" because the village druggist and two doctors had their homes there. So it was on Pill Alley in the remnant of apple orchard that we decided to locate the bookshop.

Ruth went down to look the situation over with her father and came home bursting with enthusiasm.

"It's perfect! Really almost in the heart of the village. If I go out and stand in the middle of the road I can see the hotel and the old bank building, the church, and the court-house. And the drugstore almost within reach. We'll put the bookshop right under the big apple tree close to the street." She paused a moment for reflection. "And I have a name for it already. 'The Johnny Appleseed Bookshop.' I could almost write the folder we'll have to give people, right now."

"I'm sure you could," said her father, smiling at her, "but you'll have a little difficulty, maybe, in appropriating Johnny Appleseed in Vermont."

"Oh, no. I have a perfect analogy for it. Scattering good books as he scattered apple seeds."

"Yes, but you'll have to be prepared for customers who are indignant representatives of Ohio and Indiana, demanding by what right you are using Johnny Appleseed's name in Vermont."

"I'll just give them a folder, make them welcome, and tell them Vachel Lindsay was here four years ago and read his 'Johnny Appleseed Saga' to the Poetry Society; and that this is just a way of honoring Johnny Appleseed. Not of laying claim to him."

So the bookshop's location was settled, and one might say that its birth should have been recorded in the town clerk's office; instead of which its name was duly recorded with the Secretary of State in Montpelier. Birth, growth, and maturity— these were the three stages of development of the Johnny Appleseed Bookshop covering its first thirty-five years. They went hand in hand with its three locations. Both of the other locations were visible from the orchard. That is, if one stood as Ruth said she did, in the middle of the road. One: the orchard. Two: the small additional section of building that nudged elbows with the drugstore. Three: the old brick bank building next to the hotel, at that moment being occupied by the Foster Travel Bureau and the Foster Remembrance Shop.

Among the distinct advantages of Manchester as either a summer resort or a town for all-year living were its educational and cultural institutions and organizations. The old Seminary (now Burr and Burton), a preparatory school, was Vermont's first privately endowed academy. It was incorporated in 1829, built of native limestone, and opened in 1833. Ever since, during many periods of financial anxiety, it held fast to its high scholastic standing and its classical attainments. In 1930 it was about to graduate its hundredth class. Such organizations as the Poetry Society of Southern Vermont and the Southern Vermont Ar-

tists were exerting an influence through the community and
entire valley.

Finally, the beauty of the village was in itself a factor that
drew people from all over New England and the United States
to its elm- and maple-shaded streets, its sidewalks of white
marble. To the old hotel, dating from 1853, to the inns and
homes where tourists were accommodated, they came and returned again and again.

Beyond the heart of the village extends one of the most beautiful village streets in Vermont. Close beside it, to the west,
is the protecting grandeur of Mount Equinox, rising to 3,800
feet; and across the valley, where the Batten Kill winds in and
out through its tree-lined banks, are the Green Mountains, range
upon range. Down this street in early days walked Ethan and
Ira Allen; into one of the old taverns they stepped with Remember Baker of Arlington and Peleg Sunderland of Sunderland—
all of them famed Green Mountain Boys. Down this street in the
mid-1800's the Reverend Dr. Joseph Dressler Wickham, beloved
headmaster at Burr and Burton Seminary, and the oldest living
graduate of Yale at the time of his death, drove his buggy, drawn
by Dolly, his horse, as recognized a member of the community as
the greatly respected Doctor himself. Or, at night, after he had
sat late writing important letters, he would step out into the
darkness, wrapped in his wadded dressing gown, carrying a hand
lamp for light, and slip his letters into the mail slot beside the
door of the post office, housed in what had been the old bank
building next to the hotel. Down this street Mary Todd Lincoln
walked with her sons, Robert and Tad, following her husband's
assassination. Quietly she told the hotel owner that she derived
comfort from the mountains. Here students and teachers, writers
and artists, patriots and poets walked through the years.

In the spring of 1930, as soon as snow was off the ground, we
started the building of the bookshop. As Ruth had suggested,
it stood beneath the largest surviving apple tree. It consisted of
one long room with windows above bookshelves on two sides.

It had a rough stone fireplace at its northern end, flanked by two high windows. Across the room from the entrance door a swinging half-door divided the front room from a small office with a rear door opening on what remained of the orchard.

Ruth, at college, wrote copy for the Johnny Appleseed folder she had talked of, and asked us to order bookshop stationery for her. Between classes and studying, she sent off a letter to Alfred Harcourt, whom she had met the summer before at the home of one of the Southern Vermont Artists to whom she was teaching beginning Spanish. She told Alfred Harcourt about the bookshop-to-be. She pled its cause and asked whether he would allow her to have Harcourt, Brace publications on a consignment basis. He answered promptly, with characteristic cordiality and interest, and the reply was affirmative. At the same time, she communicated with Baker and Taylor Company. She told them that she would like to enlarge the ordering which her father had been doing through the drugstore for a small Manchester bookshop of her own. Using Alfred Harcourt's generosity as a springboard, she wrote to other publishers and solicited their co-operation. At least four others were very kind in their agreement to do so.

At last she was really launched, and when she came home from college, early in June, she was ready for the hard work of getting settled so that the shop could be opened on the first of July. Her brother looked the situation over and presently appeared with hammer, saw, and screwdriver, and strength to lift and open heavy boxes of books. When the unpacking came, at the actual sight of so many wonderful books they both sat down on the floor beside the boxes and exulted in their contents.

"Look, Ruth, here's that book about the Bengal Lancers!" Then, after a moment, "Oh, these must be children's books. Here's the Van Loon *Romance of Discovery*. Remember how we read it aloud that hot summer day when we took a picnic over to Downer's Glen? We both sat with our feet in the brook, taking turns at reading. You had to help me with some of the words."

But presently they were hard at it, checking invoices, sorting books, and getting them onto shelves and tables. It was a time of glorious, exciting labor, a time of suddenly remembering dozens of small details to be attended to. Ruth kept writing memorandums and pinning them up on the office wall, and Walter, Jr., kept dashing off for some needed implement. The telephone was put in and gave the office a truly official look. The first call was to tell the drugstore that the Johnny Appleseed's *own number* was 355-J.

It was the afternoon before the bookshop's actual date of opening. Probably very few people in Manchester were aware that an epoch-making event was about to take place. Indeed, the number may well have been confined to not more than a dozen, although there must have been an announcement in the Manchester *Journal*.

When Ruth closed the bookshop door, every detail checked in anticipation of the next day, she walked upstreet to the drugstore to meet her father. Glancing at the church clock as she passed, she found it was five minutes of six. He took off his white linen coat and joined her. On the sidewalk outside lay long shafts of shadow. The trunks of the elms and maples that followed the length of the street were outlined against the white marble walks. There was a startling background radiance of late afternoon light. As the sun slipped down the sky above Equinox it bathed the village in a wash of gold. Ruth's hand nestled into her father's, and they walked in companionable silence past a few houses. Then she said, "I've been thinking how awfully glad I am that long ago you started having that table of books in the store. It's been there as far back as I can remember. Without it I might not have thought of having a bookshop. Certainly none of it could have been managed without the book table and you."

"It's a longer time than you can remember, longer than your eighteen years."

"Oh, I know. You had it before you were married. Even before you knew Mother."

"Longer still. It was your Grandfather Hard who started it. Around 1890 he moved a lot of bottles of drugs off a section of the shelves and put in books. One of the firm of Baker and Taylor Company was staying over at the hotel. As soon as Father found who he was, he was delighted. He loved to read and he never could get hold of books he read about in magazines like the *Atlantic* and *Harper's*, and in the New York papers— the *Tribune* and the *Times* and the *Sun*. This was really his chance. He began ordering. He felt sure he would find buyers for the books, for Manchester was a 'bookish' town, but he really wanted them for himself."

"The New York *Times?* That's funny. Here's a poem about Johnny Appleseed I found in the *Times*. It's by Olga Hampel Briggs. It's lovely. Exactly right. I think we ought to write to her in care of the *Times* and ask whether we may use it some-time in a folder. It would make such a nice introduction to the bookshop."

We did write, received permission, and used the poem in a folder about the shop later on.

CHAPTER TWO

The First Summer—1930

"There weren't so many, after all," she said. I had stopped in at the bookshop to see how things were going on the afternoon following its opening.

"Why, I thought there was quite a good number. Everyone seemed so pleased and interested. Fifteen or more. And Anna Buck brought those lovely wild orchids," I added, glancing at them standing on the top of the bookshelves in the July sunlight.

"Oh, I don't mean people. I mean books. When you look around it doesn't look *crowded* with books the way a bookshop should. Over there I had to stand them flat, facing out, so their fronts all show. It makes it look like more and fills up spaces."

"But that's really attractive. The book jackets are so decorative and interesting. People instantly want to look at them. I can remember when there were no book jackets. Just dust covers of Manila paper or another kind that was transparent and crackly. And there was no information about the book or author ever printed on them. You had to look inside to find out what the book was about; and then there wasn't anything particular about the author. Unless it might be a list of other books he'd written."

"Yes. I guess I want it to look busy and bookish too soon."

"It will, just as soon as the season really starts. There'll be lots more customers, and you'll begin sending orders every week."

She still looked doubtful, so I said, "Did I ever tell you that Mrs. Doubleday—Neltje Blanchan—was the one who first thought up book jackets? I mean the first colored ones. It was an experiment. They were only mildly decorative at the beginning. Just the use of color was unconventional."

"Did Mr. Doubleday tell you about that?"

"Yes. When they first bought the old Bowen place, five or six years ago. They'd had all sorts of things done to it. Partitions taken out, bathrooms added, and more windows put in. You know how few windows those old farmhouses used to have."

"Yes. All bottled up."

"Exactly. As few windows as possible to let in wind and cold."

"But summer!"

"I fancy it was *winter* they mostly thought of. Imagine that bleak Vermont farm with wind and snow rushing down over Equinox. No wonder people talk of the mountains 'roaring' in the winter."

"Mr. Doubleday wouldn't have needed to worry about that."

"No. He was worried about something else."

"What?"

"Antiques."

"*Antiques?*"

"After they were pretty well settled, he and Mrs. Doubleday invited your father and me to come up to dinner one evening. The view was gorgeous. But the house really wasn't comfortable."

"Why not?"

"Antiques. Mrs. Doubleday—the second Mrs. Doubleday; Neltje Blanchan had died in 1918—was in the midst of furnishing the farmhouse with antiques. She'd been scouring the whole region for the kinds of things she thought would have been in farmhouses. The results were mostly stiff wooden chairs and rockers that dumped you out when you sat down unless you were warned. In the dining room she had gathered together an assortment of kitchen tables. Cherry, with drop leaves. They were all the same height, which was *low*.

"When she and Mr. Doubleday were alone one table was used. When they had guests, two or even three tables were moved together. The trouble was that they were so low. Mr. Doubleday and his son, who was there with his wife, were very tall men. Well over six feet. They had big frames. When they sat down all the silver and glass on the table jumped. Their knees had lifted the tables off the floor. Finally they sat in a twisted position with knees and legs at the sides of their chairs, but facing front. You can guess how awkward it was."

"Gracious! Do you suppose she kept on that way?"

"No. I think she did something about having some length added to the legs. But after dinner, when she and the son and his wife were talking with your father, Mr. Doubleday beckoned to me to follow him.

" 'I'm going to show you the guest room I've made out of the old horse barn that was here.'

"I followed him across the lawn to the road that lay between the house and barns. There was the horse barn that I well recalled. Your father and I always passed it when we went up to the edge of the mountain each spring hunting for hepatica. But I would never have recognized it! It was all shingled, or clapboarded, with a tight roof, a window, and steps at a door in the front.

"Mr. Doubleday grinned at me, and, opening the door, ushered me in. There was a carpeted floor, luxurious twin beds, deep upholstered chairs, bright reading lights. Mr. Doubleday went about, demonstrating how soft and comfortable the chairs were. He bounced up and down in them. Then he lifted the spread of a twin bed and punched the innerspring mattress, again demonstrating features of comfort. He stood up at his full height and sighed. Then he said, 'Not a damn antique in it!' "

"Well, about those Manila book jackets," said Ruth, going back to the subject in hand. "What an awful amount of advertising space was wasted. So often it's the jacket that really sells the book."

"Well, it certainly introduces it to the customer."

"I hope I'm not going to have more experience than customers."

"They go together, don't they?"

"They certainly do! That woman from Dorset was here."

"What woman?"

"Mrs. God."

"*Who?*"

"Mrs. God. She came in this morning and brought her daughter, Miss God, with her. That's my name for them. They KNOW EVERYTHING. They took the bookshop and me apart. How is it that some people—women, especially—can be so rude and condescending?"

"Maybe she only wanted to help you."

"No. I know helpfulness. It's painful sometimes when it's frank. But it's salutary. Like a surgeon's knife. This was no desire to help me. It was a wish to deflate the Johnny Appleseed and me." She stood thinking a moment and then she smiled. "Come to think of it, people divide themselves into two groups, more or less. The 'deflators' and the 'inflators.' I think in the end the wise 'inflators' are more constructive than the 'deflators.' "

I asked who else had been in.

Mr. Schnakenberg had come. He had brought a box of candy and told Ruth that Henry was having a one-man show in New York. Ruth told him she hoped the picture he had had in last year's show, here in Manchester, was where everyone would see it. She explained she meant the one that was so different from any of the others, the one with great heads of golden wheat. It was the eye level at which it was painted that made it so arresting. It was as though one were lying in deep grass at the edge of a meadow and all the growth and beauty of earth-level things becoming magnified to sight—important in a way we so seldom see them, or think of them. There was rich, lush grass and a sense of the sky's blueness, but it was the down-to-earth wonder of "the grass of the field" that was the real import of the picture. And in the foreground those sprays of wheat, golden and full of life. It was a sermon. Ruth said that she kept think-

ing: "Wherefore, if God so clothe the grass of the field . . .
shall He not much more clothe you . . . ?"

Nat Canfield had come in and brought some of his roses.
They were by the books on rose-growing. And Miss Hermie
had sent a box of her apple turnovers, enough for supper. Ruth
wondered how she happened to be named Hermione, that beautiful Greek name. Of course, one couldn't expect Vermonters to do
anything but shorten it. But when they do occasionally use it
all, they say HermiowN. It makes us shudder.

I laughed. I thought of Miss Hermie, that staunch woman,
so full of humor and common sense, with her deep appreciation
of the fitness of things, and said I didn't believe it bothered
her. "But I do know how she happened to be named as she
was. Dorothy had told me once. It was a lovely tale, and
Dorothy knew how to weave a tale."

I told it to Ruth then—how in the 1700's two Canfield
brothers decided to move out of Connecticut. It was getting too
crowded when they could see houses within a couple of acres
of their own. They made the trek up to the Hampshire Grants,
bringing two prized possessions along with them: the plays of
Shakespeare in two huge volumes. One volume contained the
comedies, the other, the tragedies. When they came into the
Grants, one of the brothers didn't like the look of things. He
decided he'd go on into New York. So they each took one of
the Shakespeare volumes. The brother journeying to New York
chose the tragedies, and the brother who settled in the Grants,
the comedies. Dorothy said that ever after the children in
Vermont, of the Canfield family—some of them, at least—
were named out of the Shakespeare comedies.

"That was how Miss Hermie came to be named out of *The
Winter's Tale*," I told Ruth.

"Oh, Mother! It's too good a story. Do you believe it?"

I had found some evidence once, I explained. I had been
in Arlington and went into the burial ground beside St. James'
Church. All the Canfield stones, and Hard stones, too, were
there. I found several that would fit Dorothy's story: Phebe,

Celia, Katharine. Of course, I'll never cease to wonder whether I'd find Hamlet and Juliet somewhere in New York State.

Despite all that Ruth had said about the meager appearance of the bookshop it had a fairly generous representation of volumes under the different categories she had listed. She had made small cards indicating each category and tacked them at the top of each section: Fiction, Biography, Travel, Art, Essays, Current History, Classics, Dictionaries, Atlases, Poetry, Drama, Nature Books, Garden Books, Religion, Handcrafts, Sports, Cookbooks, Children's Books, Vermont Books. It was true that some of the categories couldn't boast separate sections. There had to be three or four included in one. But all subjects were carefully marked. She had made an enchanting corner for the children's books with a low table and small chairs. It balanced the far end of the room with chairs gathered in the vicinity of the fireplace.

"I think we ought to make a specialty of Vermont books," she said. "Beginning with the Green Mountain Boys, and Rowland Robinson and all his *Uncle Lisha* books to Robert Frost and Dorothy Canfield, Sarah Cleghorn, and Zephine Humphrey. Vermonters aren't just in Vermont. They live in all the states, and will want them."

As the summer advanced, customers appeared and the days became busy. Enough so that I joined Ruth and we arranged a system of shifts. "Changing Guard at Buckingham Palace" we called it, and could never refrain from going on to the rest: "Christopher Robin went down with Alice./Alice is marrying one of the guard./'A soldier's life is terrible hard,'/Says Alice."

Ruth carried the major share of the hours, but we alternated on certain afternoons and evenings. It helped the menus at home, too, not to have the same caterer for all our hurried meals. Since all four of us had work schedules and different hours, the "well-ordered home" became slightly temperamental at times. On no day but Sunday did we all sit down together to eat. I remember going home one evening around five o'clock after Ruth, fresh and smiling, had arrived at the shop to take my place. As I prepared to put on my apron, and to see what she had planned for our dinner, I noticed a large sign over the breakfast nook. Heretofore that modern supplement to the kitchen had ordinarily been used at breakfast time only. Now it served for all meals, except on Sundays. I looked up at the sign above the nook: "Please! No More String Bean Salad."

It was in Walter, Jr.'s writing. The next day being Sunday, he raised one eyebrow in a characteristic, disarming smile. "Salads are wonderful. But not string bean salad so *often*. It's lack of variation that troubles our menus, don't you think?" I agreed. "Well, I've made a list of possibilities." This, I think, was when he began to try his hand at some special dishes. Our Sunday meals became varied and exciting, as did the companionship of that day. We all wanted to exchange news about our jobs and to catch up on each other's experiences. The trouble was we never wanted to go to bed. There was too much to talk about and to discuss.

Ruth was reading *Kristin Lavransdatter* and beginning the second volume. Sigrid Undset had won the Nobel Prize for Literature two years before.

"The trouble is I'm reading such an indigestible combination of books," she explained. "*Kristin Lavransdatter* is like living in a medieval tapestry. But then I'm reading Dorothy Parker's *Laments for the Living*, Walter Lippmann's *Preface to Morals*, the new *Jalna* novel, and Willa Cather's *Obscure Destinies*."

As July advanced Ruth hit upon a new plan to arouse interest, to get people to take a special pleasure in coming into the bookshop.

"It's my 'theory of association' technique. A way to start a kind of continuing interest among customers who happen in and out.

"It's like this: I've noticed how chain reactions of enthusiasm start when you find two or three people sitting around in the shop who happen to be interested in the same author, or literary period. You remember that play about Samuel Johnson and all the people who were close to him? Like the Thrales and Garrick and Boswell. We have it in our drama section. It's the most beautiful example of bookmaking and format, the prize of our

entire collection. A. Edward Newton must have felt that was
the climax of all his devotion to Dr. Johnson. We have his
Amenities of Book-Collecting and *This Book-Collecting Game,*
too. I've managed to put them in the same locality on the shelves.

"Now this is the point. I've found at least five people who
come regularly to the shop who are all crazy about Johnson. I
mean to get them all together and ask them if they wouldn't
enjoy coming down to the bookshop some night after the closing hour, around nine o'clock, and read the play aloud. Of
course, it would have to be just certain scenes, but I think it
would be ever so much fun. It would start something they'd
enjoy, and it would start something worthwhile for Johnny
Appleseed. I'd call it 'The Kindred Spirits Reading Group.'"

"You'd have to find just the right ones to read the different
parts," said Walter, Jr. "How would you manage that?"

"Well, that fascinating Miss Booram who's staying at the
Orvis Inn would be marvelous for Mrs. Thrale. There's a Miss
Bennett who comes in from Limberlock Lodge. She's rather
stout and heavy and has a deep voice. She's awfully keen, too,
and is good fun. I'd thought of her for Dr. Johnson. There's
a Miss Colt at the Equinox House. She's clever but a little prissy.
She'd do for Miss Burney."

"Who'd do Boswell? He's terribly important."

"I'd ask Beacom Rich to come up from the Roaring Branch
Camps and do Boswell. He'd be wonderful; and I know he'd
enjoy doing it."

"It really does sound like a novel idea," I said. "Very informal, but I think it might work out."

"Informality is the keynote of the bookshop," Ruth added.
"I've even shelled peas for supper out on the front steps."

"What happens after your Kindred Spirits Reading Group
has read the play? What's the follow-up?"

"They'll be full of congenial talk about books after that;
get to know each other and become sort of wedded to the bookshop; and finally become steady customers."

"That's what I was waiting for. You can't run a business
just on congeniality and altruism."

"Of course not, but they're good self-starters."

After a little preliminary groundwork, Ruth instituted her Kindred Spirits Reading Group. The reading of Edward Newton's play, *Doctor Johnson,* proved a success, and, as she had hoped, it swelled the number of customers for the bookshop. Alfred Harcourt, who was in Arlington for the summer, dropped in frequently and eventually became acquainted with the entire personnel. Vrest Orton brought Leon Dean from the University of Vermont. I happened to be with Ruth in the shop on the morning they came. They viewed us and the bookshop with obvious skepticism. Our very apparent lack of professional know-how bored them into a state where they left us unnoticed, and conferred in undertones as to some possible suggestion that might give us a little light in our abysmal darkness. Then Mr. Orton came up with an idea. He explained that any place that sold books in Vermont should have *old* books. He'd send someone down with a load from Charles Tuttle's old books firm.

He was as good as his word. The next afternoon, a very hot one, a perspiring and disheveled youth arrived with nine or ten huge boxes of torn and dusty old books. Ruth looked at them in consternation and indignation. After he had carried in two or three boxes, dumping them haphazard on the floor, she told him not to bring any more into the shop until she had telephoned to her father.

It was not long after this experience that John Farrar stopped in the drugstore with Frederic Melcher of *Publishers' Weekly.* Walter sent them down to see Ruth and the shop. Their impression of both was evidently much more favorable than that of Professor Dean and Vrest Orton. Frederic Melcher asked Ruth to write a short account of the shop for *Publishers' Weekly* and to include some pictures. This she did, and it surprises me to find, upon reading it again thirty-five years later, that she voiced ideas we have held to steadily, except that we eventually relaxed our stand against merchandise other than books. The brief article had two pictures of the shop, one exterior, and one interior. With the photographs, it filled a page and a third. And I'm sure it gave the entire personnel a thrill to look at it.

The Johnny Appleseed is a small bookshop in a rather diminutive but altogether delightful Vermont village. We are in a building of our own, on a road that is not infested with tearing tourists, and yet is near enough to the town's center of business. We combine idealism with practicality to the best of our ability.

Manchester is primarily a summer resort, and Dorset, which is five miles north of us, is an artist colony as well. We are the only bookshop between Bennington and Rutland, so we cover a territory of fifty miles or more. We cater to all kinds of people—to the usual overnight tourist who wants a detective story or a luscious Donald Henderson Clark—to the old lady with a guimpe, who revels in Bess Streeter Aldrich—to the vacationing business man who knows his biography and his foreign affairs—and to those rare souls eager for the new Frances Frost and "Dorothy Wordsworth."

As our summer season is short—from July 1st to October 1st—we had difficulty to begin with in keeping a sufficiently large stock on hand and yet getting rid of it all by fall. Last summer, however, we secured books on consignment from four publishing houses, and will do so from five more next year. We found this a great help. The Drug Store, which is financially responsible for us, has also sold our leftovers with success.

Our lending library will include quite a bit of nonfiction, as we find that people are as dissatisfied as we are with nothing but the usual frothy summer novels.

Our newest and biggest idea for the summer is a weekly story hour for very small children, probably without charge, but with the hope of interesting the children and their parents, as well, more intimately in the Shop. One of our staff (of two) is a kindergartener, and it is perhaps her enticing way with the younger customers that draws so many to us.

A seasonal shop is, of course, a difficult proposition, especially in the summer when, we think, the general level of books published is apt to be as low as their sale. We are trying, however, by means of as judicious choice as we are capable of not only to satisfy but to stimulate our customers.

We have been as unyielding and as hardhearted as marble in our refusal to put in anything but books. We have *no* greeting cards, antiques, pottery, or gifts, though we have barely escaped knock-down-drag-out fights with customers who have insisted upon buying our Great-Grandmother's little chair and her lustre pitcher.

It is true that we will never become millionaires in the Johnny Appleseed, but business has been surprisingly good. At present we are exceedingly hopeful and enthusiastic. If one is filled with a consuming interest in books and a consuming interest in people, then it seems to us inevitable that one's place is in a bookshop, and that one will be at least moderately successful there.

This article was written after Ruth had closed the bookshop in the fall and gone back to college for her junior year. The plan for a children's story hour of which she spoke was inaugurated the next summer, but it became too difficult a situation to continue into the following year. It had, of necessity, to be held outside the shop, not to impede the progress of business within. It was held on the small space of lawn outside, where little chairs were set out in anticipation of the event. Weather, of course, was a crucial factor. However, as far as I can recall, the day always was clear. The difficulty lay in the fact that we couldn't keep the story hour within bounds. A continually increasing number of children not belonging to any bookshop clientele skirted the edge of the invited group. They hung off a little bit, then drew nearer until they were sitting on the ground well inside the sacred precincts. They listened with breathless attention. They joined in laughter and in sighs of satisfaction. When the last story was told, they departed reluctantly and returned the next week with added friends.

The rental library was a problem, too. It was largely patronized by overnight tourists. They paid their dollar deposit and left with their book. But this was the season of early sunrise, and early departures for the tourist. He wanted to return his book and retrieve his dollar by seven the next morning!

Into the hours of that first business summer came the details of getting a good mailing list, of planning regular advertising, and keeping aware of new cottagers and people at inns in Dorset and Arlington.

September came. A golden mesh of fruitfulness enshrouded the valleys and uplands. These were the days when the hands of time's clock moved from lush, green hours of summer to the benign moments of an altered tempo in earth's rhythm, the "frost-clear, blue-nooned, apple-ripening days," of which Sarah

Cleghorn wrote when her heart welled with love of this same valley and village. Presently, color blazed upon the mountains. One walked through avenues of brilliance, and all the elms and maples along the village street showered beauty upon one's head. It was hard not to pause at every step to stoop and pick up the treasure at one's feet, leaf by leaf. By the end of October, unhurried quietude would overlay the land with a sheen of bronze and gold.

Long since, people had left the inns and their summer homes. Early in September they had reluctantly gone cityward, parents to return their children to school, businessmen to return to jobs. The village street and the golf links seemed strangely deserted.

Ruth was tired, but already she talked eagerly of what we would do another summer.

"How much experience I've already had. How much I've learned! I know about invoices and statements and ordering. I'm as familiar with *Publishers' Weekly* and *Retail Bookseller* as I am with the dictionary. And people—the fussy, rude ones— don't bother me any more. After they've departed, instead of continuing in an aftermath of ruffled feelings, I pitch the whole incident into the fireplace and get out my secret talisman."

"What's that?"

"I do something *creative*. Either in my mind, or actually, if there aren't other people in the shop. I write something. Sometime I mean to try a column about people and books. Or I think up some new idea for the shop. Or maybe I just meditate about what a wonderful spot of being alive I'm in just now!"

Toward the end of the month a cold rain suddenly came at noon. Gusts of wind tore at the leaves and sent masses of them in a wet, golden downpour to the sidewalks. They lay there, their color intensified against the white marble. Inside the shop, Ruth added logs to the fire and lighted the lamps. Rain beat against the windows, and the clock ticked softly.

About four o'clock, I put on my raincoat and walked down to Johnny Appleseed to see how Ruth was faring. How short the summer had been! How soon she would be gone for another year at college! When I opened the door and went in, I found her sitting in front of the fire. A man was sitting across from her, reading aloud. She jumped to her feet and the man rose.

"Mother, this is Ray Stannard Baker. He walked up from Arlington and was caught in the rain."

I found myself looking into kind and friendly eyes.

"Yes, I've been following pretty much the same road, I guess, that my ancestor, Remember Baker, followed when he used to walk up the valley to foregather with Ira Allen and the other Green Mountain Boys at one of the old Manchester taverns. At least that's what Dorothy Canfield's been telling me."

"Mr. Baker has another name, Mother. He's been reading aloud to me from one of his own books. We had it right here on one of the shelves by the fireplace."

She reached over, smiling, and took the book from his hand: *Adventures in Contentment* by David Grayson.

"It couldn't have been more appropriate," he said, "for the kind of afternoon I've just had."

CHAPTER THREE

The Second Summer—1931

$\mathcal{R}$UTH CAME HOME for spring vacation in April. On the first morning she was outdoors at sunrise.

"I had a wonderful walk," she said as she slipped into her chair at the breakfast table. "It was like taking a sunrise dip in Equinox Pond. Cold and clean and beautiful."

"Where'd you go?" asked her brother, who was gathering his books together preparatory to starting to school. Vacations at Burr and Burton and Smith College didn't coincide that year.

"To the Pond and through the woods until I came out above MacNaughton's. Then I came back down the hill into the village. When I reached the highest part of the road I could see an almost complete circle of mountains. It looked as though the Taconics and the Green Mountains must be going to meet and close the valley. I wonder whether, way back in geologic ages, they ever did. Bromley and Green Peak and Owl Head all were flooded with light. It was like the day of Creation."

Later in the day she settled down to work with *Publishers' Weekly* and *Retail Bookseller,* making lists of books from the spring announcements. It was time to think of ordering for Johnny Appleseed.

"It's a shame," she complained, "that although we have loads of publishers' catalogues none of their representatives come to see us. It would help so much, but we're too small a business. We're just a dot on the bookseller landscape."

After turning pages for a few moments, she said, "We ought certainly to have this one. It sounds unusual. It's a novel about China. The author has lived in China all her life except for the years when she was going to college here in the United States. Her parents were American missionaries and she was born in China. It's called *The Good Earth*."

She sighed and kept turning pages. "Here's one by Agnes Repplier about the Ursuline nuns. About the founding of their Order in Quebec back in 1639. We're so much a part of Lake Champlain and French Canada that I'm sure we ought to order it. And here's a new Christopher Morley. We must have that."

For some time she was silent, flipping pages and writing down titles. Then she exclaimed, "Oh, Mother, Edna St. Vincent Millay has a new sonnet sequence, *Fatal Interview*. We must have several copies. When was it that she read in Bennington for the Poetry Society? Five . . . six years ago? I remember it was winter and terribly cold. A below-zero night. I was thrilled that you let me go. I'll never forget. . . . She looked like Jeanne d'Arc, didn't she? Her hair shining and cut short, and her dress slim and straight and made of some heavy metallic material. It looked like a coat of mail. All she needed was a great shield and a sword."

"I think she had both," I said.

"And here it says that the libretto of *The King's Henchman* is going to be published. I've simply got to have that for myself! Tonight we must get out that record from the opera and play it. We must have ever so many more books on music for the shop this summer. I wish we were big enough to have records, too."

Before it seemed possible Ruth was home once more. It was June, and she was busy getting ready to open the shop on July 1st.

Each day, even before the July 1st date arrived, friendly people stopped to talk with Ruth. Charles Crane of Brattleboro was such a one. Steeped in Vermont lore, and a veteran newspaper-man and distinguished columnist, he brought such warmth and humor as well as funds of information to any conversational encounter that just his presence added to a gathering assured a rare and unforgettable experience. Ruth came home after a morning with him bursting with pleasure and admiration.

"How wonderful you were," she said to her father, "to send him down to see me. I'm so crammed with delightful impressions and suggestions that I hardly know where to begin."

"Did he tell you about *The Mystery of Edwin Drood* being finished, after Dickens' death, by his Spirit Pen?" her brother asked. (This had all occurred in Brattleboro, in the loft of an old brick building, in strange, spooky circumstances at night. There were the finished pages, each morning! It aroused excitement all over the country, and abroad. But the thing was never solved. It was a mystery fit to go with *The Mystery of Edwin Drood* itself. For it was printed, finally, with the Spirit Pen of Charles Dickens' ending.)

"Yes. And think of it! Kipling's *Just So Stories* and *The Jungle Books* were written there in Brattleboro. Mr. Crane saw our copies of them lying on the children's table and that started him off, telling me the most entrancing story of Kipling's four years in Brattleboro. Really a saga, but a tragic one, as it ended."

Kipling had built his house for his bride, and it was like a ship—"Naulakha"—on a hillside looking across the Connecticut River to New Hampshire. His wife was the sister of his beloved American friend, Wolcott Balestier, whom he had met in London. When the friend suddenly died, Kipling, who had fallen in love with his sister, Caroline (who was keeping house for her brother), married her. She brought her husband—Kipling of the British Empire and India, Kipling of the *Barrack-Room Ballads*—to Vermont. It didn't work. After her years in London, his American wife, Caroline Balestier of Brattleboro, Vermont, had become more English in her feelings and certain social attitudes and mannerisms than her English husband. This was resented by many Brattleboro farm neighbors, and small-town business people. To them it was offensive affectation. They felt they were being looked down upon and belittled. Their weapon, and that of a highly unconventional brother, Beattie Balestier, who resided near the Kiplings in Brattleboro, was ridicule. They launched a campaign so merciless and cruel that it led to a family quarrel that became a matter of court procedure and record. The American newspapers were full of it. News reporters had a field day. The British papers also followed it. Wrecked with inarticulate wrath and humiliation, coupled with a serious illness of his own and the death of his and Caroline's first child, born at "Naulakha," Kipling and his wife fled back to London, leaving Vermont forever.

After a moment, Ruth said thoughtfully, "All of this fits in so perfectly with my 'theory of association' applied to books. It's the real touchstone to selling books. Talk about books— present and past ones. Find all possible related anecdotes, or connections with other related books, any fascinating bits of story associated with them. It's enchanting and endless."

"You seem to have an endless fund of ideas," said her father. "What else besides this 'theory of book association' are you involved in?"

"Mother's writing a kind of daily-letter-story for little Berniece Butterfield. She's been sick, you know. We see her from the bookshop office window, lying on a cot under one of the back garden trees. There's a big tiger cat that sits beside her on the cot."

The story was called "The Tangled Romance of Cordelia Tiger." I wrote and typed it in the office, during dull moments, and made colored cat illustrations for each installment of the story. I put it in a long envelope, and each night on her way home after closing the shop, Ruth tiptoed up and slipped it under the Butterfields' front door. They were all completely mystified. Berniece's sister, Barbara, had asked me if Ruth was writing it. "Oh, no, I'm sure not," I'd told Barbara. So they began asking everyone, and it became the great mystery of Pill Alley. Everyone was asking and wondering about it, and people looked all through our children's books in the store to see whether there was anything about a Cordelia Tiger.

Ruth laughed when she'd finished telling all this to her father.

"Barbara says she and Berniece and their father and mother rush downstairs every morning to find it and read it aloud at breakfast."

"I think," said Ruth's father, "that you and your mother are experts at working a publicity racket."

The Tangled Romance of Cordelia Tiger

The Small Girl sat on the doorstep. She was lonely. (Perhaps you are too.) She wished that someone would come and talk to her. Presently someone did come.

Mrs. Catt came and sat down beside her. She looked at The Small Girl out of the corner of one green eye. After a moment she remarked: "Cordelia Tiger thought that she was unhappy too."

"What did you say, Mrs. Catt?" asked The Small Girl.

"I was recalling Cordelia Tiger and her troubles," replied Mrs. Catt.

"Who *was* Cordelia Tiger, Mrs. Catt?"

"She was the daughter of Mr. and Mrs. Algernon Felinis Tiger—one of our first families, my dear."

"What made Cordelia unhappy, Mrs. Catt?"

"It's a long story, my dear."

"I should like to hear it, Mrs. Catt."

"Would you? Well, just wait a moment while I run over to the butcher's cart and tell that boy I want fish on Friday, and perhaps I'll tell you about her." And Mrs. Catt ran across the road.

"Cordelia was a charming young thing," continued Mrs. Catt, settling herself once more beside The Small Girl on the doorstep. "She was one of those kittens with a magnetic personality."

"I should have liked to see her," said The Small Girl.

"Yes. She was very lovely," returned Mrs. Catt. "But nevertheless her path did not run smoothly. And all because of her feet."

"Why, Mrs. Catt! What in the world did her feet have to do with it?" asked The Small Girl in surprise.

"Ah, a very great deal, my dear! If it hadn't been for Cordelia's feet—three black and one entirely white—Bobby Catt would never have noticed her."

"Who was Bobby Catt?"

"He was one of those independent young bachelors one meets at all the fashionable resorts."

"Resorts, Mrs. Catt?"

"Yes. Places like Lake Placid, Virginia Hot Springs, St. Moritz. And, of course, he was always in London in April. (You know that line about 'Come down to Kew in lilac time,' don't you?)"

"I'm not sure, Mrs. Catt," said The Small Girl doubtfully.

"Well, no difference. The real point is that mothers of debutante kittens didn't like Bobby Catt."

"Why was that?" asked The Small Girl in surprise. "He sounds quite attractive, I think."

"Too attractive, my dear! Too attractive by far. The trouble was that with all his attractive qualities he lacked the stable, reliable traits which make a good husband. He was too fond of prowling and roaming. Mothers did not trust him. Besides which, his family pedigree was not all that could be desired. It had a *tightrope* in it! That rather dashed his eligibility to the ground, you know."

"Dear me!" exclaimed The Small Girl. "But tell me, Mrs. Catt, how did Cordelia happen to meet Bobby Catt?"

"She met him at The Howl and Scratch-It Night Club," replied Mrs. Catt. "And, though he is a very distant connection of mine, I must admit that she met him in a very strange way. A *very strange* way!"

(Continued tomorrow)

Later in the bookshop's history, when it had moved to its quarters in the drugstore extension, what was now entitled "The Daily Letter Story of Cordelia Tiger and Her Tangled Romance" became a homemade best seller for us. With great effort and the help of a generous friend who possessed skill with a mimeograph, we produced about eighty copies, all duly bound in book form with a lovely soft green binding of cardboard and Cordelia's portrait on the front. They sold like hot cakes at $1.50 each. Two of the first buyers were Anne Parrish and Rachel Field.

It was difficult to produce in numbers by hand, and no publishers could be won to it. They complained that it wasn't exactly a *child's* story—too sophisticated, really a cat-satire of New York society. It was too much like a game, perhaps. It was a strange, off-beat idea. This was before the days of *Eloise at the Plaza* with Hilary Knight illustrations, or any of the game books.

But Ruth did write about it in her weekly advertising space in the Manchester *Journal,* called "The Apple Core."

It often seems to us, work-ridden and toil-worn as we are, that nothing would be so heavenly as some nice comfortable disease—say two weeks in bed, with constant egg-nogs and attention and masses of flowers. Only it probably isn't customary to ply invalids with gardenia corsages, which is what we want. *Anyhow,* there is now another inducement to illness; somebody might send us the adventures of *Cordelia Tiger* or those of *Mrs. Raggy Hound Dog,* which are thrilling tales, written as a series of letters, all enveloped and stamped, and ready to be sent one a day, for a week or two, like an invigorated sunshine basket. . . . Please will the next person with German measles come clasp us to his bosom?

One of the problems of the second summer that Ruth and I suddenly realized was the curtailment of outdoor hours of wandering along mountain trails, or climbing to Deer Knoll on Equinox, or to Dorset Quarry on Green Peak. We suddenly hit upon a plan. The matter of time consumed was a factor to consider. The car must serve us for speed, so Mount Equinox was out of the question, but not Dorset Quarry.

We rose at five o'clock and set out, winding along the road which led to the foot of the old abandoned quarry on Green Peak. Leaving the car at the foot, we climbed the comparatively short distance to the beautiful space before the quarry and its wall—a space like a great platform overhanging the valley, with views of Equinox to the west, the Green Mountains to the east, Mount Anthony to the south, and far below, our own white villages and the thread of the Batten Kill. Here we sat and ate the breakfast we had brought in complete communion of friendship, love, and contentment.

Gathering our things together, we went back down the trail to the foot of the mountain. Ruth was picking a handful of grass-of-Parnassus as she went, those wild grasses with an almost classic Greek simplicity of blossom, like Parian marble. When we reached the bookshop at nine o'clock, she put them in the little yellow jar with its label "Hymettus Honey" on the round table in the children's corner, and around it she placed

beautiful copies of the *Iliad* and the *Odyssey* and *Greek Myths.*
Then she looked up and sighed with contentment.

ABANDONED QUARRY

They worked these Dorset hills a hundred years ago
For marble. White as winter's first deep-fallen snow
It lies upon the mountain-side, a drift that stays
Despite the tempest of the thawing storms, the haze
Of April green appearing on the hills.

And where the mountain draws the valley to her breast,
They cut a winding road to scale the quarry's crest.
It winds past lonely farms, and high, sweet mountain-mowings,
Past upland sugar woods, and fields where late fall sowings
Of winter wheat lie green upon the hills.

Up through the dusk of woods it climbs to dazzling light
Of sudden wide-viewed clearings where one catches sight
Of the dim valley spread below, and the far ledge
Of gleaming rock above that marks the quarry's edge—
A white embattlement against the sky.

Today beside the ruined quarry children play,
Hunting the pale, sweet blossoms of the mountain May,
Or running mad with glee down the green slopes that spread
Beneath; here twilight waits the veery's notes that thread
Enchantment through the gathering maze of night.

All wild and lovely things here have their sanctuary—
The hermit thrush, frail orchid, partridge-berry,
And bronzed, sun-scented fern. How can it then be sad—
This secret dreaming place—with its great iliad
Of singing green upspringing from mute stone?

M. H.

CHAPTER FOUR

The Third Summer—1932

W HEN RUTH was graduated from Smith in 1932, Marion Dodd of the Hampshire Bookshop in Northampton knew of the Johnny Appleseed Bookshop although until then she had not realized that Ruth, a frequenter of her own shop, was its instigator. It was because of Ruth that Mary Ellen Chase took special note of Manchester's white marble sidewalks when she later spoke here at a convention of college English teachers.

No child reared in Manchester village could fail to feel those walks were as individual a beauty of her home village as the mountains rising at each side of them. When they were wet from dew or rain they held pools of reflected morning or evening light in the gentle hollows of their surfaces. In the great slabs of marble were fernlike patterns caused by intermingling deposits of different mineral substances. Occasionally, some small fossilized shell appeared, offering untold fascination to anyone interested in geological formation and the story of geologic time. Here was written a story of mountains and valleys and of this region lying between the Connecticut and the Hudson Rivers.

At Smith, Ruth became a member of Mary Ellen Chase's Creative Writing class. Inevitably, her daily themes became a continuous dissertation upon the features and fascinations of her home town: its beauties and its people. Hastily written notes from her would say, "Miss Chase gave me an A on Nat Canfield and Miss Hermie," or, "A again on Skinner Hollow."

But one day Miss Chase questioned her as she handed back her theme.

"Ruth, I don't know what village you continually write about. I know it is in Vermont, but your frequent references to light and color caught and reflected in the surfaces of the '*white marble sidewalks*' irritates me. Isn't this a poetic exaggeration? *White marble?* I think you are dreaming of golden streets and Gates of Pearl. Surely these pavements are not white marble the whole length of a village! I find it hard to believe."

Before Ruth could reply, an older girl rose to defend her.

"Miss Chase, I spend my summers in Dorset, just north of Manchester, where Ruth lives. And the sidewalks there are made of big, white marble slabs. They have been there for years and years."

Thus, by Gwen Corwin's testimony, Ruth's statement was maintained. But soon Miss Chase was questioning her again, and this time perhaps only I could have given the supporting testimony.

"Ruth, where were you prepared for college?"

"At Burr and Burton Seminary, Miss Chase. In Manchester, Vermont."

"Do they specialize in teaching Greek mythology?"

"I don't think so, Miss Chase."

"I ask because your daily themes puzzle me. There seldom is one that does not contain three or four references to some Greek myth, or to some personality contained in Greek mythology. Where did you get all this?"

"Oh! Up in Mr. Randall's pasture."

This answer must have provided Miss Chase with more puzzlement than ever.

When Ruth and her brother were nine and five years old, respectively, one of their secret kingdoms was an area of wooded upland and pastures that lay between the edge of Mount Equinox and the ledge behind our house. During afternoons in summer, this was the location of halcyon adventure. We would set forth to climb the hill behind the house. Attaining the ledge, we would take a zigzag course until we reached an upper pasture belonging to the Randall farm. Here we entered a region of provocative terrain, at least to my accompanying mind. The shallow basin of a small quarry excavation, long since deserted and now filled with a shimmer of rain water or a trickle from some hidden vein of water in a rock crevice, was where Narcissus knelt to behold his face. The gathering woods at the pasture boundary were where Pandora and Epimetheus played in innocence before Pandora opened the fateful chest. Echo answered from the face of rock high above the woods, and, looking off from the highest point in this pasture region to the north, we could clearly see the white wall of Dorset's abandoned quarry rising above the trees. Ruth already was devoted to the story of the Siege of Troy, and this location given to long afternoons of storytelling continued thus, and finally, the children reached the ages of thirteen and nine. By then, Walter, Jr., had become acquainted with all the incidents of a child's story of the *Iliad*. Now the distant Quarry Wall became the Wall of Troy. With entire conviction, he would say, "If you look carefully you may see King Priam walking there and watching the battle on the plain below." Then he added with a sigh, "I suppose I should want to be Achilles, but I don't. I want to be Hector."

This was the explanation of Ruth's reply, "Oh! Up in Mr. Randall's pasture," which Miss Chase needed.

The bookshelves in the shop began to fill up with new books —Julia Peterkin's *Bright Skin,* Ann Bridge's *Peking Picnic* were books brought home. She came filled with eagerness over having obtained copies of every one of Mary Webb's books in print, having recently discovered *Precious Bane.*

Finally, she acquired copies of William Rothenstein's *Men and Memories—1872-1900.* These books contained reproductions of William Rothenstein's great portraits of the outstanding men and women of those years, along with his memories of them. They were marvelous, Ruth thought, as enthralling as *The Amenities of Book-Collecting.* There were reproductions of drawings and etchings, as well as oils, and there were wonderful caricatures of Max Beerbohm, with all the background of events that included him. There were drawings of Whistler, and an unforgettable portrait of Rodin in his studio.

One of the accomplishments of these first summers in the shop was getting out folders and making mailing lists for Manchester, Dorset, and Arlington. It included our first advertising in the Manchester *Journal* under the heading, "The Apple Core," which Ruth wrote in an informal and gay style of her own. The heading was chosen because a book salesman from Rutland had approached her with the query, "Miss Appleseed, I suppose? Are you the manager of this shop?"

"Oh, no," she said laughing, "I'm only the core!!"

His resulting bewilderment made her ask him to sit down while she explained that Johnny Appleseed's name was not her father's. It became an almost daily process, this telling the story of Johnny Appleseed and why we had used the name. *Finally,* we received enormous assistance in the matter. The Davey Tree Experts advertised over the radio, and one day they told the story of Johnny Appleseed, but this proved confusing, too. Some people who had come in at the tail end of the program just heard the name of Johnny Appleseed. Suddenly we began to get postals: "We heard your bookshop mentioned on the radio. We hope to come to Vermont and see it." Or, a touring customer from New Jersey would smile and say, "Oh, yes, we heard your bookshop mentioned over the radio!" We were grateful, but it entailed yards of talk.

Now we began to "order every week," as I had predicted. Walter, Jr., had achieved a neat and tamed appearance at the front of the shop. A curving gravel walk, edged by old-fashioned perennials, served as the foreground for the white, cottagelike building. Apple branches hung over it, and a big elm stood at the far corner. Inside, our customers were probably bewildered by its unbusinesslike look. The impression was, I'm sure, that they were entering a living room. Surrounding bookshelves, a fireplace, comfortable chairs, and big tables covered with more books, and reading lamps furthered this impression. Vases were filled with wild flowers here and there, and a general atmosphere of friendliness prevailed. All of this was meant to create a feeling of at-homeness, with welcome to sit down, discuss books, to linger and talk, and eventually to buy some books, we hoped. It may have been good psychology, but I can see that as a beginning it wasn't perhaps the wisest approach. It puzzled some people and embarrassed others. They felt they did not know just where they were. In a private home? Or in a bookshop? Of course, there were those who liked it. We maintained this pattern in both of our future locations, but by then it had become an asset.

As fall approached and cool August nights became more and more frequent, there were blazing apple-tree chunks smelling sweetly in the fireplace. Also, bowls of apples standing about for eating. "The Apple Core" began to speak of forthcoming book reductions and to tell of the Annual Fall Exhibition of the Southern Vermont Artists to be held in the Burr and Burton gymnasium.

Here I insert some samplings of "The Apple Core." They are possibly a mixture from different seasons and years, but who has ever bought apples at a wayside orchard stand in autumn without relishing a mixture of varieties and flavors?

We have been commercial this week rather than literary—which is a state refreshing to the cash register but not, we must confess, to the soul. And we have also been haunted by nightmares: (a) of a story hour, with nothing but one disinterested and disreputable puppy present, after we had dusted under the rag rug and put on our best bib and tucker— and (b) of the Johnny Appleseed positively bulging with children, and of more sedate customers wading in, being completely swamped, and going out hastily with raised eyebrows instead of purchases.

We are also embroiled in teaching ourself German, and, in between times, when not saying "Wo ist der bleistift?" we have been absorbed in *The Epic of America,* which is splendid. We also loved *Magnolia Street* which everyone else has or should have read by this time, probably. We leavened *The Epic* with Alice Rosman's new *Benefits Received* which is delicious. . . . And *now,* we just glanced into *The Mango Tree* and we are having dutch fits for fear somebody will come and make off with it!

If we had been in Russia last week falling snow would have whistled about our ears in the dark streets, and peasants in blue smocks would have called us *"my little dove,"* and we would probably have had our head bashed in by nephews who wanted our fortune of 3000 roubles. Yes, we read *The Brothers Karamazov* all week. Every day we transport more of our merchandise home to our personal shelf, and at night we have bad dreams about these cursed dollar reprints.

We liked *A World Begins* even better than *A Princess in Exile*. It is the same story, but told with humor—and we are still blushing for our native land, which incarcerates elite exiles in back halls as governesses, and parades them as my dear countess for the benefit of out-of-town guests.

Years of Peace is beautifully written. We keep identifying it with Robert Strong Woodward's *Years of Grace* that we saw at the Art Exhibit.

We thought *A Good Man's Love* fine—but we will carefully keep it from the clutches of all "eligible young men!"

We have been hanging our intellectual legs out into literary breezes all week—holding things like *Great Winds, Heavy Weather,* and *Rain in the Doorway* in one hand and sucking plums with the other. (Pardon all metaphorical confusion.) The last two (books, not plums) actually made us forget that our parched flower beds look like After the Battle Mother. They're deliciously crazy and delirious and make one feel quite at home.

Great Winds we will not discuss at length. It's too hot to disagree with people, and everyone else has thought it one of the best books of the season. To us, it was a good magazine article padded with fictitious characters who weren't especially real, except for little Ira. He went fishing, and stood barelegged in cold brooks. . . . Yum!

All Men Are Enemies seemed self-conscious and didactic, to begin with, and some parts of it bored us to extinction. The last part, though, was pure poetry in spots, and reminded us of *The Fountain*.

Oh, why in Heaven's name didn't we take up something like yawling or polar bear trapping for a life work, instead of bookselling?

It is very wrong to talk about anything except our big sale—but here is a murmured hint that *Lamb in His Bosom* and *No Second Spring* are fine, and that Harold Nicolson's *Peacemaking* is great to limber your sluggish brain. (No slurs intended.) Heretofore we've been sure that if *we* had been invited to the Paris Peace Conference all would have been well. (Wouldn't we have been cute—long dresses and teething ring, on the rostrum.) Now we know that all the nations would have been by the ears no matter what—and the only things that can be wholeheartedly blamed are the newspapers and democracy. It's nice to have an excuse not to read the papers any more. . . .

We are planning to be overwhelmed by you all on Thursday, Friday and Saturday of this week, because everything is going to be marked down, and we will resemble Macy's, except no escalators, because we're scared of them. Mathematics have had us in their toil for days, and at last discounts are mostly figured out, but if you have any algebra books bring them on. They'll probably help.

This is our last effusion till next June, so Merry Christmas! Brrr, what a thing to think of!

Perhaps this was the year when we became most cognizant of the contribution made by the Poetry Society of Southern Vermont, not only to our entire valley, but to our bookshop also. The Society came about through Jessie Rittenhouse, who was summering in Shaftsbury at Camp Avalon on the lake there, and the scholarly and enthusiastic co-operation of Madison Bates, the headmaster of Burr and Burton Seminary, who was teaching at the same summer camp. The Society started with a group of perhaps fifty, and soon grew to a membership of over three hundred. At this time there was a renaissance of interest in poetry and modern writers of poetry spreading throughout this country and abroad. Jessie Rittenhouse's two little collections of modern poetry were being read by everyone and were constantly in demand. She had a remarkable acquaintance with the new poets themselves, as did Madison Bates, who had taught in the English Department at the University of Illinois, and afterward had headed the English Department at the University of South Dakota, finally becoming an outstanding member of the Department of English at Rutgers University.

In summer, the Society met either in Arlington at the home of Mrs. Hallie Gilchrist, patron saint of all modern poets, or in Manchester for large meetings where poets appeared, or at Camp Avalon on Lake Shaftsbury, under the sponsorship and leadership of Jessie Rittenhouse and Madison Bates, its president. In winter, the meetings were held in Bennington. Such poets as Vachel Lindsay, Witter Bynner, Amy Lowell, Robert Frost, Carl Sandburg, Hermann Hagedorn, Robert Haven Schauffler, Aline Kilmer, Edna St. Vincent Millay, Grace Hazard Conkling, Sarah Cleghorn, and Arthur Guiterman read for them.

It was at this time that Alfred Harcourt began reading

Walter's column, published weekly in the Rutland *Herald,* as
well as his *Salt of Vermont,* published by the Stephen Daye
Press in Brattleboro. He had a cottage in Arlington and he came
in to talk to Walter about publishing a book of his poems under
the Harcourt, Brace imprint. It was brought out the following
year, 1933, as *Mountain Township,* and dedicated to Madison
Bates, who had been his classmate at Williams and his devoted, lifelong friend. *Salt of Vermont* had been dedicated "To
Dorothy Canfield, who has seen to it that the salt has not lost
its savor."

During the summer, Ruth and her father both visited
Williamstown and the college. Ruth was preparing to close
Johnny Appleseed for the winter and to take a job in a bookshop
in Williamstown.

THE VILLAGE

There. From this hill look down.
That's the village.
It's like a man lying flat on his back.
The wide village street is the body.
There's an arm stretched to the east
And one lower down to the west.
Those two converging roads
Are the legs spread wide apart.
Where the head ought to be the figure fails,
Unless you make those wandering roads
Wisps of hair waving in the breeze.

There it lies
Dozing peacefully under the maples—
A church, a school, a tavern, some stores,
And a matter of fifty houses.
Somebody's hammering off to the south,
Probably mending fence.
You can hear the ring of the anvil
In the blacksmith's shop over there,
Where smoke is coming from the forge chimney.

The clock in the steeple strikes five.
The sound is a part of the stillness.

A flock of doves circles up from the road
Where a scuffling horse draws a buggy,
Kicking up a small cloud of dust.
The doves light on the Court House roof.
In a minute they are back in the road.
The East Mountain is hazy and seems far away.
It stretches as far as you can see north and south.
The winding river with the brush-lined banks
Shows silver patches here and there.

A sleepy village in a peaceful valley.
Yet, friend, there life stages its drama.
Tragedy, comedy; nobility beside self-seeking;
Petty crimes against the spirit;
The wise serenity of old age;
The rebellious passion of youth.
There the whole of life unfolds
From childhood's carefree days
To that hillside with the white stones.
Fifty houses offering the life of the race.

Calm twilight settles on the valley.
The birds are singing their evening song.
Come. It's time to go down.

W. H.

CHAPTER FIVE

The New Location

*N*OW THAT Ruth was graduated from college and had her job in the Williamstown bookshop, the question of what should be done about the Johnny Appleseed Bookshop became a matter for serious debate. Ruth hoped by another winter to find a position with a publishing firm, but Walter and I were highly averse to giving up our newly inaugurated enterprise. Not only did we delight in it and visualize it as a business with infinite possibilities, but we hoped that it might finally emancipate Walter from the drugstore business. We realized that the hope of immediate income from the bookshop to match that from the drugstore was unrealistic, but perhaps, with what we would get from its sale, plus our few investments, plus some real estate we rented, and with the new and growing income received in royalties from Walter's books and from the financial returns he was receiving in substantial amounts for the readings he gave from the books, this might eventually be accomplished. The Johnny Appleseed Bookshop, in any event, should not be relinquished, although it seemed probable that it would have to have a different location if Walter and I were going to manage it jointly.

The solution was to move it upstreet into the small extension adjoining the drugstore, once the Toggery Shop. This would be an exceedingly favorable location and the open door between it and the drugstore would prove a constant asset, not only for customers from the drugstore but to make Walter's share in its operation a matter of course.

But how could we hope to produce charm and atmosphere in a single good-sized room, with mismated measurements in walls and doorways as well as windows, such as pertained to an ancient building? For the drugstore building itself belonged to what was known as the "Equinox Junior." It had once been an old inn in the early days of Manchester's settlement.

Faced with this problem, and minus Ruth with her flair for providential suggestions, we called upon the "whenever-in-trouble-or-desperation-call-on-me" member of the bookshop personnel. It was spring vacation, and he, fortunately, was home from school and available.

He viewed the problem before him with an expression of anxiety. "It isn't what we must produce," he said, "it's what already is here! There isn't a true line, an even sill, or a correct angle in the whole place."

"Oh, well," said his father, "its original structure probably never was accurate in any way."

This comment must have seemed superfluous to Walter, Jr. "Well," he said with a sigh, "let's jot down necessities. And what already is here and of any worth. To begin with, there is the double entrance door, right here on the street, with good double screen doors. Large glass show windows at each side of the entrance, too. We'll build wide window seats under each window, with broad backs and book display ledges. Then, bookshelves on every available wall up to two-thirds of the ceiling's height. But opposite the entrance door we'll build a focal point— a fake fireplace."

"Oh!" I almost screamed.

"I know just how you feel," he agreed gloomily, "but we will make its proportions classic and have white paneling. There will be *no fake logs* burning."

"I'd die first!" I said.

"You needn't. We will have an open grate with a bed of glowing coals (electric) which will throw out real heat. On the mantel, an old clock ticking. Some nice tables—maple.

A walled-off office space in that far corner. Loads of canvas to cover any bulging, uneven wall portions that are background for pictures, paintings, and so on—and, of course, a children's corner to balance the walled and paneled office corner. Fresh paint, floor scraped, a new sign. Well, let's make a list."

During the next two weeks he worked with endless patience, coping with all the exasperating problems presented by a decadent building. His father came to the connecting drugstore door and watched as I struggled with soap and water and smoky walls.

"Never mind," he would say soothingly to his son, "it doesn't matter even if it is crooked. When the books get on the shelves and tables no one will notice."

After three or four cheering comments of this kind, Walter, Jr., drew me to one side. "Mother, can't you somehow take Dad home for the afternoon? I wouldn't hurt his feelings for the world, but I just can't do a job that way!"

I was reminded of this incident some twenty years later when Walter, Jr.'s own son, then seven years old, was spending a couple of months with us.

Having inherited his father's dexterity with tools, even at so young an age, and his love of perfection in workmanship, the matter in question was a workbench for him to use in the wide space then available in our garage. He watched his grandfather at work with an expression of growing concern. Finally, he came to me in the house and said in a troubled undertone, "Grandma, I wouldn't want to hurt Grandpa's feelings, but all of those four legs are different lengths!"

At last the Johnny Appleseed Bookshop was re-established in its new location, and despite all the preceding anguish, it did look attractive. But it was Walter's presence next door in the drugstore that worked the charm and brought an increasing number of readers, writers, and customers. Walter's growing list of reading engagements accounted for much of this. He had given readings at several Eastern colleges and universities, often with repeated engagements: Wesleyan, Williams, Harvard, Dartmouth, Bowdoin, Bennington College, University of Vermont, and so many organizations in New York, Boston, Albany, Burlington, and Montpelier that I cannot even recall them.

Homer Woodbridge of Wesleyan University, who wrote a front-page review for the New York *Herald Tribune* Sunday book review section of Walter's *Mountain Township* when it came out in June of 1933, wrote to him, "I wonder whether you realize that practically every one of your poems in this book follows one or another of the different Chaucerian meters. You are writing New England folk poetry. Therefore, I am including you in my English courses, along with Chaucer."

Professor Thompson wrote in a similar vein from Cornell, and at Cooper Union, in adult courses in Modern Poetry and Creative Writing, Walter's books were required reading.

Robert Frost came in to talk to him. "May it rightly be called poetry, Mr. Frost?" asked my husband. "It troubles many people. It doesn't rhyme and it seems to fall into no conventional verse form—free or otherwise."

"Assuredly, it is poetry," Robert Frost declared. "You have done a creative, poetic thing. You've created a true verse form to suit your need for the actual poetic expression and speech of the people and region of which you are writing . . . the essence of Vermont."

Presently Mr. Frost was paying him the honor of talking about him and his poetry on his own programs; even reading from Walter's poems along with his own. Various anthologists began to include his poems. Louis Untermeyer one summer had stopped in the drugstore, and as he moved over to the soda fountain he had eyed Walter thoughtfully and asked, "How do you manage to mix poetry and soda water?" "Both may contain considerable gas," Walter replied. But several years later, when Louis Untermeyer published his *Anthology of Thirty New England Poets,* beginning as far back as Joel Barlow, he included Walter among the thirty.

One time Walter read on a joint program with Carl Carmer before the national Phi Beta Kappa Society. Carl read from his poems, *Deep South,* and Walter read from *Vermont Salt and Vintage.* Afterward, I asked him what he had felt was the contrasting factor, the outstanding difference, between the folkways and attitudes of the people of the Deep South and those of the mountain people of his own state. Had he felt a distinguishable difference in the native attitudes of the two as he had listened to Carl's poems? Yes, he had. He thought a moment, and summed it up succinctly: "When things grow tense, and trouble brews in the Deep South, someone cracks a pistol. In Vermont, someone cracks a joke."

I, myself, have sat in the State House gallery of the Vermont Senate and observed my husband, as Senator for Bennington County, exemplify this in actuality. I have seen him rise from his seat during some heated and stormy conflict between opposing counties, and their Senators, which involved serious, even crucial, issues. As he was recognized from the floor, heads would turn in his direction. Respectful attention for the nonce would quiet a perceptibly seething atmosphere.

"I think this matter we are considering can be simply and easily clarified, its pros and cons, its actual gist and import, by the following incident that happened once, over in Beartown." He would then proceed to tell one of his stories, probably contained in one of his volumes of poems. As the climactic lines with their substance and humorous conclusion were reached, a suppressed chuckle or ripple of laughter would be audible throughout the Senate Chamber. Tempers would cool with laughter, relaxation would take over, and common sense would be restored.

Thanks to Carl Carmer's suggestion, Walter was commissioned by Rinehart and Company to write *The Connecticut* for the Rivers of America series with Hervey Allen as his editor.

When the Middlebury publishing firm of Vermont Books published his *A Matter of Fifty Houses,* Carl Carmer wrote the foreword, a foreword so discerning and intuitive that it is my desire to quote a paragraph from it. No one has understood Walter's gift so completely or expressed it so well.

The books of Walter Hard are penetrating and poetic studies [of Vermont and Vermonters]. Let no one be innocent enough to think of them as groupings of guileless and separate anecdotes. They are bound into an inseparable and continuous artistic whole by the cement of the author's philosophy. They present a likeness of a land and its people that deserves a place in the gallery of the best that has been done by the regionalists of the earth. And like that best, wherever it has been achieved, these creations transcend the limits of region. In them, physical boundaries recede and a corner of the universe becomes universal. . . . *A Matter of Fifty Houses* is a matter of a world.

One amusing situation relative to its publication and its title, *A Matter of Fifty Houses,* was that Dike Blair, the owner and publisher of Vermont Books, told Walter that he was receiving numerous orders for it from architectural firms all over the country. Walter exclaimed in amusement and astonishment, "Can't be they read the ad very far not to discover it doesn't deal with fifty architectural house plans. You don't send it, of course."

"Oh, yes, I do. And they never send it back. They order another!"

So it was in the bookshop's new location, nudging elbows with the drugstore, that *A Mountain Township,* published in June, 1933, by Harcourt, Brace, was first to be displayed in Manchester. The book immediately received excellent reviews, and almost immediately, too, Walter had a letter from the president's office at Williams, telling him that he had been proposed by Bliss Perry of Harvard, a trustee of Williams College, to receive an honorary Master's degree at commencement in June because of his writing and his contribution as a poet to Americana as well as Vermontiana.

Owing to the growing Depression that was overshadowing the entire country and to the "bank holiday" in April, the bookshop where Ruth was employed in Williamstown finally decided to close with the close of college, and thus Ruth was released to return joyously to her own Johnny Appleseed Bookshop for the summer, in its new location. In September, she joined the staff of the Stephen Daye Press in Brattleboro, and eventually became one of its editors, working with its senior editors, John and Marion Hooper. She at once resumed "The Apple Core" and wrote enthusiastically of the shop's new location. If we had known of her forthcoming return for the summer to Manchester, the apple orchard location might have been continued for another summer. As it was, it fell upon another creative career, and a distinguished one. Clara Sipprell, internationally known portrait photographer, looking for a small summer studio besides her New York one, learned of the vacated bookshop in the orchard through Dorothy Canfield and rented it from us for the summer. Thus began a friendship that has lasted for thirty-three years. The original bookshop building has long since given place to a beautiful studio with an enclosed garden, but at least one of the original apple trees remains.

By this change in events, Ruth was on hand to join us for the occasion of her father's presentation for an honorary degree at commencement time in Williamstown. It was a day of unparalleled summer loveliness, and Williamstown's main street, with its college buildings, was thronged with people. Walter was presented for his degree by Dr. Henry Wild, his former Latin professor at Williams. We listened to the citation which accompanied it with emotion that held us, son, daughter and wife, in comprehension too deep for expression. Dr. Wild had known of the journalistic studies cut short; the journalistic opportunity upon the Boston *Transcript* relinquished because of his responsibility to the family business; the immediate responsibility for an uncongenial occupation. He spoke with dignity and restraint of this man who had accepted the disappointments of what appeared a thwarted career in a chosen, dedicated field. He added that he had accepted it with determined courage and had somehow kept his creative determination alive until amid all the frustrations and attending difficulties he at last had arrived at his true goal and had achieved a recognized position as a poet, contributing to Americana and keeping alive the shy and classic muse of the Green Mountains.

We drove home almost in silence. Walter, Jr., went into the drugstore with his father to take over the five to six o'clock, before-dinnertime shift. Ruth reopened the bookshop, and I drove on home to prepare supper, too spent with inward emotion to want to do anything but sit and look out on the blue haze of evening light gathering in mountain hollows.

Presently, Ruth came home. She was very quiet.

"Daddy and Walter will be coming soon. I went in to find them at the drugstore, but they were too busy to come just yet. The store was full of people. I didn't open the bookshop. Just lit the mantel candles, framing all of Daddy's books displayed there."

She made iced tea, arranged a crisp salad.

"I know why he received that honorary degree—*the real reason!*" she said.

"Of course. I thought the citation was so wonderful, so comprehending of it all."

"Yes, but there it was all being demonstrated as I walked into the drugstore. Daddy had on his white linen coat. He was handing out Life Savers, toothbrushes, corn plasters, an occasional soda, and all with that dear, unself-conscious look. You'd never dream that anything special had happened to him—anything different, any significant honor. He was unchanged. His changeless, beautiful self."

I think I said, after a pause, "You have just conferred another degree upon your father."

The distinctly homemade atmosphere of the new bookshop location helped it to prosper. It was as convenient a place to linger and discuss books as its apple orchard forebear had been. Ruth wrote a glowing announcement, saying that soon we would be having "a party of generous proportions" in our new shop to welcome former and new friends. She combed the Manchester *Journal* and the telephone book for names of Manchester, Dorset, and Arlington arrivals at inns, cottages, and hotels, and sent forth quantities of announcements as well as asking all inns for the favor of their lobby or desk billboards. In Dorset she felt sure of co-operation at the inn, for Olive Harwood, her loving and loyal friend of Burr and Burton days, was in charge of the desk.

Ruth came into the shop with the morning's bookshop mail in her hand a few days later. She retained a long envelope and studied it with puzzled and eager attention. "It can't be! Yet it *must* be," she said. I went over to look at what she was holding. The long, white envelope in her hand was stamped Dorset, Vermont, and addressed to the Johnny Appleseed Bookshop. Along its lower edge was a continuous hand-drawn and hand-painted border. Its color and design were so familiar in style as to be instantly recognizable as the work of no one else in the world except Hendrik Willem van Loon. Inside the envelope was a similarly decorated single sheet of paper. It contained an unsigned question: "When will the Party of Generous Proportions take place?"

Ruth went to the phone and called the Dorset Inn.

"Olive, is Hendrik van Loon in Dorset?"

"Yes," Olive assured her. "He's rented the de Schweinitz cottage on the West Road." Then she laughed. "You should have heard him chuckling over your announcement about the welcoming party you are going to have at the bookshop."

Ruth took an envelope and sheet of bookshop paper and wrote, "The Party of Generous Proportions will take place whenever you arrive." This was done with tongue in cheek. Hendrik van Loon's generous proportions were as well known as his wonderful illustrations. Then she addressed the envelope to him at Dorset.

This led to another illustrated envelope and another question: "How can I come without my kiddy car? It has broken down."

Ruth replied, "I will lend you my scooter."

This back-and-forth fun continued until one day Mr. van Loon did come in, in person, but it was in September, when Ruth had gone to Brattleboro as a member of the Stephen Daye Press. Therefore, it was I who greeted him. He sat down, overflowing an armchair, and prepared to explain his request.

"I've come to see whether you can do a piece of sleuthing for me. Would you have any way of finding out the name of the remainder house to whom Liveright has sold my *R.v.R.—The Life and Times of Rembrandt van Rijn?*"

"I will try to, Mr. van Loon."

"It's outrageous!" he burst forth. "They remaindered it without even consulting me or notifying me. That book means more to me than anything else I have ever written. I feel as though

my grandmother had been thrown to the wolves. They are selling it for $1.48 a copy! It's a beautiful book, a work of art!"

"I know it is," I said in sincere sympathy.

"If you can find out to whom they've sold it—they won't
tell me—I want ten copies. I'll leave the scouting to you."

Following this conversation, Mr. van Loon sent me a letter
confirming our talk. Eventually, I did learn the name of the
remainder firm to whom *R.v.R.* had been sold, and ordered
the ten copies for him, plus one for myself. When he came
to get them, I told him, a little shamefacedly, that I had ordered
one for myself. I wanted to own it and to reread it. Then I made
bold to ask whether he would write his name in it for me. Drawing up to a table and overflowing a chair, he took the book
from my hand. Opening it to the flyleaf, he made a full-page
pen-and-ink drawing for me. It depicts Rembrandt in his final
days of life, in his studio. Having risen from what was his death-
bed, he is seated before his easel, attempting to paint. Recognizable etchings are on the walls. The entire drawing breathes
with actuality and struggling emotion. Under it, Hendrik van
Loon wrote, "Chapter 80—The End." And, at the top of the
page, "For Margaret Hard, from her obedient servant, Hendrik
van Loon."

As September had come, Walter and I were left to handle
the bookshop on a partnership basis of time, convenience, and
companionship that constantly grew in delight and satisfaction.
We waited eagerly for Ruth's letters telling us of her first contacts
with a publishing firm. John Hooper—whose father-in-law, Howard Rice, was editor and owner of the Brattleboro *Reformer,* president of the New England Council, distinguished editorialist, and
Vermont statesman—was editor-in-chief of the Stephen Daye
Press, with his wife, Marion, a devoted second. Ruth soon became a grateful and enthusiastic member of the staff and of the
Hooper and Rice families, who received her into their life with
customary kindness.

Writing of her association with the Stephen Daye Press, in
an editorial in the *Reformer* in 1950, John Hooper says:

Nearly twenty years ago a sprite of a girl came over from Manchester to serve as a Jill-of-all-trades in the new Brattleboro book-publishing firm of Stephen Daye Press. Combining intelligence, humor and a capacity for hard work, Ruth Hard was our original introduction to a writing family that has no peer in Vermont. . . . It was not long before Ruth was writing a book column for the *Reformer* and the *Phoenix* that established such a high standard and was done with so much originality that replacing it is still an unsolved problem in this newspaper.

Ruth, who had married in 1940, continued the column in the *Reformer* until the absorbing life of a mother of four children, two of them twins, ranging in age from one to seven years, made her reluctantly give up the column "until the twins are at least six." When the column again appeared in the *Reformer,* as it still does, John Hooper's announcement of its return was a picture of Ruth working in her garden with the children around her. Underneath, he explained, "These are the four reasons you have had to wait for the return of Ruth Hard Bonner's book column. But now you are to have it again."

In 1933, when Ruth was leaving Manchester to go to the Stephen Daye Press in Brattleboro, Walter, Jr., was leaving for Hanover, New Hampshire, for his freshman year at Dartmouth. Four years later, 1937, when he had graduated, Dean Bill, who was the Dean of Freshman Admissions, sent Walter the letter (required from all high school students applying for college admission, plus results of College Board examinations, et cetera) which Walter, Jr., had written when he made his original application. The required letter was to be written privately and unassisted to Dean Bill, answering the question: What experience or experiences do you feel have contributed especial value to your high school years, to your growth and maturing?

This is not an exact copy of the question, but it is accurate as to the purport of the question.

Walter, Jr., had written:

Dear Dean Bill:
The most valuable experience I have had has been working each summer during my high school years in my father's drugstore.

1. I have learned to be patient and courteous with impatient and dis-
courteous people.

2. I have learned to carry on a pleasant conversation for as much as ten
minutes about practically nothing.

3. I have learned how many times my father has to walk across the
drugstore floor to earn a dollar.

Walter Hard, Jr.

Now as I worked in the bookshop adjoining the drugstore,
I often looked in at my husband and thought how, unknown
to us, our son as well as our daughter had made a summation
of value and devotion concerning their father.

WHEN THEY ARE GROWN

When they are grown, with children of their own,
Will they remember that I once was young—
A girl who laughed and romped with them,
Who swung them high in her rejoicing arms?
Ah no! The motherhood that they recall
Will be an older and a graver thing.
Strange! When each added year my heart will cling
Close to the days which keep them young:
The time I lost him where the grass grew tall;
Her acorn teacups on the pasture wall.

M. H.

Anne Parrish (Mrs. Charles Corliss) was summering at the
Equinox House. She became a daily visitor in the bookshop. At
least once a week, if not oftener, she brought Alexander Woollcott with her. He would come down from his summer home on
Neshobe Island, Lake Bomoseen, and bring friends with him to
call on her. Sooner or later, they all would come into the bookshop.

One day, Harold Ross was with them, and Anne Parrish darted
into the drugstore to get Walter. The little shop seemed jammed
with people at the moment. There was some talk in which I
did not join but afterward I heard Walter say to Mr. Woollcott,
"I wish I could have found the right words to say to Harold

Ross. Words that would have told him how I feel about his editorship of the *New Yorker*."

"You did. You said to him what he would rather have had said than anything I can think of."

"I did?" Walter asked in surprise.

"Yes. You said to him that the *New Yorker* has given New Yorkers the feeling of intimacy and friendliness about their *city* that might belong to people living in the genial intimacy of a small *home town*."

Through this introduction Walter became really known to Alexander Woollcott, and perhaps Mr. Woollcott became as really known to Walter as was possible. He invited him to Neshobe and sent him limited-edition books, and often used his poems on radio programs.

An incident developing from this acquaintance occurred in the summer of 1944. Charles K. Field of the popular daily "Shut-In Program" on radio was known to the entire country as "Cheerio." He was a direct descendant of the famous Field family of Newfane, Vermont, of which Eugene Field had also been a member.

Cheerio, coming east from California, had restored the Field homestead in Newfane and he was now raising funds in Vermont to build a small museum in Newfane. Because he had frequently used Walter's poems on his program, he stopped in Manchester, spent a couple of nights with us, and met Walter, Jr., who was just home from his first college year. Mr. Field made contact with Alexander Woollcott by telephone and was invited to drive up to Neshobe for luncheon. It eventuated in Mr. Field's asking Walter, Jr., if he would drive him up and back in his big, open touring car.

They were gone all day, and we gathered from Mr. Field that he had not found Mr. Woollcott in a responsive mood. The next day, after he had gone on to Middlebury, we had a chance to ask for details from Walter, Jr.

"Mr. Woollcott was in a truculent mood. I was embarrassed for Mr. Field."

"Were you asked to have lunch with them?"

"Oh, yes. He recognized my father's name," said Walter, Jr., with his characteristic little raised-eyebrow smile at his father.

"Was there interesting conversation?"

"No. Mr. Field kept rowing against the tide, poor man."

"Afterward, perhaps?"

"There may have been, but I wasn't around."

"Where were you?"

"Out on the porch with Helen Hayes."

Did Alexander Woollcott have any quality of tenderness? I have often wondered. Perhaps people so gifted with sentimentality, as was he, do not have it. It fell to my lot to see him in two especially cruel verbal encounters. Surely he must at some point have given concrete evidence of tenderness to have held the affection of such women as Alice Duer Miller and Helen Hayes.

This was the summer when Walter, Jr., and I would often take before-breakfast rides, exploring back roads—as Ruth and I once ate before-bookshop breakfasts at the Green Peak Dorset Quarry. Walter, Jr., had an almost uncanny sense of direction and location and took me to the sites of mountain farms so high above the valley, and of such beauty and ancient acreage, that one did not wonder that they were being bought up by people as far west as Minnesota for summer places. In a sense it seemed sad. Yet perhaps these people from the fruitful acres of the West and Midwest carried in their blood an appreciation of what such homestead farms must have been to the families who founded them.

FARM SALE

Ben Gleason's sold the old home-place
His folks have owned a hundred years.
He doesn't care, he never worked
Its stubborn soil with sweat and tears;
And when it bore he never felt
The joy you feel to see a child
That's been a trial to all its kin
Turn steady and quit being wild.

A thousand acres if a rod!
I helped them measure every line
The time Ben's father had the quarrel
About the Black Knoll marking pine.
I've tapped his mountain sugar bush
Each spring when thaw and freeze came round;
For fifty years I've plowed his fields
And laid the harrow to his ground.

I know each sapling in his woods,
Each tree grown big by fifty rings;
For fifty years I've sheared his sheep,
And cleared his upper pasture springs;
And just as many times, come fall,
I've chopped above the Ledge log-slide,
And driven yearling cattle home
From pasture on the mountain-side.

And in the fifty years gone by
I've seen scrub acres grow to pine,
And watched the clearings on the hills
Spread up and reach the timber line;
I've reaped his crops of oats and wheat
On slopes where rock and stone have been;
I've harvested his daily bread,
And watched his children grow to men.

A thousand acres—work and sweat;
A hundred years—an endless round
Of chores and struggle. Lord! it seems
His folks must rise up from the ground.
For Ben has sold the old home-place
Those folks have owned a hundred years;
He doesn't care, he never worked
Its stubborn soil with sweat and tears.

M. H.

(This poem won the award in a state contest, the selection being made by Governor George D. Aiken of Vermont, later United States Senator.)

CHAPTER SIX

1934

SINCLAIR LEWIS came in on a rainy afternoon, when an October downpour of wet leaves made a carpet of brilliant color upon the pavements. I immediately recognized him, and was suddenly moved by his gentleness and almost boyish shyness.

"May I sit down for a while? This is a charmingly different sort of place."

"It's so crudely thrown together," I apologized. "We couldn't make it hold together any other way."

"Um-m, well . . ." He moved from shelf to shelf, tall and stooping. After a bit, he said, smiling, "Anyhow, you've some pretty substantial cement to hold it together—all the Greeks and Plato, Cicero, and a half mile of English classics. How'd you come by this idea-in-a-cubbyhole?"

I moved up a chair and began to tell him the bookshop story. Before too long I was reading aloud to him from *Vermont Salt and Vintage* and *A Mountain Township,* and he was listening intently.

"Edgar Lee Masters," he said, "without the sting and bite, without the knife with the razor edge. What became of it in Vermont?"

"I guess sooner or later it got buried with the hatchet," I replied. "There's something about Vermont that doesn't take to feuding. It's terribly hard to maintain grudges and quarrels where the whole surrounding countryside seems bent on embracing one."

He laughed understandingly and stood up.

"It's stopped raining. I must get on. I won't forget that bit about it being hard to feud and fight and hold grudges in a region where all the surrounding landscape seems anxious to embrace you. It would be interesting to test it out as a geographical, anthropological proposition."

He came over and put his hand on my shoulder.

"This is a terribly nice place," he said, and then added with the same boyish shyness, "and you're a lovely person."

"Perhaps rainy days are especially good for bookshops," I told him. "Shelter from the wet and a chance to browse and meditate." Then I told him about the rainy afternoon when I had found Ray Stannard Baker reading aloud to Ruth before the fire.

"It's a kind of wistfulness rain induces," he said. "Wistfulness and loneliness are first cousins."

I shall always recall Sinclair Lewis as shy and boyish, and for some reason strangely touching. I was glad to feel that perhaps Johnny Appleseed with its "idea-in-a-cubbyhole" had comforted him on a lonely afternoon.

Anne Parrish brought Rachel Field into our bookshop many times. Soon we sensed the peculiarly close bond of friendship between them. I recall the day when Anne Parrish told us that for some time she had been trying to convince Rachel Field that she should write for adults instead of for children. "Not but that your children's books are enchanting; but you're a novelist, Rachel. Why can't I make you believe you're a novelist —that you could write a splendid novel?"

"What proof have you that I could write a novel?"

"None, until you write it." Then she added, "Whenever you tell an episode it is never a *brief incident*. It immediately assumes a present, past, and future framework. It is then that you introduce characters—people—suppositions—concerning them, and bits of important contributing information relative to the whole story. Presently, as you talk, a discernible pattern of events begins to take shape—climaxes and crises appear."

Rachel smiled. "That sounds well, but there has to be more than that. Definite knowledge and study of novel structure, for instance. You've read widely and you have a naturally analytical mind and a keen sense of drama. You know what to leave out, what to include."

Later, when *All This and Heaven Too* was being widely read and discussed, when it was dramatized and filmed, I often thought of that conversation.

There was another interest these friends had shared in mutual, long-time enjoyment. They collected unusual small pieces of doll's furniture from odd places all over the world. One of these pieces, a toy piano found in a New York City secondhand shop, involved a coincidence so remarkable that it certainly deserves mention here. Anne Parrish told it in the presence of Alexander Woollcott. In fact, its telling was the result of a kindred predilection of theirs, a mutual enjoyment of incidents involving extraordinary coincidences.

At Christmastime, Anne's gift to Rachel Field was often some piece of dollhouse furniture found while browsing in secondhand shops here or abroad. One day while so occupied in a New York City shop, she came upon a toy piano tumbled into a basket with other articles. Upon examination it proved to be a music box. She drew it out and set it upon a table. The shopkeeper knew her of old and she was free to browse at will.

As she turned it over she found the key which wound it. Lifting its cover, she discovered a long mirror set into the dark wood. It was framed by robin's-egg-blue plush, tightly glued down with matching gimp. It was exactly the gift she wanted for Rachel. She left the shop with the toy piano tucked under her arm.

It was at about this period that the attention of the English and American public was suddenly drawn to the novels of Mary Webb through the enthusiasm of Stanley Baldwin, who had recently discovered *Precious Bane* and who felt that the work of this woman, who wrote so exquisitely and who had died so young, had never been properly recognized. Presently Mary Webb's name and her novels became known everywhere through Baldwin's articles in the British press and elsewhere, by their republication, and by articles in American periodicals.

Not too long afterward, Mary Webb's husband wrote a charming and illuminating article about her childhood and womanhood, which was published in the *Atlantic Monthly*. Reading it avidly, Anne Parrish came upon a childhood incident that Mary Webb had related to her husband and that made Anne catch her breath.

It was the story of a child's heartbreak over the loss of a cherished possession, a toy piano. She had explained to her husband that she had never ceased to mourn for it. It had disappeared during some removal from their home to a different location. Its loss seemed insurmountable to her. The beloved piano had, in fact, been a music box that played two or three little tunes. Mary's delight was to set it far back on the nursery mantel and lift its cover so that the entire length of a mirror, set into a robin's-egg-blue plush backing, was visible. She would wind the key, and, stepping way back across the room from the fireplace, she would watch her feet reflected in the mirror as she took dancing steps accompanied by the music.

Realizing that such music-box toy pianos were undoubtedly typical of a certain period, Anne Parrish nevertheless wrote to Mary Webb's husband in care of the *Atlantic Monthly*. She asked him whether there was the slightest chance of his knowing of any way in which the music-box piano could be identified as having belonged to his wife, wild as the probability seemed.

He replied that there was. Mary Webb had told him that once in an intense moment of ownership she had lifted a corner of the blue plush and scratched her initials on the wood beneath with a pin. Carefully applying the brush from the nursery glue bottle, she had stuck the plush down again.

By this time, the music-box piano was in Rachel Field's possession. Of course Anne Parrish had acquainted her with all the above coincidences and had told her of her letter of inquiry sent to Mr. "Webb." It seemed an impossible climax when Rachel Field loosened the blue plush backing at one corner of the mirror and found Mary Webb's childhood initials beneath it, but both she and Anne Parrish vouched for its veracity.

As for Alexander Woollcott, who was well attuned to coincidences, he did not even turn a hair.

There was another tale of the lost being found which Anne Parrish told, though it was less dramatic than the one concerning the music box. She said that as a little girl she had an especially beloved fairy-tale book with a yellow linen cover. At some moment of childhood it had been lost. Endless, hopeful search was unavailing. It never turned up. And, as is the case in so many similar situations, the more fruitless the search the greater became her longing for the book and the more vivid her remembrance of its attractions.

Years later, when she was in Paris, she was wandering past the bookstalls on the edge of the Seine, stopping here and there to turn over a book and study its title page. Suddenly her attention was caught by a large flat book with a yellow cover. She pulled it out. Its title was that of the long-lost fairy-tale book. She opened its cover, and there in childish scrawl was her own name.

I have never had one of these delightful, unbelievable experiences with books. Perhaps the nearest thing to it was one that befell my husband at the time he was writing *The Connecticut* for the Rivers of America series.

One of the intensely interesting stories connected with *The Connecticut* was that of the famous Smith sisters of Glastonbury, Connecticut. Their initial claim to public attention was their refusal to pay taxes unless possessed of the right to vote. They owned large and valuable holdings of property. When these were seized because of their refusal to pay taxes, no lawyer could be found to represent them in court. So they began to verse themselves in legal procedure and defended their own case in court. Of course, they lost, but their case became a celebrated issue all over the country.

They were women of rare erudition, and Julia Smith became at this time highly incensed at the way woman's position was interpreted in the Bible. Perhaps the strictures of St. Paul concerning women, as she had read them in various translations, had also been used by opposing society to lay her low and to defy her feminist viewpoint. At all events, she decided to make her own translation of the Bible. Already versed in Greek and Latin,

she began to study Hebrew, and when she was thoroughly prepared she set to work. She made what she considered a correct
and authentic translation of her own, and published it—Julia
Smith's *The Holy Bible, containing the Old and New Testa-
ments translated literally from the original tongues* (Hartford,
Conn.: American Publishing Company, 1876).

After studying all the material he could find concerning the
Smith sisters, my husband yearned to possess a copy of Julia
Smith's Bible. Through the services of the Connecticut Anti-
quarian Society he had at least seen one. One day, late in the
summer season of our own bookshop, he read in the Rutland
Herald of an auction being held somewhere in the region of
Poultney. He dearly loved auctions, and this offered a legitimate
occasion for an afternoon's holiday. Generally an auction produced some old books from which at least a few worth reselling
could be garnered.

I took over the shop, and Walter set out for Poultney. Late in
the afternoon he returned. He lifted a wooden starch box from
the car. It held perhaps a half-dozen books. On the top lay
Julia Smith's Bible.

My other coincidental experience relates to a painting which
we eventually sold from the walls of our bookshop during the
winter of 1934.

Cecil V. Grant, a New York City stockbroker by profession
and a landscape painter by avocation who had studied in Paris
as a young man, appeared more or less permanently in our
midst following the stock market crash of '29. He and his wife
and daughter had bought as a whim a few summers previously
a charming little house near the town line between Peru and
Londonderry. It was directly on Route 11 and commanded beautiful views of surrounding landscape, mountains and valleys and
great stretches of sky. In the winter, Mrs. Grant and her daughter
remained with relatives in New York and Mr. Grant returned
to what was in actuality his hide-out studio. There he painted.

One day he came into the bookshop when I was alone and
asked me whether we would consider letting him hang two or
three of his paintings in our shop for sale. "There's no market

for them in Peru or Londonderry. And I'm hungry. Dode Wilder
lets me ride down in the stage with him. Do you think Mr.
Hard would let me have a glass of milk at the fountain? I
can't pay for it yet—not until I sell a picture."

Horrified, I sent him in to Walter and with surprised delight
hung the three pictures he carried in. They were all landscapes and they captured the features of Vermont mountain winter—laden trees bending beneath deep snowfall, sunrise over
night-fallen snow, and one of falling snow through which one
gazed and gazed, discerning outlines of farm buildings almost
obliterated in drifting storm.

He had marked absurdly low prices on them. As he went
out to catch Dode Wilder's stage, I prayed that Walter had
managed to slip chocolate bars into his coat pocket, and my
heart ached for him.

The following day, a woman from Arlington came in and
fell in love with the canvas of the drifting snowstorm.

"I'll take it," she said. "I love it. Just put it on my account
and I'll come back for it."

It was marked $60. I could hardly wait to get to the phone
to call Dode Wilder. "Tell Cecil I've sold one of his pictures—
the one of the snowstorm."

Next morning the telephone rang early. It was Mrs. H. from
Arlington. "I've been thinking the matter over and I won't take
that picture after all. It was just a whim. I've more paintings
now than I know what to do with."

I stood in stunned silence. Sick and aghast, I hung up the
phone. I went in to Walter in the drugstore.

"What can I do? I know he'll be coming down with Dode
Wilder to get the money first thing this morning. Oh, Walter,
what can I do?"

He turned, and opening the safe he took out six ten-dollar
bills and slipped them in an envelope and wrote Cecil's name
upon it. Then he handed it to me and said, "It seems to me,
Mrs. Hard, that I once fell in love with you in the midst of
a snowstorm." He then added, "We can now have a really fine
picture of Cecil's."

After this we had quite a run on Cecil's paintings and he began really to establish himself. Summer after summer he displayed his paintings, large and small, on the village green across from the Equinox House, and all day long cars slowed up to view them, and presently people got out to look at them, to buy them, to have them shipped all over the United States.

The Southern Vermont Artists did not take kindly to him. They not only felt he was not a skilled painter but that he painted too many pictures too hurriedly. They were, they felt, "potboilers." But Cecil had to make the pot boil, and despite snubs and cold-shouldering by fellow-successful-artists, he stuck fast to his course. The pictures grew better. He began to sell at his house and built an adjoining studio. Mrs. Grant, his devoted companion in all this effort, came and contrived to make a charming home for him, so life began to take shape steadily. He was self-respecting and independent, and, the S.V.A. notwithstanding, he somehow painted Vermont as the Vermont traveling public saw it and loved it. I often think of the many Wall Street offices and Lake Shore drawing rooms where his landscapes hang, bringing constant comment and comfort.

As to our own painting of the falling snowstorm, it produced a personal coincidence I feel deserves a place here. Oddly enough, the picture as it has hung in our living room for over thirty-two years has elicited more voluntary commendatory praise from S.V.A. artists and art critics than any other painting we possess.

During the winter of 1942, when Walter, Sr., was in the Vermont Legislature, Walter, Jr., was in the service, Ruth was married, and I was running the bookshop alone in Manchester, struggling with fuel shortages, food rationing, and gas rationing as well, the Grants were loyal and constant callers. I suggested one night that they come out and have supper with me. We all needed company and relief from constant war talk. As we sat in the study after dinner, I asked Mr. Grant whether he had always lived in New York City.

"Oh, no. My family was from Philadelphia. We eventually lived outside the city at Torresdale, of which I'm sure you've never heard."

But I told him that I had. My father and his brother had been manufacturers of fine woolens. They owned mills in Bristol, Pennsylvania, just below Trenton and beyond Torresdale. The town was divided by a canal. The mills were on the railroad and business side of the town, and the residential section was beyond the canal running parallel with the Delaware River. The lawns and gardens of the houses ran down to the water's edge. Our family owned one of these houses, and there was always one of the brothers in residence. During the years when I was probably from six to ten or eleven, it was my father who lived in Bristol and oversaw the running of the mills. One or another of his brothers would come out for a day during the week to talk over mill affairs and have lunch with us. My own brother went to the Delancey School in Philadelphia, and soon, under his care, I was being delivered at the door of Miss Hallowell's School for little girls on Pine Street where he called for me in the early afternoon. Thus we rode to and from Philadelphia by train and daily we passed Torresdale.

"What was the name of your family?" Mr. Grant asked. "What was the business name of the mills?"

"The firm was under the name of one of the older brothers —Edward T. Steel and Company."

Mr. Grant was silent for a moment, and then he repeated, "Edward T. Steel. Do you mean that Edward T. Steel was your uncle?"

"Yes, I do."

"Do you know whether, after having been a widower for several years, he married a second time?"

"Certainly," I replied, a little puzzled. "His first wife was Anna Justice. He had two daughters just reaching young womanhood when he married again."

"Do you recall his second wife?"

"I was a very little girl—I couldn't have been much more than ten when she died. But I do remember her for a very special reason."

"What was her name?"

"Eda. My Aunt Eda."

"What had been her maiden name? Do you know that?"

I looked at him in surprise—startled. "Why, yes—Grant. Eda Grant."

"Eda Grant was my father's sister, my aunt. Your Uncle Edward Steel was my uncle through marriage."

We discovered that we had both spent days at "Woodside," Uncle Edward's home on Queen's Lane in Germantown. Both of us had been enchanted by the wild flowers growing along the edge of the Wissahickon Creek that flowed, hardly wider than a brook, through the grounds of Woodside.

"What was it that you especially remember about my aunt?" Cecil asked.

"That she was like a piece of exquisite Dresden china. She was slight, but she had great dignity and beauty of carriage. I can't remember ever seeing her dressed in anything but white. It was a whim of Uncle Edward's. In winter she wore white broadcloth and white furs. There was a long drawing room connecting a conservatory and a smaller morning room. The drawing room was furnished with Louis XIV furniture, gold-leaf frames upholstered with white satin, and there were some very beautiful French mirrors and chandeliers. An enormous white rug covered a portion of a highly polished parquet floor. Aunt Eda would stand at the center of that white rug, receiving guests. With her intensely blue eyes, golden hair, and high color, she was like a jewel enhanced by the white velvet cushioning of a Tiffany jewel box. Uncle Edward was immensely proud of her— But you, too, must recall all of this."

"I was most impressed by your uncle. I wasn't really afraid of him, but I was never at ease as a small boy."

"I'm not surprised. Yet he was possessed of kindness along with his unbending social and ethical code."

"I could never make him fit the Quaker mold, somehow," Cecil mused.

"I think that as years passed he may have found it hard to do so himself," I said, and I told Cecil about one terribly disturbing remembrance of overhearing something he said to my father in a tone so bitter that it not only puzzled me profoundly but haunted my image of him ever after.

It was during the period of what was known as "the Cleveland

Hard Times." We were living in Bristol and my father was in the midst of all the labor difficulties at the mills. It was a winter also of a typhoid epidemic in "Mill Town." Poverty, sickness, and inadequate housing were themes of which my father talked constantly, and over which he and his brothers did not always agree.

Finally, the mill workers struck, leaving unfinished web on the looms. It got abroad that the mill owners were threatening to import cheap immigrant labor. A few nights afterward, the mills were fired. The actual fire was put out, but its cause still burned.

Uncle Edward and Uncle William arrived from Philadelphia, and there was a long conference in the library following luncheon. Properly, Mother went upstairs, and I, who never had much appetite when tension was in the air, was left to myself in the dining room to finish my meal. I could clearly hear the voices in the adjoining room. Father talked in a low, troubled voice, and I imagine his brothers followed his statements with skepticism and distaste.

"Business is business. Doesn't thee know that?" said Uncle William. "We came near losing the entire output of web; the whole place would have gone up in flames except for Packer. He's a good fellow."

"The men hate him."

"Of course they do. He's on the watch."

"He's a weasel," answered my father.

Uncle William sniffed. "Weasels have their uses."

"We've been making these men walk through hell," insisted my father, "—bitter cold, sickness, poverty—"

It was then that Uncle Edward's puzzling, devastating words were addressed to my father. "Charlie, thee disgusts me! I declare! I sometimes think thee's only fit for the Kingdom of Heaven!"

Cecil moved in his chair and looked into the study fireplace where warmth glowed from a great apple-tree chunk.

"Very typical business attitude," he remarked, "in the early 1890's, as well as today."

As I recall the strange and puzzling words of my uncle which I quoted to Cecil Grant, I am troubled again. Not because their meaning is any longer obscure to me, but because I have given a picture of a side of my uncle's nature that is exact yet not entirely fair to him. He also was a loving and loyal man, to his family and to me, his little niece, in particular. It was entirely within the picture that he should be irritated beyond endurance by my father's ideas concerning social justice ("Thee reads too much of that man Ruskin!"). Perhaps he was even more aroused by my father's notable lack of shrewdness. To lack that quality, especially in business matters, was to be devoid of a cardinal quality necessary to success.

Uncle Edward always lifted me to his lap when he came to the house, and I felt the soft brush of his heavy, square-cut whiskers against my face, the good smell of bay rum, fine woolens, and immaculate linen. Invariably he brought me a book, English imprints, many of them—my first copy of Hans Christian Andersen with colored illustrations, Longfellow's poems with an appealing frontispiece of "The Children's Hour," and *Alice's Adventures in Wonderland* and *Through the Looking-Glass.*

When he would return from his many trips abroad, there were gifts for us all: a wax doll with a complete Parisian wardrobe for me; an exquisite copy of *Scottish Chiefs* for my brother, who was his namesake; several volumes of Pierre Loti for my father, who had long since exhausted the Philadelphia Mercantile Library of every volume of Loti on its shelves; and for his sisters-in-law and young lady nieces, a half-dozen pairs each of white kid gloves. I still recall my pretty mother's distressed expostulation in the midst of her gratitude.

"Oh, Edward, such beautiful gloves! But these are all size 5½ and I wear a 6!"

Uncle Edward raised his heavy eyebrows in cold disapproval. "No *lady*, Emma, wears a glove larger than size 5½!"

There it was again: that other side. It went with his question to a gay young niece, possessed of "unladylike" exuberance and activity, who was visiting us.

"How does it happen thee is downstairs so early for breakfast, Laura?"

"Oh, it's such a lovely day, Uncle Edward, I just dashed through my dressing."

There was a moment of unsmiling silence, then, "No *lady*, Laura, can bathe properly and dress in less than two hours."

The memory of those treasured books of my childhood makes me conscious of one of the most delightful aspects of bookshop routine—the ordering of children's books, an entire field in itself.

When Bob White of Harper, William Lane from Oxford University Press, and Walter Walsh of Harcourt visited us, I would feel as though through some magic spell of theirs I had been given back years of childhood. Especially was this true when I would discover that at last there was a reprint of some beloved book I had not seen for years. Walter Crane's *Baby's Opera, St. Nicholas Songs,* Laura Richards' *In My Nursery* and *Captain January.*

The appearance of harassed parents and unco-operative youngsters following in their wake always made me have a sinking feeling at the pit of my stomach, as did Book Week, when mothers came loaded down with marked copies of the current newspapers or periodicals that carried the endless lists of new books advertised for children of all ages.

Having labored to have a truly representative and catholic collection of books, displayed as enticingly and intelligently as possible, I found it maddening when obdurate young mothers or grandmothers insisted upon some book a friend out in Wichita, Kansas, or in Dallas, Texas, had written them about as "simply marvelous." Their complete refusal even to look at the beautiful selection of books surrounding them only compounded our frustration.

During one such period, a delightful episode occurred which served to lighten Children's Book-List Gloom every time we thought of it.

On a morning of summer downpour, a charming grandmother arrived in the bookshop with her two grandsons, probably aged eight and eleven. She carried a book list of selective summer reading for the younger grandson.

"Here, George, is listed a children's story about the life of George Washington. We might read that on this rainy day. Do you have it, Mrs. Hard?"

I examined the list and found that that particular story of George Washington was one we did not have, although we had two or three others from various houses.

"Oh, I'm sure that won't make any difference," the lady said, comfortingly, "we'll just take one of the others."

I spoke reluctantly. "I'm afraid that it might make a difference, Mrs. Mayfield. You see, when the children return to school and are asked to give oral reports on the book, it might induce considerable confusion and contradiction of incidents if they had not all read the same book about Washington."

Mrs. Mayfield looked dashed. The rain was coming down in a deluge outside and she was anxious to arrange a quiet, constructive afternoon at home for George.

"I'll tell you what we'll do," she said. "We'll take the one Mrs. Hard has, and then, later on, when we're in the city, we'll get the other one and read it, too."

Before George could fully grasp the situation, his older brother broke in, grasping him firmly by the arm. "No, George. No!" he counseled, loudly and emphatically. "I wouldn't advise you to do any unnecessary reading."

CHAPTER SEVEN

Emancipation—1935

Walter and I always thought of the year 1935 as his Emancipation Year. More and more the necessary division of his time between the drugstore business and his growing occupation as a writer became a personal problem. The point of saturation was reached when he began to receive so many requests to read at colleges and various societies and literary organizations, as well as to consider commissions for books from publishers, that he must either decline or slight the drugstore. His own inclination pointed in but one direction, and the urging of his family to follow it was fervent. Both Ruth and Walter, Jr., declared they were now able to stand on their own feet. Ruth was through college and on the staff of the Stephen Daye Press. Walter, Jr., had two more years at Dartmouth, but he had already achieved an earning capacity for himself. As for myself, I felt that the time for Walter to follow his true calling had come, and I felt that the bookshop, along with his writing, could become a secure backlog.

"Let's kick the ladder out," I said, "and climb under our own power."

"They're crazy," said some of the villagers. "Selling that wonderful business! Taking it right out from under that son of theirs. He'd have had a business right there waiting for him."

Precisely, that was one of the things we wanted to save him from.

"It's *her*," another contingent elucidated. "She thinks Walter's a writer! What kind of a business is *writing?* What's a *bookshop?*"

But Dorothy Canfield burst forth into song. She drove up the valley from Arlington and came into the bookshop, her face beaming with pleasure and enthusiasm.

After a few months we did complete the sale of the drugstore. We sold to Stanley Worden of Springfield, Vermont. When we drove over to Hanover to pick up Walter, Jr., and his belongings in June, at the close of his sophomore year, we carried him the deed of sale.

"It never worried me for myself," he said. "I knew you wouldn't saddle me with it. It was for Dad that I couldn't wait to see it sold."

Sally Ball, who managed the Modern Library Book Wagon business for Random House, learned the news with pleasure. She drove up to the shop with Fritz, her beautiful police dog companion, sitting close beside her. Fritz was our dear friend as well as Sally. Long ago we had persuaded her to come out with us to have supper and spend the night here in Manchester. Fritz knew that he might sleep on the floor close to the old four-poster bed where she would sleep.

We were accepted as reliable friends of Sally's. That night there was high talk of Walter's new emancipation. Bennett Cerf sent a telegram saying "Whoops!" and Alfred Harcourt's said "Wonderful news!"

This was the same week in which we had the rare experience of making the acquaintance of Lauren Ford. She came into the shop and introduced herself, saying that she felt we were exactly the people with whom she wished to discuss a plan for a book she was going to illustrate.

As she unfolded her idea it proved to concern her beautiful and original conception of illustrating the story of the Nativity with background scenes from New England rather than the customary ones from the Near and the Middle East. She felt that for children of our own country the familiar and realistic New

England setting would induce a feeling of special love and reality.

"Would it seem strange or shocking to you, Mrs. Hard," she asked, turning to me, "to see the Star of the East resting above a New England barn from whose open door the radiance of the Nativity streamed? To see Mary as a simple and lovely farm-bred girl in a New England setting and Joseph as her husband clothed as a young New England farmer? How would you feel about the starlit, snowy landscape? About having the Angels of the Heavenly Host grouped at the corner of a New England farmhouse? Would it shock you to see Christmas and the birth of Christ depicted as part of New England?"

"That is as we think of it every Christmas night, Miss Ford."

She came close to me and touched me gently with her hand.

"I have come to the right people," she said happily. "Yes, I've been led to the right people."

It is not surprising that we felt a special, almost proprietary, joy when her first book of Gregorian chants for children appeared thus illustrated.

She always remained our friend and every year she would stop to see us late in the fall on her way north to Stowe where she was taking a little black lamb from her "sheepfold" in Bethlehem, Connecticut, to Madam Trapp. Frequently, she would stop in Manchester for the night, and we had opportunities to see many examples of new paintings and drawings she was executing, always overlaid with reverence and wonder, always dedicated to the Nativity.

There is another incident connected with one of Lauren Ford's books that belongs to our bookshop's story. *The Little Book About God*, which was her first book for little children as far as I know, was our original introduction to her endearing art and her enchanting manner of depicting God's love for little folks. The book lay in its anthropomorphic innocence upon the low table inside the children's corner. I was entirely unaware of committing any error in regard to childhood's approach to an understanding of God; but one day Mrs. Loveland Munson, a remarkable woman whom I and the entire surrounding community respected and considered to be nothing short of Manchester's arbiter of moral and religious truth, entered the Shop. She told me she had come to protest the presence of a book we were displaying. Astonished, I tried to imagine what book she could mean. My mind flew to *Lady Chatterley's Lover* (the Raised-Eyebrows-Department book of the moment) but we had never even seen a copy of *Lady Chatterley's Lover,* let alone carried one.

I could hardly believe my eyes when she walked over to the children's corner and laid her hand firmly on *The Little Book About God*.

"Margaret, I highly disapprove of this book. It is anthropomorphic. It is filled with pictures personifying God. This is what we are trying to discourage, depicting God as a *person*. God is a spirit, not a person." She flipped the pages in annoyance. "Look at Him with a beard! Leaning out of heaven and watching what's going on on the earth!" (Privately, I thought He looked rather like a loving, anxious grandfather.) "And who is that person rocking that little girl to sleep and holding her mug of milk?"

"Gabriel," I said in a muffled voice.

"Well! I protest!" Mrs. Munson declared unsmilingly. Then she walked disgustedly from the shop.

It was the next day that a small and lovely customer about four years old came to the shop with her mother. Lydia Jane Bartlett was immediately seated in one of the little chairs in the children's corner; and drawing up to the table, she discovered *The Little Book About God*. Somehow, she at once absorbed some loving, comforting, and deeply personal message from the pages before her. When her mother tried to disengage her from the book her grief was so obvious that it was quickly arranged that she and the book should go home together.

The sequel to this story did not occur until the following Monday. That was the day when the famous Monday Club of Manchester was meeting at Mrs. Cunningham's.

The Monday Club was a long-established organization of women, varying in age from young mothers to grandmothers.

They met to read aloud from books that embraced a well-planned program, each book dealing with one general topic, chosen for the year. The Monday Clubbers took themselves very seriously.

It was because of this serious attitude, perhaps, that a custom was adopted to break the dignity of the afternoon's studious reading, just before the hostess of the day invited the club members to gather for supper in her dining room. Appropriately, this easeful break from seriousness to pleasant intercourse was known as "the Merry-Go-Round." Each person, in turn, told some amusing personal incident or story.

When it became Mrs. Bartlett's turn on the Merry-Go-Round, she told about Lydia Jane's sudden enchantment with the Johnny Appleseed Bookshop, and all about *The Little Book About God.* At some length she described its appeal to Lydia Jane, and how each night she went to bed with it beside her pillow.

I did not dare to look at Mrs. Munson, and was greatly relieved when we were invited to go in to supper. But somehow I found myself with Mrs. Munson close beside me as we entered the adjoining room. She drew me aside for a moment, and laying her hand on my shoulder she looked at me smilingly and said, "Well, Margaret, I think that perhaps Lydia Jane understands more about God than I do."

I frequently realize how amusing the Monday Club would have seemed to Sinclair Lewis. It would have furnished copy for his pen, a kind of understudy to the Thanatopsis Club of *Main Street.*

The readings were meted out to the various members with careful attention to convenience of date. All such matters were relative to the housecleaning, baby-teething, getting-the-stovepipe-up-or-down schedule of the year. The slight chill produced by Marcus Aurelius' lofty *Meditations* was pleasantly dispelled by proximity to Mrs. Mary Robbins' chunk stove. There was a certain ironic delight in hearing the opening pages of Gladstone's biography interrupted by Mrs. Storrs' whispered query of Mrs. Bartlett, "Did your baby eat strained spinach at six months?" and Mrs. Perkins' audible assertion to someone that "If she'd cut it on the bias, it wouldn't have puckered."

It is true that the elopement of Dr. Sharp's daughter with a young man who clerked at Bond's, and the sudden and unexplained return of Sandy Clark from college, were discussed with an appalling lack of discretion. While supper was being served, Mrs. Wyman could—and did—give exact data to prove that our village was afflicted with more juvenile delinquency than any other town of its size in Vermont! While the two women in the Club who regularly employed "help" were discussing their troubles with "maids," Mrs. Judson was making it clear that despite all that might be said in favor of Mr. and Mrs. Morse, newcomers to the village, *her* commendation of them was qualified. She could not ascertain that they were affiliated with any one of the five churches in the community.

All of these elements, so familiar to Mr. Lewis and the Thanatopsis Club of *Main Street,* were present in the Monday Club of Manchester. Gossip and scandal could be heard there, it is true. But in what gathering are they not occasionally to be found? I've yet to hear of one, from the day nursery to the Episcopal synod. These are common failings of humanity.

But side by side with us all sat Miss Hermie Canfield. Her keen eyes and calm brow had been known to the village for well over half a century, ever since the days when she was a little girl in a linsey-woolsey dress and knitted hood, trudging down the turnpike that led past her home. Nothing mean or deceptive rested comfortably in her presence. On town-meeting day I have seen a rough and noisy crowd turn silent and respectful as she rose to challenge some statement or frame some motion.

One winter day, when the snow was drifted so deep that I couldn't reach the road except on snowshoes, I resorted to the telephone for conversation with her. "You just caught me in time!" she said. "I'm going up to the Goyettes'. Minnie's been taken to the hospital and there're three children up there all down with measles. All morning I've been wondering what woman I could get hold of to go up there and help out. Suddenly I said to myself, 'Why, Hermie Canfield, *you're* a woman. Why don't you go yourself?' "

Through January and February, our months of hardest weather, she stayed with the Goyette family, cooking and nursing and settling the disordered rooms. I remember a day in summer when Walter brought news of tragedy in the North Village. Jim Blunt's eldest girl had been discovered dead in Lampson's woods. Her cheap silk blouse was drenched with blood. The more restrained inhabitants of the town stayed away from the scene of suicide, but others found reasons which led them to the grove near the North Village, and, ultimately, to the Blunts' house. The girl's mother, hysterical and incoherent, sat rocking in a broken chair. Her younger children crowded soberly about her as she wept and talked to anyone who stopped at the door.

That night Walter told me that when he'd driven out to take evidence with the state's attorney, he had found Miss Hermie there. She had walked in and taken charge of the situation. She had quieted the mother, dismissed the bystanders, and sent the children down to the brook to play. From that hour until the funeral was over, the house remained a quiet and orderly place. Decency and privacy, which should pervade any place of mourning, were bestowed on this one by the presence of Miss Hermie.

And yet, it wasn't Miss Hermie's most stalwart qualities which most impressed me. It was her unsuspected tenderness. One glowing autumn day, when I saw her for the first time after several weeks, I was convinced that she was concealing some secret trouble. The fire and fun had gone out of her talk and her expression seemed changed, somehow. Taking my way to her house one bleak afternoon, I lingered until the dusk crept down Skinner Hollow across the farm. There, by the dying fire in the low-ceilinged room, Miss Hermie finally told me.

"Ever since I was a growing girl I've had someone to look after. First, my small brothers; then, when Arthur went to college, I came home from the university. Arthur needed it more than I. Besides, Nat had been gored by a bull. We thought he'd never live. Then Mother and Father took sick and I nursed them for years. When they died, I took Bessie's little girl. Now, after nearly twenty years, she's grown up and gone to a home of her own. It's natural and right, but I feel utterly useless! I'm only seventy, and here I am, without a single responsibility but Nat. It's more than I can stand!" For the first time I saw tears in Miss Hermie's eyes.

A month later, she came to the house to bring me one of her cranberry pies. At once I was conscious of a change in her. Drawing a chair up to the fire, she settled herself with contentment. After a moment of random talk she said, "Well, Margaret, I've really come to tell you something. I've taken a little boy to bring up! He's ten and motherless. I fancy he won't leave me much time for morbid introspection. Of course, I know there are risks in doing it at my age; but then, it's risky to be an idle, discontented old woman! A lot of people will think I'm a fool, but that doesn't trouble me at all."

A couple of weeks later I started out to Miss Hermie's. A slight thaw followed by freezing wind had made an ideal crust upon the snow and I fairly flew across the meadows. Arriving at the house, I loosened the thongs of my snowshoes and, slipping out of them, I tiptoed toward the door. It would be fun to surprise Miss Hermie. It was I, however, for whom a surprise was waiting. As I passed the sitting-room windows, the dancing light on the hearth within was reflected upon the panes. I stopped, unseen, and looked into the room. Miss Hermie sat in a rocking chair by the fire, and a small boy sat on a hassock at her feet. He was whittling pine shavings into the glowing fire and pausing from time to time to stroke the dog that lay beside him. Miss Hermie was reading aloud from a book spread comfortably upon her knees.

I opened the door so quietly that they did not hear me. As I heard the words Miss Hermie was reading I smiled to think how one small, shipwrecked mariner lay in a safe haven, listening to the immortal adventures of another, older one! The book was *Robinson Crusoe*.

It was not merely the presence of Miss Hermie in the Monday Club which made it an indispensable institution. Something intangible and satisfying was contributed by its unique membership—grandmothers, widows, spinsters, those whose sons and daughters were growing out of childhood, and those whose children were still in infancy. What a wealth of human experience!

Yes, the Monday Club was a reading group. Sometimes its programs seemed incongruous and absurd, sometimes its tone descended to petty gossip, but always there was a book being read. It was a book not listed on the program; but, nevertheless, to the attentive heart it conveyed its message.

When we looked out from the bookshop on the first day of Walter's emancipation from the drugstore, we could see that color already was touching some of the trees along Equinox. Now we were having the "frost-clear, apple-ripening days" of which Sarah Cleghorn wrote, and soon the mountains would "blaze in the windless autumn."

"Imagine!" Walter said, turning to me. "We might really celebrate this afternoon by taking time off."

"This afternoon?" I asked.

"Well, all day if you like. We'll lock the door and put out a sign: 'Closed for Emancipation Day.' "

So along toward noon we took the car and climbed the Green Mountains until we reached Chester Village on Route 11. We drew up before the inn and sat in the golden, leaf-flecked silence.

"Where now?" Walter asked.

"Do you remember that old road that climbs up above the town? Where the old stage route once ran? We explored it once and I've never forgotten a phrase you used. You said it had been a *proud* hill road."

A ROAD IN CHESTER

That hill road had been a proud road.
It had gone straight up to get away from the village quickly.
It hadn't made any devious easy turnings
To get to the higher ground.
It stopped just once so you could look back at what you'd done
And get your breath to finish what you'd started.

Having got the hard part over all at once
It took its way more leisurely along the ridge.
Almost level as Vermont roads go,
It kept to the foothills
Which brace the mountains against the sky.
Then it was a cross-state road.
On it rocking stagecoaches used to go
With an extra team to get them past that first hard grade.

Now its days are over.
The village grew up in the valley
And the road followed the winding stream.
Grass grew between the ruts of the hill road.
A few old settlers who'd worked the road when they were young
Made them keep it open.
Then their sons made roads straight down from their farms
Sooner to meet the valley road that went to town.
Now, still a proud road, it climbs the hill
With enough houses near the village to keep it.
Beyond the last house it fades into the woods.
Bush-grown cellar holes and dying apple trees
Pay no taxes to keep up a road.
You can follow it now on foot perhaps
But at times you'll have to look toward the sky
To be sure you're on it.
Even the stone walls which marked the farms
Have been taken by the encroaching forest.
Here and there you'll find signs of a clearing
Where a few gray-barked patriarchal maples
Remember where the farmhouse stood.
If you look carefully you may find the two tracks
Where the iron-shod wheels packed the rocks and soil
Too hard even for seedlings to find a root-hold.
It takes years on years of rotting leaves
To wipe out a proud hill road.

W. H.

As we dipped down toward our home-valley, the chill of
autumn evening was creeping up along the edge of the mountains.
    "We'll have an open fire tonight," Walter said.

"Yes, this is the time and season I most love," I answered, "the sudden realization of oncoming winter—not for a couple of months, but soon. It is the time when our own four walls draw close to receive us, to close around us again. Such chill September nights always mean our own roof tree to me, our own fireside, and you."

THE HOUSE SPEAKS

You who have wandered far upon the hills
And drunk the mellow wine of frost-blue days,
The while you went two joyous vagabonds,
Two roaming gipsies of autumnal ways;

With the first sadness of November rain,
You will come home to me again . . . again.

You who so gaily laughed four walls to scorn,
And asked no other shelter than the sky,
Returning down some wind-blown, leaf-strewn lane,
Will shout to see your hearth-smoke rising high.

With the first sadness of November rain,
You will come home to me again . . . again.

I will have birch flames leaping in the gloom,
Touching the books and pictures with soft light,
Oh, come inside the dusk-filled, firelit room,
And shut the door upon encroaching night.

With the first sadness of November rain,
You will come home to me again . . . again.

M. H.

CHAPTER EIGHT

The Emancipation Party

*I*T WAS Dorothy Canfield's idea. It was the magnetism and enthusiasm with which she launched any of her plans that made Manchester, Dorset, and Arlington people combine in a neighborly, affectionate demonstration of good will and pleasure that is still remembered by many people as Walter Hard's Emancipation Party.

The Manchester *Journal* of November 28, 1935, carried a boxed announcement of the forthcoming event.

HEAR YE!   HEAR YE!!   HEAR YE!!!

AN EMANCIPATION CELEBRATION
in honor of Walter Hard
Tuesday Night, December 3rd
at 8 o'clock
Burr and Burton Gymnasium

Come One, Come All—Cheerful Countenances and
Brotherly Love the only requirements for
Admission for the evening.

GRAND ARRAY OF TALENT

The Dorset Players will present a play by Walter Hard,
The Manchester Band will play, as only this band can play.
Dorothy Canfield Fisher, Judge Edward Griffith and
Sarah N. Cleghorn will speak.
Interesting Letters to the Bard of Vermont
from some of the World's Notables
will be read by E. H. Goodman.

There was no formality. The Burr and Burton gymnasium was crowded. Dorothy gave the welcome. Dr. Goodman read an amazing group of messages, letters, and telegrams, all from people associated with Walter's life from high school and college years to the year of 1935: childhood playmates, high school teachers, college professors, newspaper editors, columnists, publishers, writers, artists, state and national legislators, clergy, headmasters, college presidents, businessmen, and his own people in Vermont.

Sarah Cleghorn reminisced about her childhood days with Walter when they both lived on Pill Alley. The Manchester Band saluted him and the Dorset Players presented his one-act play, *The Scarecrow*.

The Manchester *Journal* for December 12th has a long column headed "Walter Hard Is Duly Emancipated." Judge Edward Griffith, the Probate Judge of Manchester at the time, had written what purported to be an official proclamation of Walter's "emancipation." Clever and amusing, the tone set a happy keynote for the evening, and Walter was immediately put at ease by Dorothy's initial assurance that he was not going to be asked to make any responding speeches. Finally, the center of the gymnasium floor was cleared for square dancing, and cider and doughnuts and cheese were consumed in generous quantities.

The following is a copy of the purported "Official Proclamation" of Walter's "emancipation," written and read by Judge Griffith:

WHEREAS, for one score years and ten, cruel slavery has existed in Manchester whereby one who is, and has been for many years past, destined to fame in the realm of letters, has been shackled with fetters of bottles and jim-cracks, and his talents confined to The Manchester Journal and The Rutland Herald, while his soul has yearned for freedom and for a more abundant life; and

WHEREAS, the Village of Manchester recognizes and maintains that such a person should be henceforward and forever free and unencumbered; and that no person or persons should do any act or acts to repress such a person in any effort which he may make for his actual freedom;

NOW, THEREFORE, I, Andrew E. Martin, President of the Village of

Manchester, by virtue of the Power & Authority in me vested by that municipality; and as a fit and necessary measure for the welfare and delectation of the United States of America; do, on this 1st day of December, in the year of our Lord One Thousand Nine Hundred and Thirty-five, Publicly Proclaim; and by virtue of the power and purpose aforesaid;

I do solemnly declare that Walter Hard shall henceforward and forever be free, and that the State of Vermont, and especially the municipalities of Manchester, Dorset, Arlington and Sandgate, and the people thereof, will recognize and maintain the freedom of this person;

And I hereby enjoin upon the said Walter Hard, so declared to be free, to abstain from all sordid mercantile pursuits and especially the vending of drugs, soda water, lipsticks and rat poison; and I recommend to him that, in cases when allowed, and when he feels like it, he labor faithfully for reasonable compensation in the fields of literature to produce large crops of verseless verses;

And I further recommend that there be no restriction of such crops by any laws or regulations, and no plowing under of each third line of such verses to the detriment thereof;

And I further declare and make known that said Walter Hard shall be received into good standing in the fellowship of authors and poets, regardless of his previous efforts to make an honest living, and I enjoin upon the cult of literature to abstain from all reference to his former long period of servitude.

And, upon this Act, sincerely believing it to be an act of justice warranted by the great need of real talent in the field of literature, I invoke the considerate judgment of mankind, and the gracious favor of God.

IN WITNESS WHEREOF, I hereunto subscribe my name and command the seal of the people of Manchester to be affixed.

Done in the Village of Manchester, this first day of December, in the year of our Lord One Thousand Nine Hundred and Thirty-five.

[*Signed*]   Andrew E. Martin,
         PRESIDENT OF THE VILLAGE OF MANCHESTER

         By the President
         [*Seal*]

                                        E. Griffith, Clerk

It was not long after this that Alfred Knopf considered finding a Vermont author to write a travel book about Vermont. He sent a "feeler" to Walter. Meanwhile, the Stephen Daye Press came to us with a contract for Walter and me to write a Vermont travel book together. Eventually, Mr. Knopf chose Charles Crane to write his Vermont travel book, *Let Me Show You Vermont*. He couldn't have made a finer choice.

There was an amusing coincidence here. Charlie Crane was the brother of Ephraim Crane, who owned the Stephen Daye Press.

It was at this time that we acquired a new piece of bookshop equipment. The word *new* is a misnomer. It was an ancient, two-wheeled cart with two handles at one end and a steadying support, for use when not in motion, at the farther end. It was deep and capacious. It took Walter's fancy at some auction and he brought it back in triumph.

He painted its box bottle-green and its wheels bright orange. He made a hinged cover for it that, when lifted, supplied space for book jackets, book reviews, et cetera; and he designated it as the "apple cart" and filled it with tempting bargains. He then wheeled it out to one side of the bookshop entrance.

It was his pride and joy, but even at so early a stage I had a feeling of doubt regarding it. I was not wrong. It soon became a bone of contention—not between us, and not on the part of the buying public, who loved it, but on the part of our devoted and efficient village president—not the one who had written Walter's official proclamation of "emancipation," but a new "from-another-state" one whose determined purpose was to Keep Manchester Beautiful. He didn't think the apple cart was beautiful, and he soon made an ordinance that dismissed such unsightly adjuncts to business, or businesses, from the legal realms of permissibility in Manchester. Before we knew it, the Case of the Apple Cart had become the rallying cry for those who felt their rights as merchants were being infringed upon and for those who felt any extraneous objects outside one's place of business were dangerous and sure portents of a future blight upon the town's beauty. There was truth and justice in both points of view.

Eventually, Walter was allowed to keep his apple cart by

sending a written request to the president of the village with a specified statement as to its purpose, a diagram of its size and placement, and an agreement to renew his request each year, when it would be legally considered.

Probably, over the years, the apple cart became a bookshop landmark responsible for an untold number of bargain and secondhand book sales. I recall one amusing incident connected with it which is worth telling.

A summer patron of ours appeared in the shop one morning, after having browsed through the apple cart.

"There aren't enough of them there," she said in a troubled voice to Walter.

"Not enough?" asked Walter, slightly puzzled.

"Oh, of course, you don't know what I'm driving at!"

She then explained that she had recently rented a cottage that had an appalling number of unfilled bookshelves. "I can't fill them all with bric-a-brac. It makes it look like a gift shop. And, heaven knows, I can't afford to buy enough new books to fill them. I really don't particularly want so many books up here in the country. It's the look of all those empty shelves that bothers me. They look so *needless*."

"I've an idea," said Walter. "How about secondhand 'sets' of books?"

"Oh, wonderful! Scott, Hawthorne, Dickens?"

"Well, yes, I could find some of those for you. But I was thinking of a different kind of sets. Not really sets, but series. I just acquired a lot at an auction. They'd really be conversation pieces—great fun, I think. You see, they're old-time children's 'series'—the *Rollo* books, all of Horatio Alger's 'luck and pluck' series, and, believe it or not, sixteen volumes of the *Elsie* books. They must contain enough sentimental tears to warrant a rain bucket. Want to come into the back room and look them over?"

Before long, Mrs. Palmedo was opening the back of her car for Walter to pile in load after load. He even added a series of Henty books, *The Five Little Peppers,* and all of Louisa M. Alcott available in the shop.

One day, a few weeks later, he asked Mrs. Palmedo how she was getting on with the books.

"Oh, they're a tremendous success. All our guests are so intrigued. But funny as it sounds, it's our daughter, Betty, and her friends who are especially crazy about the *Elsie* books. Did you ever hear anything like it! They're all around twelve or thirteen, and they're reading the entire sixteen volumes, one after another, and just wallowing in sentimental anguish."

These girls were already playing golf and tennis. They rode and swam and skied with dauntless practicality. Yes, it *was* funny. I joined Walter to listen as she continued her story.

"I came home the other afternoon and found Betty looking woebegone. Her face was all tear-stained. 'Why, darling!' I said, gathering her into my arms, 'what's the matter? What's happened?'

" 'Oh, Mummy,' she sobbed, pressing her face against me, 'she almost died!'

" 'Who, darling? Who almost died?'

" 'Elsie!' "

Whether there were any similar repercussions from the Horatio Alger books I never heard, but I somehow doubt it.

Presently the rental library, as we then conducted it, became an almost menacing problem to me. The problem was the mystery story section, and the menace was a gentleman from Philadelphia who was renting the cottage beyond the Equinox Junior on the bookshop side of the street. He was a high-strung, nervous invalid and he would read none but British-written mysteries. Our supply was very limited, in his eyes, and he complained bitterly of our inadequacy. This was the period when we did not have plastic covers to protect the book jackets, so each book jacket was removed to a large folder for safekeeping, and a plain Manila book jacket, stamped with the bookshop name, replaced the regular jacket.

One day, in an attempt to assure him that he was being made aware of every British-written detective story we had, even those that were "out" in another reader's hands, I opened the big folder of jackets and handed it to him so he could truly see all the titles of the mysteries the shop possessed. In angry impatience, he jerked the folder out of my hand and all the jackets were flung over the floor. He walked out in a tantrum, and I gathered up the jackets, or had started to do so when Walter appeared and completed the task.

A rental library customer of the opposite sex also made my life miserable, and again, it was the mystery story with which she was involved. She was a spoiled and pampered elderly woman whose daughter rented one of the large houses on the Street. I used to suffer with indignation when she came in with her browbeaten "companion," a timid, elderly woman who must have desperately needed this employment. One day Mrs. C. came in alone and asked at once for a popular mystery story that was "out," taken a couple of days before by another customer.

"How can it be *out?* You told me that yesterday."

"It still is out. It hasn't been brought back."

"I believe you're hiding it. Probably reading it yourself."

I did not reply. As I stepped aside, she suddenly began to lash me about the ankles with a flexible cane she carried.

Walter was grim after these two incidents. He said that he would "handle" them. I told him that I would gladly let him see to Mrs. C., but I begged him to let me "handle" the Philadelphia invalid. I had a plan. Following another day of thought, I wrote him a note. I explained that presently he would begin to get a daily installment of a mystery story, laid in England, which I hoped he would enjoy. Although it was not written by a British-born writer, it was, I understood, written by a descendant of Lord Anson, who, according to records in the New York Public Library, had at one time been a privateer—in fact, a *pirate*. I then settled myself to the job of writing a portion of a daily mystery story, on the plan of "The Daily Letter Story of Cordelia Tiger," in which my Philadelphia invalid appeared as the Chief Detective. Each night I got the bellboy next door to the shop to slip it under Mr. E.'s door. After two or three days,

Mr. E. and his wife appeared in the shop. She smiled at me hopefully as he walked over to me.

"Are you the descendant of that pirate?" he asked.

"Yes," I said, smiling.

"Well, by Jove! I like him!" He held out his hand and shook mine, and as long as he lived, we were friends.

Later, I observed Walter's handling of the case of Mrs. C. I was safely hidden behind the panel of the small office when she entered. I slid farther behind it as Walter stepped out into view. I watched through a knothole in the wood.

Before Mrs. C., who was carrying her cane, had a chance really to get into form, he stepped close to her and said something to her very quietly. I could not hear his words but I could see her face. Her expression was one of astounded unbelief. Then her face became scarlet. Gently and firmly he removed her cane from her hand. He turned her about toward the street and, taking her by the elbow, he led her to the double entrance doors. Pushing them open with his shoulder, he conducted her outside to her car. As her chauffeur jumped out to open the car door for her, Walter literally lifted her into her seat. Then, turning to the chauffeur, he handed him Mrs. C.'s cane and, smiling in friendly recognition, he said, "I believe Mrs. C. wishes to go home."

I wonder whether rental libraries are not the bane of all bookshop keepers. There are never enough copies of a new and popular book, although frequently we have put in as many as three copies under compulsion and desperation.

There are always people who have forgotten their glasses.

There are always people who "have read all those books before."

There are always people who expect two new whodunits to be put in the library every day.

There are always people who "finished that book days ago. It's just been knocking around in the back seat of the car."

There are always people who take a book home and find they'd read it twice before. ("Why, then it should have showed that you had it on the card." "Well, maybe I read it somewhere in a friend's house—perhaps Bermuda, or Miami." *Two* friends, we wonder.)

There are always people who can tell us how we should run the rental library.

There are always people who tell us about that *wonderful* rental library in Rockville Centre.

Well—there are always People. *People,* and *people,* and *people.*

Any bookshop that is really "business-minded" carries greeting cards, gift wrap, novelties, notes, and Christmas card albums. They deserve what they get.

What do they get?

Hoards of women who make a pastime of ranging through all the greeting-card racks and pulling the cards out and jamming them back at will, in all the wrong places.

"No, I didn't see anything I liked."

"No, I didn't find anything *different.*"

Hoards of women pulling all the gift-wrap packages apart.

"There was one here last year with chartreuse wheelbarrows on it. What did you do with it?"

"There were some terribly cute little jumping beans. Well, I *thought* I saw them here. Maybe it was in a dime store."

"No, I want one of those *unusual* notes. The kind that has something cute written across the corner like 'Who ever heard of you?' or 'Hi, Pal, I'm sick of the sight of you. So I write.' "

And the Christmas card albums.

The people who come in in July and say, "Haven't you got your Christmas cards out yet?"

"I've *always* bought my Christmas cards here. I'm sure you had all the albums out by the Fourth of July last year."

"What on earth are Christmas card manufacturers thinking of? So *few* skiing Christmas cards to choose from. And in Vermont, too. What can they be thinking of?"

"Maybe they're thinking of Christmas," we say defensively to a blank stare.

And then there are those who come in on a sopping wet day, drag out all the twelve or fourteen Christmas card albums, and have themselves an afternoon of lazy pleasure, sprinkling cigarette ashes over everything and leaving daubs of lipstick here and there.

"Oh, no—I was just *looking*."

"It's too early yet. I really can't get the Christmas spirit until just before."

"Sort of sickening, really, to see all this Christmas stuff around so *early*, isn't it?"

And then, interlarded with all of this, are the special orders for special books for individual customers, to be ordered in time to be mailed (maybe overseas) as Christmas gifts.

We begin to plead with people, personally, by telephone, and through our advertising media, as early as November 1st to send in their Christmas gift orders as early as possible. We will do our very best for them, but *time* is the crucial point. As time shortens and the telephone queries about ordered books increase, we dream of titles and dates and customers' names by night. Dream? No, we have nightmares about it. We telephone or telegraph queries to publishers, imploring information regarding certain orders. They are polite and as helpful as possible, but they must be having nightmares, too.

The customer says, "But, Mrs. Hard, I ordered that book a *week* ago."

"Yes, I know. I have a carbon of the order to the publisher right here in my hand. I'll call you the minute it comes. It does have to come from Los Angeles, you know—one of those small art publishers."

"My husband says to tell you he wants to know why in the *devil* that book he ordered doesn't come."

But then, there are those who come in smiling. Who say (sniffing our balsam wreaths), "How Christmassy it smells in here! *Real* Christmas greens. No gilt and silver paint to spoil God's green as it grew."

"How lovely the mantel looks. Beautiful books, just enough, perfectly arranged."

"And the children's books! They grow more wonderful every

year. Did you hear that little boy over there, singing to himself?
Just for happiness?"

"Oh, I like that long line of beautifully printed words you
have over the door, so you can see them from outside, too, with
the light behind them."

> God rest ye merry, gentlemen,
> Let nothing you dismay,
> For Jesus Christ, our Saviour,
> Was born upon this day.

So many Christmas Eves, Lorraine Kelton stopped in to wish
us joy and leave us a loaf of her Christmas coffee cake; and
so often Kay Duke came in with a loaf of her fresh bread, still
fragrant and warm from the oven. How much has happened
and altered for us all over the years, but—

> Let nothing you dismay,
> For Jesus Christ, our Saviour,
> Was born upon this day.

CHAPTER NINE

Fall of 1935—We Journey
through Vermont

THE FUTURE PLANS we had talked of as we climbed the old hill road in Chester on the first afternoon of our freedom naturally involved discussion of the Vermont travel book which the Stephen Daye Press had asked us to write together. Its title already was part of our thinking: *This Is Vermont*.

We wondered what such a title would convey to people. To Vermonters it would mean home, the farm or village or town where they happened to live. But maybe the word Vermont would mean more than that to them. It might stand for a certain kind of living, or for a type of people. Perhaps it would bring some particular picture to their minds, some memory—a certain stretch of winding road closed in by stands of spruce and hemlock; a certain valley with farms nestled beneath trees, or high upon clearings that ran up to meet the timber line. Or a quiet village street with white houses and an old church grouped about a small green; or the unbelievable blue of Lake Champlain with mountains piled up on one shore line and peaks reaching up from the plain on the other.

Or again, it might be a day they spent in the woods, climbing a hill road, fishing a stream, or scaling some mountain height where, far below, the whole world seemed spread out to bless their eyes. Or still again, it might be the talk they heard at some crossroad store, or the story they listened to beside the fire in a farmhouse; the anecdotes and tales told in the gathering room of some inn. To everyone Vermont would mean something different, yet to all of them something that is the same.

But how should we put all of this on paper? The book was not to be a history, although of necessity it would contain history. It was not to be a regulation guidebook, although of necessity it must contain data as to roads and route numbers. It was not to be a geography, although it would deal with mountains and valleys, lakes and water courses. While it must incorporate sufficient accurate factual material to be of practical use, it must be capable of taking its readers upon a journey of the spirit as well as upon a journey in the flesh. We hoped that it might prove, when the reader laid it down, that he would find old memories and new longings stir within him, and would close its final chapter with the lingering impression of something so dear to his heart that he would be able to say, "Well, this is Vermont." Yet, to write such a book there had to be a plan, a definite procedure whereby the ultimate impression would be accomplished. Could we do it?

Our procedure included weeks of journeying, from September into December, in cold and stormy weather, along main thoroughfares, and along back roads and byways. Sometimes we left our car turned off in the grass below some mountain trail, and climbed to a summit, or wandered along a stream. Sometimes we stopped to eat our lunch on the steps of a small, country store where old men sat about in the sun and where we fell into conversation with them. We knocked upon unfamiliar doors to find them opened, not grudgingly, but with kindness when our errand became known. "Why, yes, that old house stood there, I've heard, in the 1700's." Or, "No, it was Jacob Bayley— Isaac Bayley's father—who first came up the river to the Oxbow. Yes, yes, do come in. There's some fine old paneled wall you might like to see."

And then the pungent talk of some old fellow, stopping his horse and calling out to us, "Lord, no! This is *Cambridgeport*. Used to be a thrivin' village. Say, do you folks know how many there was went up from here to Stratton to listen to Dan'l Webster, time he spoke up there durin' the Whig campaign?"

Or some quiet-faced woman, giving us a glass of milk at a mountain farm, would say, "Yes, it is pretty hard getting in and out of here in winter, but it's beautiful. You can look into fourteen different townships from our upper meadow. It's worth the climb, I always say."

Such journeying, undisciplined by too insistent timepieces or a too exacting calendar, led us up the western side of the state. We made frequent stops at points where the chief highways were joined by roads that cut crosswise over the Green Mountains to the other side of Vermont, or ran farther eastward to the Lake boundary. These stage routes of long ago, now good roads, led us to back mountain country, wilderness farms, small villages, and towns in which historical personalities had once played a part—a fact so surprising as often to seem almost unbelievable. On and on we went, our course continually northward, but always interwoven with these cross-journeyings to bind areas together. When we at last reached Canada, snow was thick in the air. As we came down the eastern side of the state, the White Mountains across the Connecticut River Valley glistened with snow, and we knew that Mount Mansfield, which we had climbed a few weeks before, must now wear blazing crystal upon its summit.

So we made a circle, a circle continuously intersected by cross-state journeying on roads which often joined each other. Finally, we were driven indoors by bitter cold and biting wind, by depths of snow and ice-glazed roads. Then it was that we sat down to write, to tell the story of our journeying, to try to capture in the concrete phrase the elusive mood of joyous freedom, permeated by the presence of overwhelming fact, fleeting impressions, and indescribable beauty.

How did we write? Day and night. Two people working steadily in a room hung with maps, piled with reference books, and invaded by the deafening clack of two typewriters hammering out our story. Thumbtacked to each desk were our respective plans of operation, for we did have a method in mind. Starting at the Pownal line, where we had commenced our journeying, one of the natural points where people visiting Vermont might frequently enter, we divided our trips so that each one of us should cover certain alternating, connecting portions of the journey.

So we set to work. Not until the final words of the book were typed did either one of us see, or hear, the other's chapters, although we sometimes made queries.

"What time did you say we reached Danville in your chapter? Yes, that's right. I was telling about our supper there, and the next morning when we went on to Peacham. I want to be sure it fits together perfectly as to times of day."

Into the chapters, inevitably, went our own personalities. We weren't thinking about any audience when we wrote it (and I suppose that's very bad authorship as well as salesmanship). No, we were thinking only of our journey. Remembering its days of marvelous sunlight, its days of slanting gray rain, its nights of enveloping fog, and its nights of brilliant stars. We were recalling some village with old houses, some village so beautiful that it seemed that an architect would be carried away with the enchantment of its quiet, elm-shaded street; we were following stretches of mountain road, mile on mile, with only the sound of a rushing brook and wind stirring in trees to accompany us. We were listening to stories, anecdotes, and tales; remembering our hours of companionship.

Trying to get such memories into words, we forgot to be formal, forgot to be exceedingly careful and conservative. We forgot that, outside this world of our memory and happiness, there was a world of very practical people waiting to read the book. If we had remembered them, would we have put in more route numbers and fewer stories, less poetry and more geographical facts? I don't know.

Finally, it was written. Late one March dusk we sat down by our fire and read it aloud to each other; just as we hoped other people might sometime read it aloud. How much of the spell of Vermont did we capture? How much of its worth and beauty did we retain or lose? Those who read it would say. How far short of our love of Vermont it fell, only we could know.

Of course, some people spoke at once of its shortcomings—
the special home village we didn't say enough about; the mountain we misnamed; the river we made flow into the wrong place;
the great-great-grandfather we designated as a captain instead of
a general. Indeed, there were days when we dreaded to open
the mail!

Yet, there was mail of another sort, letters so generous, so
full of pleasure from people all over our country as well as from
abroad, that it was impossible to feel other than happy about
the book. One really couldn't feel downhearted after such letters.

This Is Vermont was published in June, 1936, just as the
bookshop opened for the summer season. It had good reviews
and was a Book-of-the-Month Club recommendation. Bernard
De Voto made one objection. "They have a nasty habit of re-
ferring to each other as *he* and *she*." He evidently didn't know
that all mountain farm husbands and wives are apt to refer to
each other as *he* and *she* in Vermont.

Dorothy Canfield, writing about it for the book section of the
Herald Tribune, was characteristically generous. The book, she
said, gives "the flavor and savor and scent and sound of the
sleepy villages in the valleys, and the lovely uplands with their
sparse grass and encroaching white birches. The authors 'make
you 'quainted' with some of the Vermonters they met, some
queer, others not so queer, all of them handmade, not the result of mass production, and almost without exception . . .
preferring to live where they are rather than somewhere else.
They tell you enough old stories and local legends and pungent
anecdotes located in the towns they mention to make you realize
that in all the others, asleep in the sun though they may seem,
there is a similar accumulation of human life, crystallized into
stories, axioms and proverbs. Most of all—the eating which
proves this pudding—the journey of the Hards through Vermont makes the reader long to follow in their tracks."

The book went into seven printings. People came into the
bookshop with it under their arms from as far away as California,
Indiana, Kansas, Florida, Texas, and Canada. It proved a bo-
nanza for the Johnny Appleseed. But there were dejections as

well as elations. I was found to have changed the course of a river, and Walter moved a mountain. And "Why didn't you come to *me* for material about White River Junction? I know *all* there is to know about White River Junction."

But there were problems about knowing *too* much as well as about not knowing enough.

One of these problems was Arlington, and a second one concerned Stratton Village and the Daniel Webster monument. The Arlington problem fell to Walter. He was charted to write the chapter about Arlington. In our plan it was listed as Chapter Three, and headed as follows: "We go north from Bennington through Shaftsbury—to Arlington."

I presently became aware that Walter seemed to be avoiding the Arlington chapter.

"What's the matter?" I asked.

"Well, how on earth can anyone but Dorothy Canfield write anything about Arlington? As she'd put it, she's lived there ever since Arlington was granted a township. It makes me feel tongue-tied even to think of it."

I could understand, but I kept being anxious about it. Then, one day it seemed to solve itself after I'd been into our Manchester Library and had fallen into conversation with Anna Buck, our librarian, who has always been able to help me with problems.

"Anna, weren't there *two* Charles Bucks who lived in Arlington at the same time?"

"Oh, yes," she said, "there were *three*. There was Charlie Ed (the son of Edward Buck), and Charlie Ans (the son of Anson Buck), and Charlie-on-the-Green (who lived on the green)." As I left the library, Anna's words kept ringing in my ears like a refrain—"Charlie Ed and Charlie Ans and Charlie-on-the-Green."

That night I said to Walter, "You needn't write the Arlington chapter."

"No? How's that?"

"I'll do it. I've an idea that I think will help us get away with it. Arlington history is going to burst into verse."

That evening I did some stiff research on Arlington's early history; and then I sat down and wrote "A Ballad of Arlington," with sixteen verses and a refrain following each verse.

A BALLAD OF ARLINGTON

Red Mount and West hold fast the line
Of Arlington's fair village,
As in the days of Yorker raids
And title-granting pillage—
Those times when Hampshire Grants were held
Of no account by Tryon.
Though truth to tell, some settlers proved
Quite willing to rely on
Whichever hand with lawful seal
Would guarantee their common weal.

Then sing a song of Arlington,
        of Arlington's fair scene;
Of Charlie Ed, and Charlie Ans,
        and Charlie-on-the-Green.

The date was one and seven first,
With sixty-four thereafter,
When Captain Hawley, stalwart soul,
Raised high his roof-tree rafter.
He called his neighbors to attend
A sort of village meeting;
They gave the trust of Public Rights
Into his worthy keeping.
Remember Baker followed him
And built two mills by East Brook's brim.

(Refrain)

But Baker was a fighting man;
He loathed York men like sin,
His blood ran hot for liberty—
He was Seth Warner's kin.
And now new folk to Arlington
Were flocking by the dozen—
The Hards, the Bucks, the Canfield clans—
And each one brought a cousin.

Hawleys, Hards and Canfields mated,
Fam'lies soon were all related.

(Refrain)
Two mills were built, some fields were sown,
A road cleared through the town,
Three rods in width at east and west
And four rods up and down.
Jehiel Hawley then was sent
To treat with Indian bands,
Related to some Stockbridge tribes,
And thus made safe their lands.
But Yorkers then stretched out their hands
And made their proud and hard demands.

(Refrain)
They sought to tear these settlers all
From homestead, kin, and farms,
Unless they owned the Yorkers' claims.
So for this cause their arms—
Their flintlocks and their powder horns—
They took from out the corner,
And Baker was the fiercest one
(With Allen and with Warner)
For he was bold and unafraid;
And thus, alas! his fate was made.

(Refrain)
The villainous and dastardly
King's Justice, named Monroe,
Laid hold of Baker at his home
And caused his blood to flow.
Arrested, he was carried out
A wounded, prisoned man.
Then loyal friends his rescue made—
The Hawley Hurlbut clan.
Then hardy blood did freely flow
And bitter was the pain and woe.

(Refrain)
'Twas then that faithful Loyalists
And Tory-minded folk

Were watched by a suspicious band
Who weighed each word they spoke.
These Loyalists were cursed afar,
Yet, one or two debarred,
Still held respect of other men,
And such was Zadok Hard.
He lived with simple, honest grace
And neighbors liked his kindly face.

(Refrain)

Esquire of his broad pleasant lands,
He treated all his kind
With tolerant and friendly hand.
And so, although they fined
Him for his British loyalty,
His love for Crown and King,
They let him bide and often sought
Protection 'neath his wing.
For life was an uncertain thing
And friends were few to which to cling.

(Refrain)

Esquire Canfield still retained
His Loyalist affection
But Baker's sturdy men, despite
This British predilection,
Esteemed his character so well—
His faith in all good part—
That never questioned were his acts,
Which warmed his fine old heart.
For he was brave and gentle too,
A sweetness in life's bitter brew.

(Refrain)

But now the skies grew black with storm
Between the warring factions.
Brave Phineas Hurd was carried off
And bitter were the actions
That followed on this sad, sad deed,
For he did ne'er return.
His widow suffered every wrong,

We from the records learn.
Oh hard was fate of friend and friend,
And woeful was the tragic end!

(Refrain)

The tragedy of Mallory
When Adams shot him down,
The confiscated flocks, of folks
Once thrifty, in the town;
All marked the deeds of those sad days
On which the skies looked down,
Where villages to east and west,
And on that turnpike once were blest.

(Refrain)

Marauding soldiers roamed about
Through kitchens here and there,
And many tales of housewives' wit
The Loyalists declare.
In Arlington, one brave "Aunt Ann,"
The wife of Andrew Hawley,
Belabored them with broom until
They fled with cries right brawly.
She would not have them steal her bread,
No, not if it should mean her head.

(Refrain)

She walked with bold and fearless step,
A Loyalist proclaimed;
Her brave and sturdy, ample life
Still in the town is famed.
Jehiel Hawley—saintly man—
The founder of the town,
Was hounded for his love of King
And black threats broke him down.
He fled a broken, weary man
And soon was cut his sad life's span.

(Refrain)

His faithful friend of better years
Named Stoddard, Justice, scholar,

Had lent his aid to build the church
For those who once in Parlor
Had met to hear Jehiel read
The Book of Common Prayer;
Jehiel honored God and King
As all did know when there.
His spirit towered high, apart,
And yet they stooped to break his heart.

(Refrain)

Then Vermont's honored Governor,
Tom Chittenden by name,
Moved into Hawley's once dear home—
It was a wicked shame.
But Chittenden was kindly too,
Though faced with deeds of war,
When famine threatened Arlington,
He equally gave store
To Mountain Boy and Tory too,
So hearty praise to him is due.

(Refrain)

The tale that's writ of Arlington,
Except for 'Member Baker,
Must be a tale of Loyalists
True to their King and Maker.
And even the Green Mountain Boys
Might pause with true regret
To honor Hawley, Canfield names,
Hards, Hurds, and Stoddards, yet.
Their heritage of heart and mind
Should with brave hemlock be entwined.

Then sing a song of Arlington,
        of Arlington's fair scene;
Of Charlie Ed, and Charlie Ans,
        and Charlie-on-the-Green.

The second problem, concerning Stratton Village and the
Daniel Webster monument, was apportioned to me, and was
dealt with in the final portion of Chapter Seven. As this matter

involved the story of the "Tippecanoe and Tyler, too" Presidential campaign of 1840, when Webster spoke for the Whig cause at a great demonstration in Stratton Village, I soon found myself involved in endless dry facts and research. In the process, I fell on a note in an old Rockingham town history: "first meeting of Rockingham Tippecanoe Club was holden at Cambridgeport, Saturday, June 13, 1840, at 4 o'clock P.M."

I needed some way of enlivening all the pages of dull paragraphs I had absorbed in the research about this famous campaign. So I invented a roadside encounter with an old inhabitant of Cambridgeport who burst into talk when we remarked on what a deserted village it was, and wondered what on earth had ever been its activity in its palmy days. I had him break into an account of Cambridgeport's glorious part in the Whig campaign of 1840, with full details of the hectic excitement on the day when Daniel Webster spoke to fifteen thousand people.

It made a pretty good chapter. The old fellow with his Yankee speech and excited rehearsal of the epic event carried it through in great form. Not until the book came out on June 26, 1936, did I have trouble. A telegram came to us from the Boston *Globe:* "Please supply name of old man in Cambridgeport who gave you the story of the Daniel Webster speech at the Whig Convention at Stratton. Wish to send a reporter to interview him."

All we could do was to telegraph back: "Sorry. He died."

CHAPTER TEN

"Believe-It-or-Not in Vermont"

*A*FTER *This Is Vermont* had been in print for a couple of years, I had a letter from Howard Hindley, the editor, at that time, of the Rutland *Herald*. He was recovering from a recent heart attack and he asked me whether I would take over his own weekly double column of personal comments and "oddments" and pinch-hit for him for a time until he was better. He left it to me to fill it with anything I chose. It had never, of course, been a column of a political nature, purely personal and entertaining, as I recall it.

I do not know whether I was more excited by his amazing confidence in me (although, come to think of it, he probably trusted in Walter's judgment to steer my course safely beyond rocks and eddies), or by the pleasure I anticipated in writing the column, for I knew what I wanted to write about.

I think I have spoken in a preceding chapter about the astonishing number of unusual incidents, and personalities connected with them, which we discovered in the course of our travels through Vermont. Inevitably, many of these had to be sacrificed because of lack of space. I used these surprising discoveries of incident, place, and personality for the weekly column in the Rutland *Herald*. Mr. Hindley dignified it by the name of "Vermontiana." I, myself, think that although it truly *was* Vermontiana, founded upon honest research, it might more properly have been called "Believe-It-or-Not in Vermont." In all, there were about twenty columns, and I did have great pleasure in writing them.

Peacham's Bell

One of the finest churches in the state stands in Peacham. Not that it has architectural beauty such as the Old First Church in Bennington, or the one that stands at the head of the green in Middlebury, but it has, nevertheless, nobility. Its main structure and the belfry and spire that rise above it have the dignity which exists in most of the New England churches erected in the Colonial period. Aside from thinking that it is a nice old church you could easily pass it by. Associated with it, however, is an incident that should make you pause and look up at its bell with reverent interest.

Here, on the 2nd of December, 1859, Leonard Johnson, young and ardent Abolitionist member of the *Juvenile Society of Peacham,* an organization given to debate, stood hatless, and breathing deep, as he tolled Peacham's church bell for one hour without stopping. No funeral procession wound up the hill, but Leonard Johnson did not stop the slow, deep tolling of the bell which reverberated through the whole village and echoed in the hills beyond. He was tolling out the soul of John Brown who was being hanged in Charlestown, Virginia.

Those were days when the question of abolition was hotly debated in Peacham. Its *Juvenile Society* had been organized as early as 1810 and young men felt a thrill of pride to see their names written on its roster. In 1854, Leonard's name appeared with those of four other Johnsons in the membership lists. He could claim relationship to Oliver Johnson who was the clerk of the Executive Committee of the Vermont Anti-Slavery Society, organized in 1834. Garrison referred to the Society as the first State body of the kind "regularly organized in this country for the immediate extirpation of American Slavery." Its president was Asa Aldis of St. Albans, and the chairman of its Executive Committee was Rowland Robinson of Ferrisburg. Later, Oliver Johnson went to Boston and there founded the Anti-Slavery Standard with Garrison and Wendell Phillips. So young Leonard had it in his blood to espouse the cause of abolition.

It was a cause that was indigenous to Vermont. In 1777, when Vermont drew up her Constitution as an independent Republic, she included the prohibition of slavery as one of its articles. In 1828, Garrison found congenial viewpoints in Bennington where he lived for a year and edited a sheet called *The Spirit of the Times.* The state was honeycombed with stations of the Underground Railway used to assist escaping slaves on their way to Canada. There is hardly a town of any size in Vermont which did not have a family who was a member of this great system. Dozens of houses still stand in which the secret "slave room" may be seen. The Rev. Joshua Young of Burlington defied certain influential members of his church, unsympathetic to John Brown, and preached his funeral sermon. It was an act of heroic conviction for which he was forced to resign his pastorate in the Burlington church. For while Vermont bred Abolitionists, there were many who bitterly opposed them.

With all this in mind, we can see young Leonard Johnson quite clearly on that December day, tolling Peacham's bell with tears and excitement in his eyes. For he believed John Brown to be a martyr. And at that very moment, on a Groton farm near by, lived a boy named William Scott, the sleeping sentinel pardoned by Abraham Lincoln on September 9th, 1861. The marker which tells of him can be seen on the highway between Groton and East Barre.

But already on that day in 1859 Vermont was keenly alive to her part in the great debate concerning slavery. She could have named a Vermont Abolitionist for every toll of the Peacham bell as it responded to Leonard Johnson's hand.

Night Train through Ferrisburg

In 1860, Vermont had 556 miles of railroad track which in layout was essentially the same as today except for a few cross-lines to the north. Other states developed railroad systems earlier than Vermont because of better terrain and a larger traveling population. However, in the years between 1833 and 1860, Vermont had a railroad which superseded them all. It carried hundreds of passengers to one destination—the Canadian line. It was the famous Underground Railroad which transported escaping slaves to freedom, and whose secret stations lay along two trunk lines on the east and west of the state with connecting branches linking them.

Vermont had always been pledged to the gospel of freedom for all of the human race. Its Constitution (as an independent Republic), framed in 1777, prohibited slavery. Ten years later, it passed a law which levied a heavy fine upon anyone transporting a Negro from the state for purposes of sale. In 1788, Lemuel Haynes, a mulatto preacher, became one of its most influential and revered citizens.

In 1819, the first State Colonization Society in America was founded in Montpelier. Its object was to transport all free and enslaved Negroes to Liberia. Thus slavery should be abolished in our own country and civilization brought to Africa. The Society, however, began to fall on difficult days as the Anti-Slavery Movement gathered force in the North. From 1833 until 1837, alone, sixty-eight Anti-Slavery Societies were organized in Vermont. Garrison, who had lived in Bennington for a year in 1828, and who had published his *Spirit of the Times* there, knew that Vermont was soil where the seed of emancipation for the Negro would grow into a mighty tree. In Burlington and Montpelier, Randolph and some other places, there was strong slavery sentiment. Anti-Slavery gatherings were broken up and slave hunters were aided. Feeling in Vermont was strongest and the Courts sympathized with such emotion and upheld the cause of escaping slaves.

The Underground Railroad began to flourish. It was the great, unauthorized system of help to the slave. It did much to precipitate the break between the North and the South. It threaded a secret way that ran like a malignant fever through the body of the land, carrying infection to its entire system. Rowland T. Robinson, who might have been called the head engineer of the Railroad in Vermont, lived in Ferrisburg. There was a "slave room" in his home. It adjoined an eastern bedroom, far back beneath the eaves, by a low door. Slaves were secreted there during the day. At night, when it was safer, they were taken to other stations of the Railroad until they finally reached Canada. Many a wagon stole through Ferrisburg at dead of night, loaded with a cask or box containing black freight, for Vermont was the black man's white hope in those days. In later years, Rowland Robinson's son wrote stories that have become famous lore of Vermont's past, and some of them are thrilling tales of the Underground Railroad.

From Albany and Hoosick, the western trunk of the Underground Railroad in Vermont ran through Bennington, Manchester, Wallingford, Rutland, Brandon, Middlebury, Weybridge, Vergennes, Ferrisburg, Charlotte and Burlington. It continued, with numerous branches, to St. Albans and Swanton, and thus to Rouse's Point and the Canadian line.

There are many houses upon its length which still stand. Go to "Rokeby," the old Robinson homestead in Ferrisburg, and see the "slave room." Look with reverence at the other relics of that time, still cherished in the family home—the proclamation of the Great Anti-Slavery Convention to be held in Ferrisburg at the Friends' Meeting House, at the writing and portrait of Garrison. Then climb to the ancient Quaker cemetery above the hill. An incomparable view of Lake Champlain and the Adirondacks will meet your eyes. At midday, there will be no sounds except the hum of insects, the stir of leaves. But should you go there at dead of night, and let a century slip by you, you would hear the ominous rumble of a night train passing through Ferrisburg.

Lord Byron's Sword

It is a far cry from Vermont of 1939 to Greece of 1824. But, believe it or not, the sword which Lord Byron, the poet-liberator, used in the cause of Greek independence at Missolonghi now lies in a case in the museum of the Vermont Historical Society in Montpelier. It is due to that Society's efforts that we can partially unravel the tangled thread of events which connects Byron's sword with Vermont incident, and brings so valuable a relic to our state.

Vermonters of the early 1800's were particularly sympathetic with oppressed minorities. To fight for independence was traditional with them. So there was nothing surprising, they thought, in young Jonathan Miller of Montpelier espousing the cause of the Greeks who were suffering at the hands of the Turks. It was a cause which was talked of in every home where newspapers were read.

Aided by a Committee of Boston sympathizers in the cause, Miller sailed for Greece. Arrived, he enrolled in the army. Eventually, he was made a Colonel in the Legion which Lord Byron had organized and trained before his death in 1824. After the siege of Missolonghi in 1826, Colonel Miller returned to this country to raise funds and supplies for the distressed Greeks. When he went back to Greece to distribute these gifts, he found that the young Greek soldier named Loukas, particularly beloved of Byron, had been killed.

Shortly before his own death, Byron had given his sword to Loukas. It was a family possession, having belonged to Lord Byron's forebears. Its mountings were of gold, and upon its hilt was the coronet and initial of the Byrons. Engraved upon its blade was an Arabic inscription. This sword Colonel Miller bought at the auction of Loukas' effects which was held in the Forum at Athens. He brought the sword back with him to Vermont, but later loaned it to Mr. Castanis, a native Greek lecturer, by whom it was carried back to Greece.

Twenty-six years later, when Colonel Miller's daughter, Mrs. Abijah Keith of Chicago, was traveling in Greece with her husband, she learned of Mr. Castanis' whereabouts. He was living on the Island of Syra, Greece. Through the assistance of the United States Consul, the sword was recovered. That it was the identical one owned by Lord Byron and given to Loukas was vouched for afterward by Mr. George Finlay, the eminent Scottish philhellene, who knew Lord Byron well. It was also identified by Colonel Miller, and Mr. Finlay gave a written certificate as to its being the sword he had often seen in Byron's possession.

At least one more adventure befell it before it came to rest in the museum at Montpelier. Mrs. Keith left it at her death to her intimate friend, Mrs. Henry King of Chicago. The sword was to be hers during her lifetime, but was to be sent to the Vermont Historical Society at her death. During the great Chicago Fire Mrs. King lost everything—everything but the Byron sword which she rushed back into the blazing house to save.

Last year, the sword was sent by the Vermont Historical Society to Harvard University in the hope that someone there might assist in translating the Arabic inscription on its blade. Miss Whitehead of the Harvard Library staff translated it as follows, explaining that it was a quotation from the Koran: "And for him who putteth his trust in Him will God be all sufficient. God truly will attain his purpose. For everything has God assigned a purpose."

Someday, if you chance to take the trip to Montpelier you will want to go to the Historical Museum and look at Lord Byron's sword. As you journey there you will see many things to remind you of events in Byron's life. Narrow valleys with rushing streams pouring from their uplands will make you think of his Scottish heath. A height of land with an overhanging elm will recall the knoll where he loved to climb as a schoolboy at Dulwich, a secluded spot where he could read and dream, and yet overlook his small world. And the Lake—that surely will remind you of the day when he paced beside the burning pyre where drowned Shelley lay on the shores of Spezia. Finally, the Greek dignity of the Vermont State House will seem especially fitting to overshadow the resting place of Byron's sword.

Bee Keeper of Jamaica—1936

Miles of mountain road where deep woods alternate with glimpses of open valley lead one to Jamaica. A strange name, Jamaica, for a little village which rubs elbows with such places as Londonderry, Townshend, and Windham, places settled in the 1770's by Scotch-Irish people. The Irish countryside could hardly have been lovelier than this green, surrounding world in June. The sign at the entrance to Jamaica was startling, it looked so new and "on the map." JAMAICA . . . POINTS OF INTEREST: COLLEGE HILL—THE SALMON HOLE—BALANCING ROCK. But the Bee Keeper of Jamaica, because of whom this pilgrimage had been made, was not mentioned.

Anyone passing through Jamaica during the last twenty-five years would have seen his bee hives set under the trees, deep in the flowering grass, behind the house where he lived. The house stands close to the road at the entrance to the village from its Winhall end. It is a small, white cottage, built into the sidehill, with a long roof sheltering a narrow porch. There is something indescribably different about it from the two or three small farmhouses that are neighbors to it. It has a certain atmosphere of peace that is devoid of conscious thrift and bustling efficiency. Here, while Reuben Grout lived, there was a sign with the word HONEY painted in large letters. Since last winter it and Reuben have gone.

A friend and neighbor said that Reuben Grout cared more for his bees, by far, than for the honey that they made. He bred Queen bees and sold them for $5.00 apiece, making as much as $500 in a summer from their sale, without taking into account a drop of the honey which he collected from his homemade hives. One hive would produce as much as one hundred pounds of honey in a year. Mr. Grout had different kinds of honey— goldenrod honey that was dark and heavy, raspberry honey, of heavenly fragrance, and basswood honey with a delicate tang and practically no color.

Stored in Mr. Grout's mind were the observations collected during hundreds of days of bee keeping, and through endless hours of patient experimentation. He corresponded with bee keepers and scientists throughout this country, and bought native and foreign books on bee culture. "Somewhere," his friend thought, "he must have written down all the things he knew about his bees. He was like that. He'd have kept a record somewhere. He used to say he'd discovered things about bees that he'd never read of in books. He didn't have any family, he was an old 'bach,' and after he died last year, things got scattered. But I've got his books. I don't know much about bees—not like he did—but I wouldn't have anything happen to his books. He was eighty years old when he died but he stood as straight as an arrow. There was Indian blood in him. Maybe that's why he had such a way with wild things. He used to be a sawyer up at the Grout lumber job in Stratton. He had a sawmill of his own when he first came down here, but it was bees he cared about. He couldn't keep away from working with them. When he went up to Montpelier to the Legislature, once or twice, he could hardly wait to get back home to his bees. He was an all-fired Republican, and death on liquor and tobacco— called them 'danged cussed nuisances'—and he'd get excited and shout when he talked about politics; but when he was telling you about his bees his voice was low and gentle, like he was talking to a child. He had a way with sick people, too. Folks who were bad off or helpless seemed to know he'd handle them just right. Bees and folks both trusted him."

Reuben Grout's friend sighed and glanced at the little house that nestled into the sidehill, its door closed to the summer sunshine, its windows blank with drawn shades. By the road lay a great pile of discarded hives. Up the hill, behind the house, a few wild bees hovered above the white clover.

Victorian Mood at Clarendon Springs

When Victoria came to the English throne she revived old virtues. It became fashionable to be modest, religious and sensitive. Soon, however, these virtues became ends in themselves. Prudishness and piety began to overflow in a sea of social smugness and hypocrisy. The sea rose so high and spread so far that presently it lapped American shores. In so remote a spot as Clarendon Springs, Rutland County, Vermont, Queen Victoria and her virtues exerted a powerful influence upon the CLARENDON HOUSE.

In 1830 visitors were coming to Clarendon Springs to drink the waters. Indeed, in 1781, George Round built a large log house near the springs and took summer boarders. In 1798, he expanded his endeavors and put up a frame house and opened a hotel. By the time 1830 had arrived there was an imposing brick hotel, the CLARENDON HOUSE. Its long, white verandas, commodious parlors and dining room, its fountain playing upon the tree-shaded lawn, marked it as a resort which only the elite would seek. Curving roadway, graveled paths, gardens and croquet grounds added to its elegance; and springhouse pavilions and summer houses dotted about its lawns gave assurance of its gentility. Yes, those were the Victorian words that described it.

But its real claim to distinction lay in the exceptional medicinal virtues of its mineral springs. Thompson, in his *Natural History of Vermont* (1842) says, "These waters resemble most nearly the German Spa water. For their curative properties they are believed to be indebted wholly to the gasses they contain. They are highly efficacious in affections of the liver, dyspepsia and all cutaneous complaints, rheumatism and inveterate sore eyes."

There were accommodations for "as many as 500 visitors" in the vicinity of the springs, he also states. The Rutland *Herald* of 1835 carried the following announcement: "CLARENDON HOUSE—the subscriber has opened this recently erected Boarding House at the Clarendon Springs and is prepared for the reception of company. The House is well furnished in every department and no exertion will be wanting to those who visit the springs. The House being large and commodious is well adapted for the accommodation of individuals, and families—the valetudinarian, and parties of pleasure. The wants of all who call upon him shall be consulted and by strict attention he hopes to merit the patronage of the public. Thomas McLaughlin."

The patrons of the CLARENDON HOUSE came from Boston, New York, Philadelphia, and points south. They brought their trunks, nurses, and personal maids. Invalids reclined in lawn chairs and rode out in open carriages. Elderly ladies and gentlemen took "constitutionals" on the verandas and nearby paths. Discreet fathers and mothers studied the names and appearance of other guests, and investigated their social standing. Introductions were accepted or declined according to a system of which Queen Victoria would have approved.

Meanwhile, young girls in voluminous merino "outing dresses" and broad-brimmed hats tipped over their faces so as to display curls and "waterfalls," chignons and braids to full view picnicked and drove about to Chippenhook and the Clarendon Gorge. Young men in linen pantaloons and skirted coats, stocks and tall beaver hats accompanied the young ladies on such expeditions, always under the watchful eye of their chaperones. In the late afternoon, when the sun's rays were less devastating to delicate complexions, yards of dainty flounces were lifted to just the correct height while small and exquisitely shod feet were placed firmly upon opponents' croquet balls. In the evening, the CLARENDON HOUSE twinkled with lights. Music and laughter, the swish of stiff silks and satins, of crisp poplins and embroidered muslins, floated out among the fireflies to mingle with the plash of the fountain on the lawn.

If you drive through Clarendon Springs today you will see the old CLARENDON HOUSE. Its day of glory is past. It stands empty and forgotten. If you go there some summer evening you may still catch some of the Victorian illusion that even now clings to the famous old resort. There are no voices, no laughter. No carriage wheels turn upon its graveled roadway; no water splashes from its fountain. The summer houses and springhouse pavilions are gone. It seems like the stage-set for some mid-Victorian play. Only a few more properties are needed. The actors must be waiting for their cues in the wings. Why doesn't someone turn on the footlights? Why doesn't someone ring up the curtain?

CHAPTER ELEVEN

Robert Frost Writes an Introduction—1936

*I*N 1936 we added a substantial number of volumes on music to our music section in the bookshop. This was partially because Walter, Jr., and one of his Dartmouth classmates were planning to go to Europe that summer, working their passage on a ship from Montreal. The major intent of the trip as far as Walter, Jr., was concerned was to go to the Salzburg Music Festival and to hear Richard Strauss conduct his own tone poems in Munich.

At this same time we made a brief and interesting contact because of our books upon music, although they seemed a painfully inadequate collection in my eyes. A middle-aged man came in one day and lingered for some time, looking over our music section. I apologized for its inadequacy, and he responded that, although the books were not a great many in number, they were exceedingly well chosen. I then asked his opinion as to record players, explaining that we, ourselves, for a long time had been building a library of recorded music and were in the process of deciding upon as good a record player as we could afford.

"Have you decided?"

"Yes," I answered, giving him the name of the one we had chosen.

"Oh! I think you have chosen wisely. That is the kind of machine which both my brother and I have." Then he added,

"Perhaps in your personal library of music you have some of my brother's recordings."

I looked at him questioningly.

"My brother is Eugene Ormandy. I, myself, am a cellist in the Philadelphia Orchestra."

Walter, Jr.'s working passage from Montreal landed him and his friend in Wales. Having long enjoyed the chorus of Welsh singers who came to Manchester each summer to sing (descendants of Welsh slate miners who had settled around Poultney, Vermont, years before), he was eager to see Wales. It was not until 1940, four years later, that Richard Llewellyn wrote *How Green Was My Valley,* but if there are Welsh families living in Vermont, they, too, can say, thinking of a Vermont boyhood rather than of one in Wales, "How green was my valley!"

From Wales, Walter, Jr., and Jack went to London. Jack's father had been president of the English-Speaking Union, and the boys had some fine letters of introduction and unusual opportunities because of this.

Before they left for their trip, Walter, Jr., had said to me, "It ought to be you and Dad who are going on this trip. I think you could be set down in any spot in literary Britain and know almost at once where you were. Where do you want me to go for you, especially?"

"To Hampstead. To the Keats Memorial. Bring me back a photograph of the Keats life mask—not the death mask; and do one other thing for me. Walk across Hampstead Heath toward evening. You see, I ask this because of a particular reason. There is such a touching letter from Keats to Fanny Brawne that I am thinking of when I ask you to do this for me.

"One day Keats wrote to her, saying, 'You will have a pleasant walk today, and I shall see you pass. I shall follow you with my eyes over the Heath. Will you come towards *evening,* instead of *before dinner?* When you are gone, 'tis past—if you do not come till the evening, I have something to look forward to all day.' "

When the boys returned in September, just before college opened, they were unable to get working passage on the same boat. Walter, Jr., finally managed to get a job as a deckhand on a German-American liner leaving Antwerp. He had liked the German sailors and carried in his wallet a certificate from the steamship company stating that he was "an able-bodied seaman." He looked so brown and lean and strong that I felt he must deserve such a rating.

He had accomplished his desire to see London and the lovely English country. He had heard Richard Strauss conduct his tone poems in Munich and had attended the Salzburg Music Festival, besides doing much else in England, Austria and Germany. He saw the Olympic Games in Berlin and the sudden appearance of Hitler upon the balcony of the chancellery, at which there was what Walter, Jr., felt was a terrifying, almost insane, demonstration from the crowds in the street below. Escorted by a cavalcade of storm troopers, Hitler's car had stopped before the chancellery, and not only Hitler, but Rudolph Hess, Göring, and Himmler, who were accompanying him, got out and later appeared with him on the chancellery balcony.

Walter, Jr., had brought me the photographic copy of the Keats life mask, and for himself—a love of tea. "You can't turn around anywhere in England that there isn't someone standing at your elbow with a cup of tea."

Home news included the election of his father as Representative to the Vermont Legislature of 1937 from Manchester, Bennington County. Also, there was a new book in the bookshop that held vital interest for us all. *Threescore: The Autobiography of Sarah N. Cleghorn, By Herself,* with an introduction by Robert Frost, and published by Harrison Smith and Robert Haas. Sally was a loved and respected, but controversial, figure to all our village: friend and neighbor, a writer of distinction, and a firebrand and leader in many causes that brought her trouble and dangerous, unfortunate prominence and publicity as well as admiration, albeit reluctant, at various points. Even her dearest friends, Dorothy Canfield and Robert Frost, felt this keenly, but it was Masefield, the poet, who reached his hand across the

sea to encourage and praise her *Ballads and Poems of Protest,*
who really understood her.

I have a thousand intimate memories of her, colored by deep
affection, troubled irritation at her stubborn unreason in the face
of actuality, along with a tremendous admiration for her gift
as a poet and for her fearless statements, couched in such beautiful
English and spoken in one of the most crystalline voices with
the purest enunciation I ever heard.

In reviewing my knowledge and impressions of Sally's life,
for no one who really knew her called her Sarah, I know that
the only reason it covers almost the full span of the sixty years
of which she has written is because of my husband's close association with her and her family since his own childhood. They
had been diagonally opposite neighbors on Pill Alley. Perhaps
Walter and Carl, Sally's brother, two years younger than she,
had been most congenial because at so early an age Sally was
continually admonishing them on the subject of fishing, regarding what she considered was wanton cruelty and injustice. These
two deep concerns, cruelty and injustice, so evident in her course
through life, even in early childhood, were a seal—and an unusual one—set upon her almost from babyhood. A psychological
study of what might, so early, have set her upon such a life
course that she followed continually and fanatically would be
interesting to develop.

There is a reference to her awakened concern for humanity
and for social welfare as early as Chapter One in her autobiography, when she was only six years old. Following their mother's
sudden death, their father brought his three children, Fanny,
eight, Sally, six, and Carl, four, to live with and be brought up
by their two aunts, sisters of their mother.

The incident concerning Sally's six-year-old recognition of
social welfare and happiness is told by her, concerning a surprise
of fresh strawberries prepared for the children by their young
Aunt Jessie.

There were three big saucers of strawberries set on the steps.
Sally says that she felt an onset of pleasure which the strawberries alone couldn't account for. She was enraptured by the

unexpectedness of the treat. It had come on a weekday morning. It seemed to her almost inexcusable kindness! She felt that it gave her a kind of standard in life. Was this the way people ought to be treated?

When Sally was thirteen, she experienced agonizing initiation into man's hideous brutality to man. She used to read the *Tribune* on her way home from the mail. One day she read something strange and fearful. It was an account of the burning alive of a Negro by his white neighbors in the South. This ghastly thing was the most sickening event she had learned of up to that time, yet the *Tribune* had strangely put it into an obscure and very tiny news item not over an inch long.

She wondered how the rest of the paper could be so calm and so cheerful. Burning people alive was what Bloody Mary had done; and it was mentioned in the histories as an instance of the evil nature of Indians. She recalled that it was what Nero had done to the Christians; what Joan of Arc had suffered. Why, she asked herself, was it considered unimportant now—this week —that a Negro had been burned alive by us—an American by Americans?

It was then that she felt her first overwhelming onset of wonder and rage that the sufferings of others could be so calmly contemplated by those who considered themselves good. This was her painful graduation from childhood.

The summation of Sally's autobiography by her publishers gives memories of her rather than concrete events. *Threescore* is an intimate and charming record. It is the kind of book one does not often encounter. An early childhood in the Middle West was tragically terminated by the death of her young mother. Sally's next years were lived in a Vermont village, with her mother's sisters. She left Manchester for various reasons, but always to come home to the serenity of the Green Mountain countryside. Dorothy Canfield was her neighbor. Sally went to Cambridge, to Radcliffe College; later, to Pauling to teach at the Manumit School (her story of this socialist experiment in education is fascinating). She took up the cudgels against vivisection and engaged in other social crusades. During all these years she was composing poetry—much of it appears throughout her book.

From this autobiography a picture of life, now almost gone, emerges. Sally herself is the most interesting person in the book. Sally once wrote:

THE GOLF LINKS LIE SO NEAR THE MILL

> The golf links lie so near the mill
> That almost every day
> The laboring children can look out
> And see the men at play.

Robert Frost used to emphasize that Sally's great hunger was for the righteousness of goodness and mercy. A student of hers once spoke of her "strange obsession with Masefield." Are people still stirred by *The Everlasting Mercy?* I am. I came under Sally's "strange obsession" and echoed it:

JOHN MASEFIELD

> Democracy's best pen, with passion vowed
>   *"To maimed and halt and blind, in rain and cold,"*
>   Three mighty epics of the poor hath told:—
> The Dauber, freezing to the sleeted shroud:
> The Widow kneeling in the gallows crowd:
>   And that great idyl of the windy wold,
>   The drunkard walking where the dawn unrolled,
> And with changed eyes beholding one who plowed.
>
> Again, Immortal, yoke that share divine,
> And fix our eyes *"forever on that sign"*;—
> Plow deep our souls, that can with mirth endure
> Ease to ourselves and burdens to the poor;—
> Convert us wastrels; O undying pen,
> Harrow our hearts, that we may *"flower to men."*

It also explains the fact that Sarah Cleghorn soon heard from Masefield and that he had become a champion of many of her "poems of protest" and considered her *True Ballad of*

Glorious Harriet Tubman to be an American classic. Harriet Tubman's achievements, which this ballad relates, have been verified. It was she who led more than three hundred Negro slaves to freedom from the South through constant peril of her own life before and during the Civil War.

When Masefield came to New York City after his publication of *The Everlasting Mercy,* he was invited to be the guest of honor of the New York Poetry Society. Louis Untermeyer, its president, wrote, asking him to make a choice of an American poet he would like to have sit at his side. I have often thought how astonished Untermeyer must have been by his reply: Sarah Cleghorn. And Sally went, wearing her soft, black chiffon home-made dress, her mass of fair hair piled high upon her head.

I sometimes think that among all the carefully cherished historical or Colonial markers attached to some of the oldest houses in the village, the choice of Sarah Cleghorn and the recognition of her as a poet by Britain's Poet Laureate should be recorded. This fact about "the Pink House," as it is known now in the village, seems so much more interesting and compelling to any literary and cultural records than the date of its building, or its early eighteenth-century ownership.

One day she and I walked along the edge of the mountain for an autumn glimpse of our valley from Deer Knoll. We rested by the Equinox spring and she told me she had brought her most treasured possession to show me. It was contained in a leather envelope: all of Masefield's sonnets which he had written out in longhand for her and had signed with special words of admiration for her.

It was the next year that Masefield and his wife wrote, inviting her to come to England and spend several weeks with them. But her invalid aunt would not agree to her absence, and it was to be expected that Sally's sense of duty would override her longing to go.

For years, Sally's *Portraits and Protests,* published in 1917 by Henry Holt, has been out of print and has never been republished. Because of this I am including some of the poems, so

many of which originally appeared in the *Atlantic,* and so many
of which speak not only of the landscape of Vermont but of
the landscape of her heart and its convictions. Each one of them
I could repeat by memory, but Sally herself typed out each of
them, and many more, for me, even in quantity, hoping we
might sell them in the bookshop, since her actual book was out
of print and Holt could not be convinced it would have further
sale. How many times ever since we have been asked and asked
for it in the bookshop!

DOROTHEA (DOROTHY CANFIELD)

Young is she, and slight to view
    In her home-made cambric dresses:
Are her sweet eyes gray or blue?
    Shade of twilight are her tresses.
Fairy-fine at first she seems;
    But a longer look confesses
She's more wholesome stuff than dreams!

(Yet I mind an April moon
    Shining down an orchard alley:
From one book, companions boon,
    There we read "LOVE IN THE VALLEY";
And I saw bright phantoms race,
    Thousand phantoms fleet and rally
All across her lighted face.)

Once, within the ancient ground
    Where her fathers all lie sleeping,
She, beside a recent mound,
    Still and tender, but not weeping,
Stood: that picture on my heart
    Fair am I forever keeping:
With that look I would not part.

O but in her maiden days
    How she led the children trooping
Through the old familiar plays!
    Up her sash and flounces looping,
If the tiniest lost his cue,

To his side she ran, and stooping,
Caught his hand and danced him through.

Met you her in Hemlock Wood
    In the white midwinter weather,
When the pine's a tufted hood,
    And the fern's a crystal feather?
Heard you then her yodel sweet
    And a far reply, together
Float in echo where they meet?

Ariel voice, from range to range
    Lightly tossed and sweetly flying!
All her notes to murmurs change
    When the winter light is dying:
All in magic murmurs she
    Laps and lulls the wee one lying,
Pearl of twilight, on her knee.

MARGARITA SINGING BALLADS

Dark her eyes of tranquil wonder;
    Dark her smoothly banded hair;
Broad and calm her brow and bosom
    Rising white in shadow where
Tall she stands by the valley window
    Singing soft to the evening air.

Hush! 'tis the tune of sweet *Ben Lomond,*
    Poignant sweet and timbrel clear.
Now when falls her wistful cadence,
    O that forest and field could hear!
—Thrilling rise and tender cadence,
    Low and long in the dreaming ear.

Pause not yet: the sands are fleeting:
    Fast, too fast, the moments run.
Lo, the strains of *Allan Water;*
    (Amber tears in April sun).
She breathes; and sings *The Bailiff's Daughter,*
    The wayside lover of Islington.

Yield the charm, melodious hour!
　　Distant valley chimes, forbear!
Hark the rainbow shower of grace-notes,
　　Fall of sounds how light, how fair!
Is it a voice of earth or elf-land
　　Singing *The Lass with the Delicate Air?*

THE INCENTIVE

I saw a sickly cellar plant
Droop on its feeble stem, for want
Of sun and wind and rain and dew,—
Of freedom!—Then a man came through
The cellar, and I heard him say,
"Poor, foolish plant, by all means stay
Contented here: for—know you not?—
This stagnant dampness, mould and rot
Are your incentive to grow tall
And reach that sunbeam on the wall."
—Even as he spoke, the sun's one spark
Withdrew, and left the dusk more dark.

VERMONT

I

Wide and shallow, in the cowslip marshes,
　　Floods the freshet of the April snow;
Late drifts linger in the hemlock gorges,
　　Through the brakes and mosses trickling slow,
　　　　Where the mayflower,
　　Where the painted trillium, leaf and blow.

II

Foliaged deep, the cool midsummer maples
　　Shade the porches of the long white street.
Trailing wide, Olympian elms lean over
　　Tiny churches where the cross-roads meet:
　　　　Fields of fireflies
　　Wheel all night like stars among the wheat.

III

Blaze the mountains in the windless autumn,
 Frost-clear, blue-nooned, apple-ripening days;
Faintly fragrant, in the farther valleys,
 Smoke of many bonfires swells the haze:
  Fair-bound cattle
 Plod with lowing up the meadowy ways.

IV

Roaring snows, down-sweeping from the uplands,
 Bury the still valleys, drift them deep.
Low along the mountains, lake-blue shadows,
 Sea-blue shadows, in the snow-drifts sleep.
  High above them
 Blinding crystal is the sunlit steep.

NOCTES AMBROSIANAE

From Windward Mountain's barren crest
The roaring gale flies down the west
And drifts the snow on Redmount's breast
  In hollows dark with pine.

Full in its path from hill to hill,
There stands, beside a ruined mill,
A lonely house, above whose sill
  A brace of candles shine.

And there a lonely bachelor
And maiden sister full threescore
Sit all forgetful of the roar
  Of wind and mountain stream:

Forgot the wind, forgot the snow,
What magic airs about them blow?—
They read in wondering voices low
  The "Midsummer Night's Dream!"

And reading, past their frozen hill
In charmèd woods they range their fill
And hear the horns of Oberon shrill
  Above the Plunging Tam:

Yea, long beyond the cock's first crow
In dreams they walk where wind-flowers blow:
Late do they dream, and liker grow
                To Charles and Mary Lamb.

THE OLDENBURYS OF SUNDERLAND

Turn again into the wooded Hollow
        By the fabled Tory-hunter's well,
Where the strange and bookish Oldenburys
        On their wasted patrimony dwell.

Rowland plows to the sound of Celia's fiddle:
        Celia sews with her Milton on her knee:
Young Miranda goes forth to gather berries
        Singing the song of Ariel by the sea.

When the dusk falls downward from the landslide,
        Through the bush they drive the cattle home:
They see the shadows of the first Crusaders
        And hear the sibyl at the gates of Rome.

In the northward, in the southward village
        Brisk steps hasten, the busy hours fly fast;
But the clocks are slow in Oldenbury Hollow,
        Where they chime with the voices of the past.

MR. WILLOWAY

His beaded waistcoat and his silvery hat,
        His large-tailed coat and russet pantaloons,
Down the long, solitary marble street
        Come twinkling late on Sunday afternoons.

Twig-like his limbs, the slender bachelor:
        Loose on him hangs his coat of bygone blue.
He carries, from his weedy garden plot,
        A bunch of pansies and of feverfew.

He enters at the cemetery gate
        And Lovers' Lane he follows up and down,
Past all the sagging weather-eaten stones,
        The tombstones of the founders of the town,

Until he comes out on a hill-top green,
    Spreads his coat-tails, and seats himself beside
One "LUCY WATERS, AETAT TWENTY YEARS"
    Born in the Baretown Hollow, where she died.

HEMLOCK MOUNTAIN

By orange grove and palm-tree, we walked the southern shore,
Each day more still and golden than was the day before.
That calm and languid sunshine! How faint it made us grow
To look on Hemlock Mountain when the storm hangs low!

To see its rocky pastures, its sparse but hardy corn,
The mist roll off its forehead before a harvest morn;
To hear the pine-trees crashing across its gulfs of snow
Upon a roaring midnight when the whirlwinds blow.

And she whose narrow shoulders the trembling fever shook,
As daily came her health back, more wistful grew her look.
Within her eyes the picture how well we came to know!
The woods on Hemlock Mountain where the windflowers grow.

Tell not of lost Atlantis, or fabled Avalon;
The olive, or the vineyard, no winter breathes upon;
Away from Hemlock Mountain we could not well forego,
For all the summer islands where the gulf tides flow.

COME, CAPTAIN AGE!

Come, Captain Age,
With your great sea-chest full of treasure!
Under the yellow and wrinkled tarpaulin
Disclose the carved ivory
And the sandalwood inlaid with pearl:
Riches of wisdom and years.
Unfold the India shawl
With its border of emerald and orange and crimson and blue,
Weave of a lifetime!
I shall be rich and splendid
With the spoils of the Indies of Age.

COMRADE JESUS

Thanks to Saint Matthew, who had been
At mass-meetings in Palestine,
We know whose side was spoken for
When Comrade Jesus had the floor.

"Where sore they toil and hard they lie,
Among the great unwashed, dwell I.
The tramp, the convict, I am he:
Cold-shoulder him, cold-shoulder me."

By Dives' door, with thoughtful eye,
He did tomorrow prophesy:—
"The Kingdom's gate is low and small:
The rich can scarce wedge through at all."

"A dangerous man," said Caiaphas,
"An ignorant demagogue, alas.
Friend of low women, it is he
Slanders the upright Pharisee."

For law and order, it was plain,
For Holy Church, he must be slain.
The troops were there to awe the crowd:
Mob violence was not allowed.

Their clumsy force with force to foil,
His strong, clean hands he would not soil.
He saw their childishness quite plain
Between the lightnings of his pain.

Between the twilights of his end
He made his fellow-felon friend.
With swollen tongue and blinded eyes
Invited him to Paradise.

Ah, let no Local him refuse!
Comrade Jesus hath paid his dues.
Whatever other be debarred,
Comrade Jesus hath his red card.*

* In the '20's, it was the Socialist who carried a "red card," *not* the Communist.

CHAPTER TWELVE

A Winter in Montpelier

WALTER AND I spent the winter of 1937 in Montpelier, beginning with the opening of the legislative session in January. John
Fisher and Dorothy Canfield Fisher were also in Montpelier, as
John had been elected State Representative from Arlington. They
had rented a house on the hillside behind the State House and
Walter and I stayed at the Walton Homestead. There were
other legislative guests there as well as ourselves, although I
cannot recall whether they lived there or merely had dinner there.
Senator Leon Gay and his wife added immensely to the pleasure
and interest of that winter for us.

Mrs. Walton was very elderly, but she and her housekeeper
conducted her dinner table each night as though a group of
distinguished guests were being entertained. She was a gentle
and kindly lady, but had reached the age when she was easily
confused and forgetful. One of the social maxims she tena-
ciously held to was that no lull in conversation should be allowed
to last. The ball must be kept rolling, and a pause in talk, of
even the briefest sort, at once urged her into action.

Many times Senator Gay was the victim of this belief of hers.
Having paused for a moment in his conversation (when he was
explaining or enlarging upon some point that he was making),
he would suddenly find himself cut short by a new and completely irrelevant topic tossed into the pause by Mrs. Walton.
He would look around in startled and frustrated annoyance, com-

pletely thrown off balance; but Mrs. Walton had her topic
well launched into the stream of the former conversation and
was entirely unaware of his irritation and balked thread of
thought.

I remember that long after this I happened one day to be
standing near the Plaza park entrance in New York, when a
mounted policeman emerged from the park on a beautiful horse.
He reined the horse in and came to a standstill while some
traffic passed before him. Meanwhile, a very elderly white poodle
appeared from nowhere and began to travel in and out between
the horse's feet. The horse looked down, bewildered and in-
sulted. Suddenly, he gave an infuriated snort. Watching, I was
vaguely reminded of something. What was it? Of course! Senator
Gay and Mrs. Walton.

Being a member of the Montpelier legislative family was not
as interesting as I had anticipated. It took so awfully long to
pass a bill. Such pulling and hauling, as I sat listening in the
gallery. Even when one learned all the regulated courses of
procedure, it seemed a limited affair for the mere onlooker. I
wanted to be present to hear the debate and argument that
followed in the committee rooms!

Most of the wives of the legislative members seemed to have
any number of social pleasures—endless bridge games, tea
parties, and luncheons together; and evenings of frankly absurd
fun—spelling bees and improvised take-offs on certain good-
natured personalities at the State House. But in all of this I
was a failure at the start because I didn't play bridge, was anxious
not to put on weight, and was the sort of speller that would
make any editor want to jump off the dock. Finally, in desperation, I sought out Dorothy.

"Dorothy, give me a job! Anything you can trust me to
do for you."

"Do you mean it?"

"Yes. I'm bored with being an unoccupied woman."

It ended by my having a kind of secretarial assignment with
Dorothy, really nothing important, just helpful. I would go up

to her study each morning while she opened her mail, an unbelievable quantity of letters. She would read each one.

"I *always* read them through. They may seem unimportant at first glance and then prove otherwise in the last line. I could never do what Robert [Frost] does. He just sits and throws them into the wastebasket or fire after reading only the opening sentence or two. He thinks I'm crazy."

By the time the letters had all been opened she had made jottings on them, notations. Finally she handed me a couple of dozen or more. "These few I must answer myself. These others I'll send to my regular secretary in Arlington for regulation replies; she'll understand. But these I'm giving you are letters involving things you'll have to do *actively* for me."

From that moment I never felt I was "an unoccupied woman."

The activities in which I became involved were varied. They included arranging an educational schedule for the ten-year-old daughter of a naval officer stationed in Hawaii, whose wife and little girl were living on a nearby small island. For a few weeks I was in communication with the University of Hawaii, with officials who furnished me with the regular boat schedules running daily to the different "outer" islands, with textbook publishers, and possible tutors and teachers who might be available for the child. Another assignment involved me in interviewing the Jehovah's Witnesses parents of a little girl who had been dismissed from one of the Montpelier public schools because of her refusal to salute the flag.

I marvel now that Dorothy should have thought I was qualified to undertake such a task. I found the father and mother at home in a small, scantily furnished tenement on a side street. The little girl sat on the floor of an inner room, drawing with a broken piece of crayon on brown wrapping paper.

"She likes to draw," said the mother.

"There are so many nice chances for children to draw at school," I said. "Tell me all about why it is that you do not want your little girl to salute the flag. I want to hear *your* side of it, too."

But almost immediately I wondered whether I did; such a volley of impassioned words was opened upon me. Somehow, in the midst of all the quoting of Old Testament Scripture, I found myself raising my hand and saying firmly, "Now, listen to *me*." And to my own, almost unbelieving ears, I began to quote the Scriptures myself. How had I ever retained so much in my memory? Psalms, Isaiah, the Gospels and the Book of Revelations poured from me in such a torrent and with such concentrated conviction that my opponent listened in almost stunned silence. It ended with the parents agreeing that I might at least come and take the little girl to one of the free W.P.A. craft classes in drawing held in the afternoons, where no salute to the flag was required! Every couple of days I went for her and took her home. I grew quite fond of her and my only fear was that, because of my exhibition of scriptural knowledge, her parents now looked upon me as a possible convert.

Montpelier began to seem a busier and more acceptable place following Dorothy's provision of an occupation for me. And not only I began to fit into the picture but Walter was rapidly doing so. One day as I was returning from delivering to her house some carbon copies of letters I had written for Dorothy, I heard her and John's voices as they came along the street below their house. It was John's voice speaking Walter's name that arrested my attention.

"I was perfectly astonished," said John. "I never dreamed Walter Hard could speak that way. He stood up there, completely at ease, and was so clear and convincing that he just demolished the opposing arguments of seasoned committee members. Everyone is talking about him. I believe he can make the Senate if he ever wants to."

(Later on, Walter was elected each of the three different times he ran for the Senate.)

In June, Walter, Jr., was graduated from Dartmouth and Walter took him the first copy of his new book, *Vermont Vintage,* which the Stephen Daye Press published and which he had dedicated: "For my son, himself a heartwarming vintage."

This was an especially happy month for us, because the June,
1937, *Atlantic Monthly* contained two of Walter's poems.

But the difficulties of the first Depression years soon became
painfully realistic for Walter, Jr. His hope was to find some newspaper, or a publishing house, that would give him a job. Vermont had no openings for him and he went to New York, for
over two weeks beating the pavements, with no employment to
be found. Who would engage a young man just out of college
with no actual newspaper experience when experienced men were
begging for work?

The Depression was a bitter, frustrating time for young graduates who seemed to find that the four years of conscientious
study had not really fitted them for such a situation. It was
more bitter still for their parents that eventually it was *war* that
offered occupation!

Meanwhile, Walter, Jr., opened a branch of the Johnny
Appleseed Bookshop in Bangor, Maine. It was a losing battle
for him since the cut-rate drugstores and news stores seemed
to carry all the reading matter people wanted. The big library,
of which he had been hopeful because it had a notably large
book fund, bought through other channels. After a year he took
down the sign from his store door and came home so thin and
worn that we were frightened about him. He worked in our
own shop and took on every available short-time, fill-in job that
offered. The fact that we knew many people were saying, "If
they'd kept the drugstore . . ." was an added distress, and
yet, it wasn't. Even as things were, we did not regret the sale,
Walter's opportunities for writing were so increased.

Skiing areas had begun to be developed around Manchester,
notably Big Bromley, and it offered promise for employment
and at once brought new people to the region. Suddenly we
had new business at the bookshop and Walter, Jr., got some
newspaper assignments because he had been a skier at Dartmouth
and could cover news of the new winter sport growing rapidly
in our region.

It was at this time that I came upon a small calfskin-bound
book while looking through some old papers in a little trunk.

It proved to be a diary that Walter's father had kept as a boy while living in the family homestead down on the river road. It was written in a delicate, precise penmanship, and gave an intimate picture of the life of the farm and the family during the Civil War years. Constantly recurring are the words: "Father and I." Suddenly I realized that in this Hard family of mine, the relation of father and son, of "Father and I," seems to be an established devotion repeating itself from generation to generation. *Vermont Vintage* with Walter's words of dedication to his son that instantly bespeak the relationship and companionship existing between them; this little diary written by his own father, with the recurring phrase of "Father and I"; and my own constant observation of the continuous companionship and devotion existing between Walter, Jr., and his two sons of twelve and thirteen bespeak a heritage from the past that has its roots in unshakable understanding, companionship, and devotion.

This little diary, written during the Civil War years, throws a brief but vivid light upon the home which its young writer knew. Often I turn its pages, trying to fill in the picture. This little boy leaves out so much which I long to know! One expression, however, recurs constantly—an expression which seems to be the keynote of all his boyhood—"Father and I."

March 30th, 1863—Father and I went up to the sap house to-day and carried around about 200 buckets. This afternoon our cow had a pair of twin calves. It has snowed very hard all this afternoon. We heard today of the famous spring near Yorktown, Va. It is said that it broke out and ran freely for three months before the Revolution and stopped three months before its close. It also burst forth three months before the war of 1812 and ceased three months before its end; and it also commenced to run three months before this Rebellion and stopped running a few days ago.

March 31st—Father and I went up the mountain this morning and drew a load of logs. It began to snow at noon and has been snowing all the day. Mother and Grandmother have gone a-visiting at the village. Gathered the sap in and boiled it down this evening and had two pails full.

April 5th—It rained this morning and we shall not go to meeting. We went to the barn a little while ago and found a little bossy, it belongs to old White. Father and I can soon take the banking off the house.

April 10th—Went over to the sap woods this morning and found some of the buckets running over. Will sugar off tonight. Father and I went over to see Mr. Pettibone's sheep, mud very deep in the roads to the village.

April 19th—It is very pleasant today and the birds are singing and it seems like Spring. Father and I are very busy with the lambs. We have three pairs of twin lambs and we have to raise four lamb cossets. One of the little lambs is dead. I did not go to meeting this morning. Had a toothache and my face is beginning to swell tonight.

April 27th—Father and I sowed oats this morning—that piece across the river, and Father harrowed this afternoon while I took care of the lambs. We lost three lambs today. Walter helped draw stones this afternoon.

April 28th—Father and I went down to mill this morning and got the grist. Harrowed over the oat piece this afternoon. Mother went up to the village to-day to sit with Uncle Curtis who is very sick. Walter and I drew out two loads of manure onto the garden and set a hen on eight turkey eggs.

April 30th—Father and I finished plowing and sowing on the hill this morning. It rained this afternoon pretty hard and I went fishing and caught three trout. Mother says Uncle Curtis is very sick to-day. Tonight I cleaned out my gun and Father went up to watch with Uncle Curtis.

May 4th—Father and I took our cattle up to pasture to-day and Walter drew over a load of rails to mend fence. Father set out some apple trees this afternoon. Carried Mother and Sister Katie up to the village to call on Aunt Sarah.

May 25th—We heard to-day that the stars and stripes are floating over Vicksburg. Got up this morning at sunrise and went over the river and shot at a crow. Father and I washed the sheep to-day. Sold our cosset lambs to-day for $10.

June 3rd—Father went up to court to-day but was not drawn on the jury. Sowed our Injun wheat and harrowed it. Walter and I cleaned out the corn house and washed up the carriage. Mr. Temple sheared our coarse wool sheep to-day.

January 1st, 1864—Joe DeMarr came home last night. He has enlisted for three years more. There was a donation at the parsonage tonight and we all went—Mother, Walter, Willis, Sister Katie, Father and I.

January 4th—I went to school to-day and skated all the way on the river. Walter was taken sick to-day and Willis' face is swelled up. Father and I went up to Dorset this afternoon after sheep and I went up to the village to Singing School tonight with Sister Katie.

February 13th—School does not keep to-day and I chopped wood all day except when I was in the house. Mother went up to the village to a ladies' meeting. Sister Katie and I went up to the village to a Spelling Bee tonight.

March 23rd—Father and I went to the stone mill this morning to get some marble for an arch. When we got home I tapped a few trees. This afternoon we tapped about 200. Sap runs first rate.

March 24th—Father and I went over to the sap woods and found a good many buckets full and running over. Father fixed the arches and we gathered 15 barrels of sap. Boiled until about nine o'clock.

April 13th—Sold 50 lbs. of sugar to-day at 14¢ a lb. Have an order for 180 lbs. at 18¢ a lb. Walter is sick and I have all the chores to do. Father and I went up to the village tonight.

April 14th—Heard to-day that Grant had been put in command of all our army. Walter is better to-day and I guess he will be out soon. I hope he will. Have had to work hard and feel very tired tonight.

Here the diary ends—the only written record of the valley farm and its household during the war that changed its life so radically. There is no mention in the pages of this little book of the tragedy which the war had already brought to the peaceful home. I find no rehearsal of the fate of Cyrus, the eldest son, who in 1861 enlisted with the first regiment of Vermont Volunteers.

He had been barely more than nineteen at the time, a slender boy with his mother's winning smile. His letters had come frequently at first—brief descriptions of encampments and military programs, interspersed with bits of whimsical humor—poorly veiled attempts at light-heartedness. As I read them over now, they give but one impression—longing for home. News traveled slowly in those days and the boy had been dead for weeks when the family learned that he was "missing." Even now, years afterward, I sometimes stand in the room where he once slept, and imagine, with a sudden gripping of the heart, how he must have longed for the peace of this same room. As he lay dying of fever and infection he must have prayed for water from the cold streams he knew, for a breath of mountain air upon his face. For him heaven could have meant but one thing—his mother and the valley farm.

All this philosophizing about fathers and sons recalls to my memory the two months when Walter, Jr.'s older son, Crosby, then seven years old, was with us while his father and mother were in Europe—the little boy who, I have earlier explained, was troubled over his grandfather's rather inexact carpentry.

It was not until the third day of his visit to us that I realized something was wrong. He had been loving and tractable and very quiet. I awoke on the second night to the more or less frequent sound of his coughing. His room was just across the hall from mine. In the morning he still coughed. Suddenly I thought I recognized all the symptoms of measles. I called him to me and opened his shirt. His chest was covered with rash. When the doctor came I had put my little boy to bed. He lay, his face turned away from me, looking small and bereft. I gave the doctor a list of varied information concerning him which my daughter-in-law had given me. The doctor went upstairs alone. He thought a man-to-man introduction might be best. He was downstairs in a very few minutes.

"He hasn't measles, Mrs. Hard."

"He hasn't? What is it, then?" I asked anxiously.

"That boy's *homesick*."

"But that rash!"

"The list his mother gave you says he was inoculated for measles ten days ago. He has held such a tight rein on his emotions, his homesickness, for fear of disturbing you, that it has made the inoculation 'take' as though he briefly had measles. If you can comfort him I think all these symptoms—rash and cough—will be gone by tomorrow."

I could have wept.

But my grandson had not improved. He lay with his face turned from me, listless and silent.

"Darling, the doctor says that you *haven't* the measles."

There was no reply. I went and sat on the side of his bed and put my hand on his cheek.

"Darling, if you can hold on just a day or two longer, then everything will be all right."

Then came the relieving tears.

"Is there anything that you can think of that *I* can possibly do to comfort you?"

He sat up in bed, his face wet with tears, and pulled himself together.

"Do you have a book called *The Wind in the Willows?* That's my father's and my favorite book. If you could read it to me . . ."

I tore downstairs to the living room and came back with it. I read, hardly knowing whether the book was bottom-end up, or right-end up. Presently, his grandfather came, went over and drew him into the curve of his arm. They listened together. Then I explained that his grandfather and I would take turns at eating luncheon so that he need not be left alone.

"Oh, no, Grandma. It'll be all right now. You and Grandpa go down *together* for lunch. I wouldn't want to *worry* you, Grandma."

The doctor was right. By the next day there was no further sign of either cough or rash.

We finished *The Wind in the Willows*—"my father's and my favorite book"—and began *The Tanglewood Tales*.

"Which one of the stories do you like best, dear?"

"Well, I thought at first the one about Mercury and the Flying Slippers. But oh, Grandma, the one about the Flying Horse—about Pegasus. That's the most wonderful one of them all!"

In his next column of "Hard Times," in the Rutland *Herald,* Walter wrote:

The Vermont section of the Grandchild Front has been reunited and moved back to its northern base and our recent visiting share of it has left a great emptiness. The day starts less early but less shiningly, and moves through hours filled with none of the recent innumerable activities and joyous surprises. A small flying figure in a red shirt no longer marks our landscape, or, full of serious business, awaits the finishing of each letter to get it to the postoffice without delay. And now, in the starlight, Pegasus no longer waits outside his window to carry him to a wonder world of fancy. "But Grandma, I'll surely be back in the morning."

At seventy, one has learned to discard many things that once seemed superlatively important. But at seven, one has not yet accumulated all these things and yet lives in the world of fundamental truth. Seven and seventy have much in common.

CHAPTER THIRTEEN

The Depression and
Legislative Years—1939–1940

$\mathcal{D}$URING THE Depression one of our final experiences in the winter of 1938 in Montpelier was an evening spent at Craftsbury Common with Elliott and Kay Merrick. Walter had written the introduction to Elliott's book *From This Hill Look Down,* which the Stephen Daye Press published in 1934. Elliott Merrick had explored the Labrador Peninsula and had written about it in his book *True North,* published by Scribner. He had met his wife, then a young Australian nurse who was performing heroic service, at the Grenfell Mission.

When the Depression came, they found themselves in New Jersey in a tight financial trap. My husband says in his introduction to this book (long out of print):

John Dacey [*really Elliott Merrick himself*] like thousands of others lost his job and pounded the pavements in a vain search for work. Then one day he made the break. He moved his wife and small son and his household goods to a rented farm on the Vermont shore of Lake Champlain, there to turn his toil directly into the necessities of life—into food, shelter, and warmth, without the need of much cash.

In doing this he came on some things which apply to many seekers after a new way of life. He found he had to give over the idea of the market place, that "time is money." What if it did take him twice as long to get his wood cut as it did his skilled neighbor? He had plenty of time to spend and, when he had absorbed the idea that he was rich in time, much of the strain and worry fell away.

Furthermore, he decided that he preferred a dinner of green herbs, gathered by the sweat of his own brow, to a stalled ox furnished by a charitable government.

Statistics showing that there are thousands of homes without the benefits of modern plumbing do not cause him to shudder. Here is what he says in a conversation with a special friend: "I would like to see every man who can't work for somebody else move heaven and earth to work for himself."

This story is a cross section of a small Vermont community. You get to know the people as the author knows them. You feel that, as his body has been nourished by and become a part of the soil, so his spirit has breathed in the beauty of conquering life. He is not disguising philosophy in the form of fiction. He is writing with the sweat of toil. The story is wrested from the soil by hands which know labor. Elliott Merrick writes with the insight of a native. This story is as stark in its truth as Rockwell Kent's drawings, and withal it shows beauty, as they do, seen through the eyes of a poet.

How graphically Elliott Merrick has recorded the compensations of the country is beautifully illustrated in the chapter, *The Rain*. The last load of hay has been rushed into the barn when the heavens open. And the refreshing torrent floods down on the thirsty earth. John Dacey goes out on a high hill and as the rain drenches his sweaty body he cries, "Good God, I am a crop as good as oats or garden truck. The rain is rain, and for me and my lips and body. The transplanted has indeed taken root in good earth."

It was at this same period of the Depression that Walter wrote an article for *Survey Graphic,* at John Farrar's request, entitled "Vermont, a Way of Life." John Farrar had stopped to see us at our Old Square House and as he sat with us he kept remarking that he had not found the atmosphere of desperation and despair, attendant upon the Depression, anywhere in Vermont as it existed in other states. He wanted to know why there was this difference. Walter replied that, for one thing, Vermont was still a rural and farming state as compared with the industrialized states. The average Vermonter never had had any money with which to "speculate." His small farm provided his physical needs—root vegetables in the cold cellar and canned green vegetables, apples, a small wood lot, or a share in one, for fuel, a cow and chickens for milk, butter, and eggs. Some small business and thrift accounted for the serenity of most of the people living in the villages and towns. Vermont had few *cities.* This situation, Walter explained, was exemplified by an ad he had recently seen in the Rutland *Herald:* "Wanted: a family cow in exchange for an automobile." One obviously could walk if necessary.

It was in May of 1938 that we returned from Montpelier and Walter's first session of the Legislature (for, although representatives were elected for two years, a session was called only for the first year unless a "special session" was called during the second year to transact some special state business).

The lilacs were in their glory all through New England, and especially so in our valley. Walter and I had driven up to Rutland to do a few errands and noticed a poster announcing that Carl Sandburg would be speaking at Green Mountain College in Poultney that evening. With eagerness we drove over to the college and asked Dr. Bogue, the president, whether there would be any possible arrangement by which we might be allowed to come and hear him. Dr. Bogue reassured us by saying that Carl Sandburg had asked him by phone that morning whether there was any chance that Walter might be there. A mutual friend had given him two or three of Walter's books and he was eager to meet him and to talk with him.

So we returned around eight o'clock and had a rare experience. Carl Sandburg had just completed his last volume of *The War Years,* and talk of Lincoln, with amazing poetic commentary, flowed from his lips. He held the students and faculty who crowded the auditorium in rapt attention. Later, we met him in Dr. Bogue's study and Mr. Sandburg asked Walter whether we were driving back to Manchester, and whether, if so, he might drive with us and telephone from there to friends at Bennington College where he was to speak next day. They would meet him at our house and take him on to Bennington.

He was very tired and chilled after having expended so much effort and emotion in his talk. "I just had to give those young people everything I had! They were such a fine, appreciative audience."

When we reached our Old Square House surrounded by ancient lilac trees in bloom, I said to Mr. Sandburg, "Why don't you stay with us tonight? You are very tired. Walter will drive you down to Bennington College in the morning and it is really a shame for you not to see this beautiful valley by daylight."

"I believe I will. If I go on now I'll just stay up all night talking."

He telephoned to the college while Walter made an open fire in our study and when he came in and relaxed in a chair before it, I said, "If you were home, you would have something to eat now. What would it be? Let me get it for you."

"Yes, but I doubt you'd have it. Goat's milk cheese, rye bread, and orange juice brought to the boiling point." As a matter of fact, I had all three.

Soon Mr. Sandburg was relaxed, warm, and comfortable. He talked again of Lincoln and I explained to him that because my father had been twenty-two years older than my mother he had been a young man at the time of the Civil War. I told him that I had been brought up to cherish two episodes concerning his adoration of Lincoln.

My father had heard Lincoln when he spoke at Cooper Union in 1860, and in 1861 he had slept all night on the ground close to the edge of the platform where Lincoln was to stand when he raised the flag at dawn over Independence Hall in Philadelphia when he left that city on his way to Washington for his first Inaugural. There was an extra family slant for me to this episode. When Lincoln started to raise the flag the rope became tangled in the pulleys. My father leaped to the platform, and, untangling the rope, placed it in Lincoln's hand.

"Every Philadelphia paper of that date," said Mr. Sandburg, "includes that little incident. But reporters were less omnipresent in those days. The young man's name was not given. Now, after—how many years?—I come to Vermont and the young man's daughter tells me the name."

I also talked with Mr. Sandburg about young Leonard Johnson of Peacham, Vermont, whose brother Oliver had helped found the *Anti-Slavery Standard*. "I found an old Peacham town history," I told him, "that said that Leonard Johnson tolled the Peacham Church bell for one hour on the day that John Brown was being hanged."

"I've always felt I'd like to own a copy of the *Anti-Slavery Standard*," said Mr. Sandburg, "but I guess they are all among archives now."

Or in trunks, I thought to myself, knowing I had two copies in a trunk in our attic.

It was almost three o'clock when the fire died down and Mr. Sandburg went to bed.

The next morning, when he came down to breakfast, I had a copy of the *Anti-Slavery Standard* folded beside his breakfast plate for him. As it was, he did not get off with Walter for Bennington until almost noon. There was more absorbing talk and then he went all through our bookshelves. He not only autographed his own books for us but wrote personal messages in them. As he stood on our doorstep saying good-bye to me he looked up into one of the lilac trees that reached above the roof of the house and said, "When I woke up this morning in that old room with the fragrance of lilacs coming in at the windows, I said to myself, 'Carl Sandburg, how did you ever get into a room like this from the stockyards?'"

In November of the following autumn the Stephen Daye Press held a book fair in Brattleboro. In the afternoon Governor George D. Aiken spoke, as the author of *Pioneering with Fruits and Berries, Pioneering with Wild Flowers,* and *Speaking from Vermont,* Walter spoke as the author of *Salt of Vermont* and *Vermont Vintage,* and I spoke as a collaborating author of *This Is Vermont.*

In the evening there was a dinner followed by a shorter session of speakers, not necessarily authors of books published by the Stephen Daye Press. I remember especially enjoying the presence of Lewis Gannett, Ralph Flanders, and Charlie Crane.

When the session of evening speakers occurred, Frederick Van de Water, as I recall it, followed Lewis Gannett and Ralph

Flanders. He was unfortunate in what he said, for he proceeded to heap belittling statements upon the Stephen Daye Press, its authors, and its guests. He began by saying that he could not conceive of any reason why a small, unknown firm like the Stephen Daye Press should have a book fair and that as he had read the names of its authors and guests he realized that there was not a truly professional author or writer among them; that, as far as he knew, he was the only one who could correctly be placed in such a category. His audience—it was a large assemblage—fairly gasped. Perhaps that was the reaction he had been aiming at. Charlie Crane was the next speaker. With humor and amazing finesse, he took Mr. Van de Water over the hurdles in a manner that caused his listeners to laugh aloud and break into applause.

It was during this same week that Walter read at the Boston *Herald* book fair which was held in the Boston Public Library. Certainly, it was an august and impressive affair, but somehow, for us, it lacked the color and pleasure of the Stephen Daye Press book fair. Perhaps it was because it lacked Frederick Van de Water and Charlie Crane.

This was the autumn when Walter was elected to the 1939–40 Senate of the State Legislature. I decided not to go to Montpelier with him but to try keeping the bookshop open during the winter. The new skiing developments were giving us a winter season as well as a summer one. It would be a challenge to run the bookshop alone, and to be alone out on our hill. This would be the start of maintaining an open-all-year bookshop. Walter would be coming home every Friday night from Montpelier to stay until Monday morning. I couldn't go too far wrong in a week's time and he would be back to reassure me on weekends.

When he left me for the opening of the Legislature during the first week of January, it was snowing heavily and I felt like a pioneer as I walked the mile through the thick snowfall. Rather silly, because our almost two-hundred-year-old house had a modern heating system besides its four comforting fireplaces. If the snow became very deep I could get a taxi at night.

But I found pioneering did not begin at our Old Square House but at the bookshop. Mr. Worden, who had bought the drugstore, did not supply any heat, "to speak of," in the bookshop. He opened the glass door between it and the drugstore to allow a small, very small, proportion of the heat from his quarters to filter in. When there was a stiff wind blowing, the proportion was slight. I would huddle as close as possible to a chilly radiator. Perhaps this explained why I had so many *men* customers and so few women. The men came dressed in ski clothes or bulky mackinaws and sweaters, heavy trousers, and high boots, and caps with protecting earflaps. By half past four, when it began to grow dark, I would decide to call it a day and phone for a taxi. But I soon found that no taxi was to be had at that hour. The available ones were limited under all conditions, and in the early morning or evening, when my need for one occurred, they all had been previously engaged by skiing parties to climb up the mountain to the ski areas and back to Manchester. No taxi could be expected to seek a one-mile run when those to ski areas, much longer, brought in large fares. So, at five o'clock, I would put out the lights and walk the mile home in deep snow, the street lights diminishing as I reached the end of the Street. Next morning, I would leave at eight thirty, wearing my ski clothes. Only for me they were more often snowshoeing clothes. When I got home, along about five thirty, the snow would be drifted over the fence, so I just lay down on the drifted top and rolled down to the front door and burrowed my way in.

Were there many customers? Well, not exactly.

But I was too cold and worried to think about the small number of customers. What was worrying me? The credit manager at Doubleday's. I had written Doubleday & Company a letter explaining that I was going to keep the shop open *all the year* now, to accommodate winter skiers. I asked permission to keep their "on consignment" books instead of returning them.

I received a *stern* printed form from their credit manager. I was told that the books were overdue and that they must be returned *at once* or they would be charged to our account. I was horrified. I packed the books up immediately and called the expressman, and he came and took them away. On the next day I received a letter from someone in a different department saying that I might keep the books in question, and wishing me well in my new venture!

So I wrote another letter, saying that I had already returned them because I had had a *stern* letter from their credit manager about them which had scared me out of my wits.

Then came a second letter from the first credit manager, who was much annoyed with me. Didn't I know enough to know that a publishing house had more than one department? He knew nothing of my letter asking if I might keep the books. He was merely minding his own business as credit manager.

So I wrote an apology. I got out my Gilbert and Sullivan opera scores and I wrote a parody of "A Policeman's Lot Is Not a Happy One," and mailed it to him.

Presently came a reply saying that he had had it framed and it was now hanging over his desk. All was well.

That was a good weekend. Walter came home and reassured me, and talked with Mr. Worden and got more heat for me in the bookshop.

I read *Publishers' Weekly* every night and tried to send well-selected book orders. The skiers having at last discovered the bookshop, our business began to increase. This also meant that we began to have an international group of customers. Some of them were barons and baronesses, fleeing from Europe and Hitler's wrath.

Dr. Max Bondy and his wife (also a *Dr.* Bondy), trying to escape Hitler's Gestapo and his dictum regarding their school, had come to this country. Eventually, they re-established their famous preparatory school in Manchester, which added greatly to our contacts and business. What a step up in our book inventory! There were children of sixteen different nationalities at the Bondys' school. Governor Aiken and Dorothy Canfield had been instrumental in bringing the Bondys to Manchester. Soon we were asked almost to become a part of the school. They *trusted* us. It was like receiving a Distinguished Service Medal.

I said this once to Dr. Bondy, and he replied that he and his wife felt that our bookshop *was* giving them *distinguished service*. I began to sense that we were making a deeper contribution in our human relations to anxious, bewildered people than that of the books alone for which they asked. Race prejudice, the values of various ethnic groups, became a daily portion of our thinking.

It was during this winter of 1939 that I wrote a letter to Alfred Harcourt. In it I suggested that Walter had written enough new poems for another book since they had published *A Mountain Township*. He wrote back to me in agreement. Walter was too busy in the Senate to do anything about collecting them, so Mr. Harcourt wrote that he would trust my judgment in selecting them and in preparing the book manuscript.

I typed them out at night after the bookshop day was ended and in a few weeks sent them to him. Following another week I received a contract from him to take to Walter, and thus *Vermont Valley*, a companion to *Mountain Township*, was published in the summer of 1939.

In 1940 Walter had a letter from Stephen Benét at Rinehart saying how pleased he was to ask Walter to write *The Connecticut* for the Rivers of America series. Stephen Benét was the editor of the series at that time.

Another date of special importance on our 1940 family calendar was Ruth's wedding in July to Norman Bonner. The day and the garden were perfect, and Walter, Jr., almost brushed and combed the lawn to make it look its loveliest. But none of us looked at anything, after all, except Ruth and her husband and their radiant faces.

During the winter of 1941 Ruth and Norman occupied an apartment in Leominster, Massachusetts. This seemed singularly appropriate for Ruth since Johnny Appleseed was born, or lived, in Leominster before his trek to the Ohio country. The particular part where they lived was known as "French Hill." Norman and his brother, who were chemists, had a small experimental laboratory in the town. French Hill was inexpensive as to rentals, and picturesque, from his viewpoint. Many of their neighbors were of French extraction, and before a month was gone, Norman, who was possessed of the most genial and lovable approach toward people, knew the stories of all of them. Ruth shared his feeling. This was a kind of French habitant living. Their apartment consisted of a large room, both kitchen and living room, an adjoining bedroom, and bathroom, spotless and ventilated by numerous windows along whose ledges Norman made bookshelves and shelves for window plants. There was a huge wood-burning kitchen stove, so highly polished it would reflect one's face, a tall dish cupboard with doors holding small panes of glass, and copper and brass cooking utensils hanging nearby. A wooden rocker and a wooden armchair were drawn close together. They stood in informal comfort between the warmth of the stove and the table that served both for a writing table and a dining table. The little place, after Ruth had taken possession of it, became gay with bright window curtains, plants, and earthenware dishes. In later days, when they were living in much more conventional comfort, I have often heard Ruth say that she never met a young wife hurrying home at dusk with her arms full of suppertime groceries and her face full of love that she was not instantly transported to Leominster and French Hill.

It was in the same winter of 1941 that these children of mine suddenly had a most horrible attack of New England conscience. Walter, once again, had been elected to the Vermont Senate. They suddenly decided it was all wrong for me to plan to stay alone in Manchester and run the shop. They announced that Ruth would come from Leominster to live with me during her father's absence and that Norman would join her on weekends. I was troubled by such a plan, and reluctant, but they were firm. Ruth arrived with all her impedimenta. All afternoon, after Walter's departure for Montpelier, they sat in the study silent and already bereft. I had realized how little they had eaten at dinnertime. Finally, as darkness came and the hour approached when Norman, too, must leave, I could bear it no longer. I went in and stood before them as they moved apart on the sofa, their faces frankly woebegone.

"Ruth," I said, "go upstairs and get your things. I want you to go home with your husband. I just won't stand for any more of this! I'm perfectly able to look out for myself. All this 'take care of Mother' nonsense is needless. I *want* to be left to manage my own affairs. I don't *want* you! Now go home with your husband, where you belong."

There was instant joyful rushing about—clattering up and down stairs with suitcases, banging of doors, and laughter, a great amount of hasty hugs and kisses were bestowed upon me as they drove off.

Next evening in the late mail there was a note from Ruth:

"We can't see how you knew. It was heavenly driving back. But how did you ever guess how we felt?"

Did their father and I really seem that old to them?

It started me thinking of all the dislocated households that legislative sessions produced, and of one of Walter's poems.

A PUBLIC SERVANT

He got directions to his lodgings
And, carrying a small black bag,
He walked from the railroad station.
The searching wind penetrated his thinner Sunday clothes.
His neck missed the soft, wool shirt he usually wore
And he hunched his shoulders
As he faced the cold on State Street.
Even the solemn dignity of the lighted State House,
Where he'd been sent to serve his town,
Distracted his shivering attention for only a moment;
About now, he thought, I'd be going to the barn
To do the milking, if I was home.
It seemed weeks ago he'd left there.
He thought of the warmth of the waiting cows.
He could hear the rattle of the stanchions,
The rustle of the hay,
And the rhythmic swish of the milk in the pail.
He shivered as the stinging wind lashed his face.
He looked at the lights in the houses.
At home he'd have been going toward the light
Streaming from the warm kitchen.

She'd be putting things on the red-clothed table.
His chair would be waiting by the glowing stove.
He stopped before a strange house
Peering in the dusk for the number.
He stood looking at the place he'd stay in
Which wasn't home.
He straightened his shoulders
And went up the steps.
—*Damn politics anyhow,* he muttered
As he pressed the bell.

CHAPTER FOURTEEN

The Growing Storm
and War Years—1940–1945

WORLD WAR II already had begun in Britain. In the tempo of its increasing involvement, the bookshop became a kind of clearing house. People came in from the drugstore. There was a constant interchange of opinions and apprehensions. And at once we became aware of a horrid accompanying wave of suspicion in our own village. Mrs. Bondy came to us in tears. "How can people suspect *us?* We, who have lost everything because of Hitler. Our school, our home, our country!"

Nevertheless, we found there was a well-established vigilante committee among a group of the "summer people." There were whispered reports of heavy cases that were delivered almost daily to the Bondy School. What was in them? Bombs? No, only groceries bought at a wholesale house. Even more electrifying was the report of a strange light that appeared in one upper window of the school late at night when the midnight train passed through the valley below, on its way to Montreal. What was it? Code messages? To be delivered to the enemy? Carloads of vigilantes went down along the Lower Road, and looking up at the Bondy School waited for this strange, moving signal light to appear. And invariably it did. What was it?

It was the little grandson of the great scientist Wassermann, who had become intrigued with the study of moths. During the night they would collect on his window screen and he would get up and follow them, one by one, with his flashlight pressed against the screen, examining them and making notes. My husband decided that this kind of persecution must stop. Next day, he and Louis Martin, one of our town officials, drove to Albany to interview F.B.I. officials. They were disgusted and infuriated.

"This sounds like half-baked Gestapo stuff. Don't they know anything? Why, that school and the Bondys themselves are well known all over the world among educators. They ought to realize the good fortune of a place like Manchester to have such people among them. If they weren't complete numskulls, they would feel terribly important to have such wonderful educators there. Churchill himself vouched for them, and for their school. Their son-in-law is a distinguished Englishman. Their school was sought by many world diplomats in Germany. We have separate 'clearing' files on every teacher and student in it. We'll come up and put the fear of God into your vigilante committee. They'll find themselves in Federal courts presently for libel!"

The F.B.I. did come to Manchester and read the riot act to the vigilantes; but I've an idea that many of them simply continued their activities underground.

I am proud to say that the headmaster of Burr and Burton Seminary, Ralph Howes, and his wife co-operated with the Bondy School and supported it in every aspect.

After the distressing discovery of a local vigilante committee, it was like a refreshing breath of air cleansing the atmosphere to have Charles F. Speare, of Bound Brook, New Jersey, come into the shop, and to make his acquaintance. He was a wise and thoughtful man. He proved to be one of the regular writers and consultants for the big New York newspapers on financial matters and he owned a summertime farm in Sudbury, Vermont. He was not only an authority upon finance but a naturalist as well. To hear him talk of the brook which flowed the length of his farm was like reading a page from John Burroughs, for he was of a philosophic and poetic turn of mind.

I asked him whether he had never written anything for publication about his brook, about his farm. He confessed to a few privately printed booklets for the pleasure of his family and friends.

"You ought to do more with them," I insisted. "You are really a naturalist. These would make a fascinating small book, authentically and charmingly written."

After several visits, I persuaded him to go to see John Hooper at the Stephen Daye Press, who was delighted to publish it as *We Found a Farm*. In it, Mr. Speare said, "We bought a farm but, unwittingly, someone gave away with it a hundred varieties of wild flowers, rare orchids among them. When the cowslips blossom in May, there is a golden border by every spring run and pool on the place, and silver covers the mountainsides as the maples and poplars start to leaf out. There were no cattle in the trade but deer come stealing at twilight into the orchard or stand in the early morning hours on the edge of the brook, drinking and listening. Nothing was said of a claim for the gorgeous sunsets that may be had by stepping out of doors, of the moon that bursts suddenly over the near peaks and floods the yard with light, or of the innumerable stars, in the clear northern atmosphere, that bewilder and humble the gazer below. All these intangibles were unconsciously thrown in with buildings and barns and stubbles as measuring little in the dollar appraisal though they are really what one comes to realize as the priceless items of his new home inventory."

TO JOHN BURROUGHS IN APRIL
(Born April 3, 1837)

How could he spring from any soil but this—
This warm red Catskill loam he loved so well?
Here he was native as the trillium
Or his "trout lily" whose pale yellow bell
Rang April through the woods.

He was indigenous to these high hills
As the black mountain-birch or hermit thrush;
Inherent in his simple nature lay
Some quality as healing as the hush
Of woods or falling rain.

Kindred he was to the enduring earth,
To fields he plowed, to sugar woods in spring;
He wandered worshipping upon the hills
And wore the mark of their transfiguring
Through all his steadfast years.

April returning to these hills he loved
Shall never find him gone. The secret art
Which made him one with birds and streams and trees
Holds him forever in the waking heart
Of the resurgent year.

M. H.

That same summer there also came another distinguished
writer, accompanied by his tall son. It was the son who asked,
"Do you happen to have a copy of *The Nazarene?*"

"Surely. Ever since it came out last year we intend to *always*
have a copy."

"Then I think you would like to meet my father—Sholem
Asch."

Then, a few days later, we were shocked to learn that Stephen
Benét had died. A new editor would now need to be appointed
for the Rivers of America series. Walter thought the story of the
Connecticut River, all the history bordering its banks, far too
important and dynamic to "simply hit the high spots," as Carl
Carmer, the general editor, had originally suggested to him. So
he settled on a course of conscientious research destined to cover
many months of work.

A pleasant man came in the shop one day about this time.
Taking out a few books here and there, he had little to say,
except to speak again and again of the beauty of the village,
and to ask how we managed to get sufficient business to run
the shop through the winter after the hotel had closed.

After he had gone, I began putting things in order and discovered that all our copies of *Anthony Adverse* had been autographed. Oh, dear! I could have found so many more interesting
things to talk of to Hervey Allen than the bookshop! How
many questions he could have answered for me concerning

Anthony Adverse, had I but known his identity. And it was he who became Walter's editor for *The Connecticut.*

As the war in Britain and Europe more and more harassed everyone's thoughts and lives, we tried to arrange a shelf of suggested reading for evenings after the dinnertime war report on the radio made any more war subjects unbearable until next morning, if one was to sleep at all. We finally included Jane Austen, Trollope, Daudet, Sarah Orne Jewett, Willa Cather, Hopkinson Smith, and biographies; and asked everyone who seemed of a thoughtful and understanding nature for suggestions.

It was during this period that I was working on a book which Henry Holt & Company published in 1944. The book served me as a certain respite from all the continual distress of the war. The Selective Service came in 1940, and in November Walter, Jr., enlisted as a volunteer and left for Fort Devens. He was placed in the 26th Infantry, based at Fort Devens. Roland Palmedo recommended him for the (Ski) Mountain Troops, and, eventually, he served with the 87th Regiment of the 10th Mountain Division in the Aleutians (Kiska) and in Italy. While Walter, Jr., was serving in both the Asiatic-Pacific and the European theaters of war, I set my thoughts of him in a poem.

TO LEARN THE ART OF WAR

For the first time you will not see these hills
When the green tide of May has reached their crest,
Nor watch the tender spreading green that thrills
Along wood roads to shield the swinging nest;
They wait your eager step in vain this spring
The while the vireo and white-throat sing.

The orchard, heavy with the hum of bees,
Where once you lay for hours with your book,
The quarry ledge, far-flung above the trees,
Where once you climbed for sake of a last look
Upon your hill-rimmed world at break of day—
Now they must know that you are far away.

Those words that ever whisper in my ear!
RIFLE and BAYONET and AMBUSHED FOE . . .
The icy wind, the targets that you fear
To miss . . . "because they could be men, you know,"
The bayonet and rifle charge, the drills—
For you who walked with love on these green hills. . . .

I can bear autumn with its sighing rain,
I can bear winter with its storm and reek,
But spring! Spring is so YOUNG. Oh, once again
To find YOUTH in your eyes and on your cheek!

While attending a concert in Rutland on Sunday, December
7th, we learned of the Pearl Harbor attack. The telegraph office
was just across the street from the bookshop. Unbelievable telegrams began to come from the War Department concerning boys
we had seen grow up among us. Distraught and grimly silent
people came in and out of the bookshop—parents, young wives,
and members of dislocated families. Local war relief agencies
and Red Cross classes were immediately formed and conducted.
Blackout curtains were installed, and every twenty-four hours
brought fresh knowledge of the anxiety and loss people in our
own community were suffering. Into this first war year of 1942,
when our son was in training, our first grandson, Daniel Hard
Bonner, was born on Armistice Day, November 11th. When we
had grasped this news of a grandson born to us and that his
mother, our Ruth, was safe, we went outdoors and stood looking
up at the multitude of stars filling the sky over the peak of
Equinox. Which was his star? This newborn child, the symbol
of peace and love, born in the midst of war.

"I know what I want to do," I said to Walter as we came
indoors. We went into the study and I took down the *Oxford
Book of English Verse*. Walter sat down beside me, and my
hand fell naturally into his as I began to read aloud Milton's
Hymn on the Morning of Christ's Nativity.

> . . . No War, or Battails sound
> Was heard the World around,

The idle spear and shield were high up hung;
The hookèd Chariot stood
Unstain'd with hostile blood,
     The Trumpet spake not to the armèd throng,
As if they surely knew their sovran Lord was by. . . .

Heav'ns youngest teemèd Star
Hath fixed her polisht Car,
     Her sleeping Lord with Handmaid Lamp attending;
And all about the Courtly Stable,
Bright-harnest Angels sit in order serviceable.

In the early summer or spring of 1944, Henry Holt & Company published my book, *This Is Kate*. They called it a novel. It was hardly that, I think. It was the story of a child, meant primarily for adult readers, and I had letters from an admiral, bankers, soldiers and sailors and marines in all the different branches of the armed forces, old ladies, WAVES and WACs, twelve-year-old girls, even Princess Elizabeth. There were well over six hundred letters.

It was all very confusing. My close friends were so frank. "Margaret, Florence Broebeck knows *exactly* what is wrong with your book!" And, "It's such a nice book to give to an invalid. Of course, Mrs. Hawley's mind is gone, but she just loves it." Or, "We read it aloud in bed but we never get very far. We always fall asleep."

Perhaps because of these remarks I wrote anxiously to William Sloane, then at Henry Holt & Company, and asked him fearfully how *he* felt *Kate* was getting on. He was terribly annoyed with me. He wrote me brusquely that he didn't have time to give to answering such questions. He pointed out to me the small importance of my little book among the large group of important books they were handling, and the serious shortage of paper in wartime. Eventually I was amazed to learn through *Publishers' Weekly* reports that the entire first printing had been sold prior to publication. It went into five printings within a year, and then they printed no more because of the paper shortage. I received royalties from France and Canada, where it had been sold, but I never received a hopeful or kind word from Mr. Sloane. And when he would occasionally stop in at the bookshop later on, on his way to Bread Loaf Writers' Conference, he would curtly recognize Walter's presence but never mine, although Walter spoke to me as "Margaret." What was it? Was I really obnoxious, an offending woman?

It was on June 6, 1944, that Robert Frost came to Manchester to be the Commencement Speaker at Burr and Burton Seminary. He was devoted to Al Henry, now the headmaster, and his wife, Ruth, having become very close to them at the Bread Loaf Summer School. He had said, "Remember, Al, whenever you want me to come down to Manchester and talk to your students, I'll be glad to do it."

So this was one of a number of times when he came. It suddenly occurred to the Henrys that they would have to be at the school banquet festivities in the evening. Robert Frost would not enjoy them, as he had been seriously ill the winter before and tired easily. If they sent him to an inn or to the hotel for dinner, he would be recognized and doubtless annoyed by unwelcome attention. What to do?

Since I only went to Burr and Burton banquets as the wife of a graduate, and since Walter, as president of the Board of Trustees, need not necessarily have me with him, I suggested that if it would seem helpful in the situation I would be delighted to have Mr. Frost have supper with me. I wouldn't bother him or give him elaborate food he could not eat. He could lie down for a rest. In short, he could do just what he wanted to do.

The Henrys thought it a fine plan and said as soon as the banquet festivities ended they would come home with Walter and take Mr. Frost back with them for the night. So everything was decided until it occurred to Walter that probably Mr. Frost would most enjoy spending the evening and having dinner in Arlington with John and Dorothy Fisher, his friends for many years. So Walter called and explained the situation to John, because Dorothy was in New York at a Book-of-the-Month

Club meeting. "We thought you and Dorothy would probably like to have Mr. Frost have dinner and spend the evening with you."

"No, we wouldn't!"

John's tone was so emphatic and blunt that Walter almost dropped the phone. "Well," he said, rather lamely, "I guess that settles it."

"It does!"

Next morning, while we were still at breakfast, Dorothy called on the telephone.

"I hear John had a rush of frankness to the head last night," she said. "I must explain. We are both very irritated and out of sympathy with Robert. John is simply fed up with him, he's so terribly anti-British. He insists that Churchill is trying to get us to pull their chestnuts out of the fire again.

"I'll tell you what I'll do. I'll come up and have supper with Margaret and Robert at *your* house. That will bridge the difficulty, and maybe make it easier for Margaret. I'll be going up, anyway, for the Burr and Burton commencement exercises."

It seemed a fine idea to me also, and so I had lost any sense of concern when Mr. Frost came to our house around four o'clock. He had his big sheep dog with him, and asked at once whether he could give him something to eat out in the kitchen. I was delighted when Mr. Frost began to open cupboard doors and peer inside. "Oh, yes—here's just what I want." He took down a big box of Shredded Wheat biscuits and, reaching for one of the largest mixing bowls on the workshelf, crumbled four or five biscuits into the bowl. Then he opened the refrigerator door and took out a bottle of milk, pouring it over the Shredded Wheat until it filled the bowl. The dog ate contentedly until not a drop remained.

I asked Mr. Frost if he would like to go upstairs and lie down.

"No, no. I want to be with you. How about Walter's book room we came through?"

So I led the way back into the study. Mr. Frost sat down on the couch and looked around the room, which everyone who comes to the house seems to love. The fireplace with its low crane, the window looking out across the valley to the mountains, the cherry secretary with its Queen Anne doors and drawers that had belonged to Walter's great-great-grandfather, paintings, books, music—all these things supplied peace and the needs of thoughtful enjoyment of friendship.

Mr. Frost sat down on the couch; then, looking up at the ceiling-high bookshelves at his left hand where we kept all our New England books, he drew out a volume and, patting the couch beside him, he said, "Come and sit here with me. I'm going to read to you the ones *I* especially like."

It was his own book, *Come In, and Other Poems*. So he read to me for more than an hour. Then Dorothy came, and leaving them together in the living room, I went to put supper quickly on the table. It was a simple supper, carefully planned for one not too strong after the previous winter's illness—tea, warm corn bread, fresh-made applesauce, scrambled eggs, some thin slices of the Harrington ham Dorothy had brought with her, and what I call "a baby dessert," Floating Island, satin-smooth, with the meringue islands delicately browned. It seemed as though peace should surely preside at such a meal. But it didn't. Suddenly, Dorothy had begun a bitter denunciation of Mr. Frost's commencement address to the Burr and Burton graduates.

"Robert, I was furious with you! How could you say the things you said to them, about Britain and the present war situation? There they sat, drinking in your every word, swinging incense before you. You're a lost leader, Robert. A lost leader! I was *ashamed* of you!"

He appeared undisturbed by her attack. He began to fling provocative statements toward her. She brought her small fist down on the table with a force that made the glasses and silver shiver. Looking at him, I had a strange, almost certain, impression that he was deliberately baiting her. I tried to introduce a change of subject. They brushed me off as though I were a chance fly, and were fast at it again. When I brought the Floating Island, Dorothy stirred hers so furiously and rapidly that I thought it would overflow its saucer. Finally, in desperation, I rose from the table and suggested that we go back to the living room. Maybe a change of scene would help. But it didn't. Mr. Frost sat in the big winged chair by the fireplace and Dorothy in one diagonally across the room. For a moment I thought all was going to be well. Mr. Frost began to discuss what were his best hours for work.

"Morning's the time to write, the earlier the better. Then you and the day are both new. After that, it's best just to push your poem to the back of the stove and leave it to simmer."

But the conversation didn't continue in this vein. I don't know how it happened, but Dorothy managed to interject some challenging remark about the war, and they were at it again.

Finally, Dorothy stood up, shaking herself like a ruffled bird ready to take flight. "I've got to go. I'm chaperoning the senior dance at the high school in Arlington." She went out to the front hall, followed by Mr. Frost. She gave me a slight pat on the arm as I handed her the basket with its remaining ham. She smiled at me absently and, opening the front screen door, stepped out upon the broad marble flagging and down to the grass. Mr. Frost followed and stood on the step above her, framed in the doorway. She turned and looked up at him indignantly. "Robert, what makes you behave so!"

Suddenly he leaned down to her. Taking her face between his hands, he looked at her gently. "Couldn't you see I was teasing you?" he asked.

She gave a shrug of her shoulders and walked off across the grass to her car, unmollified.

It had turned chilly, as it often does in early June in Vermont. When we came back to the living room I lit the open fire but no lamps. Just quiet and firelight in that comfortable old room was what he needed, I felt. He sank into the big armchair and drew close to the blaze.

"I know I behaved badly," he said. Then he added wearily, "I went down to the first Shaftsbury house this morning, and since then I've been walking with death all day."

I didn't speak, but for an instant I reached over and laid

my hand on his. After a minute or two, he began to talk, unburdening his heart to me. So many unexplainable griefs! How did one meet them? Why had he had to survive the past winter's sickness? Why was he still here? I tried to comfort him by understanding silence and only an occasional word.

A little while later he suddenly spoke about my book, the one Henry Holt had recently published. "I read it. I enjoyed it. It was refreshing and honest. You didn't *pretend* to anything. How do you come to understand a child's thoughts so well?"

"I had two years of child psychology with John Dewey, and perhaps that's why."

When I told him how annoyed William Sloane had been with me, he said, "Don't let Bill Sloane bother you. He's always trying to lead *me* around by the nose!"

Along toward midnight, after Mr. Frost had talked to me of his own methods of writing; of what aroused the creative, poetic urge in him; of how he could awaken it; and especially of his disturbed realization that he still harbored bitterness toward certain people because of critical and caustic attitudes during his "years of hard plowing"—along in these late hours Walter came with the Henrys, and Mr. Frost went back with them for the night.

And then one of those tragic griefs that assail people came to Dorothy Canfield Fisher and her husband. News came of their son's death in the Philippines. Captain James Fisher, of the Medical Personnel, 65th Ranger Battalion, during the attack that freed five hundred American prisoners from a Japanese concentration camp, had been shot. After three days of desperate attempts to save him, he died. The people of Vermont, and of our own valley, walked with bowed heads. All over the world, people to whom Dorothy's name was a deeply humane and beloved one, were stunned by knowledge of her and her husband's loss. "Can there be any grief to match this, the death of a brilliant, only son?" they asked. Again I heard Robert Frost's question: "So many unexplainable griefs! How does one meet them?"

CHAPTER FIFTEEN

1945–1949

A SEQUEL to Robert Frost's and Dorothy Canfield Fisher's controversial evening in our house came several years later when John Kouwenhoven of Columbia University, who was one of the friends who spent summers in Dorset, brought Lawrance Thompson, Professor of English at Princeton University, to the bookshop.

In 1939 Robert Frost had requested that Professor Thompson should become his authorized biographer. Mr. Frost had asked him to come to me to get me to verify his own recollection of the confrontation with Dorothy in our home. He evidently felt the incident was of sufficient importance to be considered by Professor Thompson in relation to the future biography, perhaps because it had a distinct bearing upon his changed relationship with Dorothy and John at that period.

I asked Professor Thompson not to tell me the incident as Mr. Frost remembered it but to let me tell it to him in the way in which I recalled it; then he could ˙judge how closely my account followed Mr. Frost's. When I finished, he said that they were practically identical, even to the words used in the heated conversation. This was valuable confirmation for me, also. All the conversation of mine with Mr. Frost which occurred *after* Dorothy's departure upon that evening, as I have written it in the preceding chapter, is equally valid. In fact, before I slept that night, I wrote it down to save for future use should

I sometime write the story of the unusual friendships Walter's life as a writer and our joint sharing of bookshop contacts brought to us. I had begun this habit of keeping such notes as long ago as when we first had the bookshop in the remnant of the apple orchard. All of this long-kept material has been invaluable to me in covering the bookshop's story for thirty-five years.

I asked Professor Thompson whether he had visited the Robert Frost Room in the Abernethy Library at Middlebury College, and told him that Mrs. Arthur Davids (Corinne Tennyson Davids), who had given the collection of Frost treasures to the college, lived across from us and was our neighbor and friend. I found he had not seen the room and told him that it was by Mr. Frost's own choice that this unique and valuable collection had been placed at Middlebury.

I then suggested that I would call Mrs. Davids by phone and ask her whether I could send Professor Thompson out to talk with her. Thus a meeting and a friendship came about which has been of long and happy duration.

All of this now brings back to my mind another incident in which Mr. Frost was concerned, of such characteristic quality, with such a humorous slant, that I must include it here. It concerns a meeting of the Poetry Society of Southern Vermont which had gathered on a smotheringly hot summer afternoon at Hallie Gilchrist's home in Arlington. Since Madison Bates, the Society's president, had left Vermont to become identified with Rutgers University, Mrs. Gilchrist had headed the Society.

John Walter Coates of North Montpelier at this time was printing a small poetry magazine of his own called *Driftwind*. He printed it on a hand press, monthly, in the back of his little general store. He had among his writers a group of women he referred to as his "Little Garland of Poets"—and there were good and serious writers among them. Mr. Coates for a long time had wished to read from his amassed material which had appeared in *Driftwind,* before the Poetry Society of Southern Vermont. On this particular hot afternoon, he had been scheduled to do so.

The room was fairly well filled with people, and present

among them were Robert Frost, Sarah Cleghorn, and Carl Ruggles, of Arlington, noted composer and painter who had been elected to the American Academy of Arts and Sciences. He was a close friend of Robert Frost and they sat shoulder to shoulder, watching intently as Mr. Coates came in carrying a staggeringly high pile of loose manuscript and a few books. He set the pile down on the floor with a resounding thump, beside the table where he was to stand.

Mrs. Gilchrist introduced him, and he began to speak and to read aloud from the toppling pile at his side. It was rather harrowing to listen to him, as he would pick out a sheet from the tower of papers beside him and say, "Now this is an ode, one of the most beautiful in the English language." (One's mind instantly supplied "Thou still unravish'd bride of quietness.") "It is written by one of my Little Garland of Poets." I shuddered as he read. Not necessarily because of the poem itself, but at his extravagant statements regarding it, which most certainly would have caused its author to blush painfully.

After quite a little of this, during which his audience moved restlessly in the hot room, he paused and shuffled some more sheets in his hand as though uncertain how to proceed. Then he said, "Well, now, I'll say something about Sarah Cleghorn. Of course it's too bad she's never had any real recognition as a poet, but I'll read two or three of her poems." As he reached for a book, Robert Frost shouted, "Let Sally read them herself!"

Mr. Coates was thrown off balance. He apparently had not recognized Sally or known she was present in the group of people before him. The room was becoming very dark as a gathering thunderstorm was close at hand. Rising to her feet, Sally said, "No, I won't read myself, but I'll turn on the lamp near Mr. Coates so he can have a little more light."

"God!" shouted Carl Ruggles, "no one needs it more!"

By this time Mr. Coates was completely frustrated. He dropped the book in his hand and decided to remedy the situation by introducing another subject: Robert Frost. "Of course, there's Robert Frost," he said. "I might read that thing about mending wall, but everyone's heard it. Besides, he isn't really a Vermonter."

There was a blinding flash of lightning and a crash of thunder. Under cover of the uproar Mr. Frost bounded to his feet and, followed by Carl Ruggles, he bolted out of the room and into the street. The whole meeting broke up. I never did know who remained to comfort Mr. Coates. Probably, Sally.

It was fourteen years after this happening that Madison Bates told us that one afternoon as he was waiting for a train in the big waiting room of the Grand Central Terminal, he saw Robert Frost plunging through a crowd of people toward him. Mr. Frost and he had long had a mutually congenial and affectionate friendship. He told us that almost without any introductory greeting, Mr. Frost clutched him by the arm and said, "Do you know what that idiot, Coates, said about me at that Southern Vermont Poetry Society? He said I wasn't a Vermonter!!"

Madison Bates said that he was divided between amusement and surprise—amusement at the absurdity of Mr. Coates' statement, and surprise that after such a lapse of time Mr. Frost was still remembering it with rankling indignation.

It is too bad that Mr. Coates did not live long enough to hear Robert Frost proclaimed Poet of Vermont by action of the assembled Vermont Legislature.

Carl Ruggles, internationally acknowledged genius, composer, and painter, still lives in Arlington, a famous and beloved resident. Though possessed of a habit of violent speech bordering upon profanity, he has a mellow and generous inner strength. He goes his way and lets people be absurd if they are so constituted. On March 11, 1966, Carl Ruggles was ninety years old. He had made his home in Arlington for forty-three years. A festival in his honor was held at Bowdoin College during the three-day weekend of January 28th. "The most salient impression emerging from the weekend Festival," according to Lisa Tate of the Bennington (Vermont) *Banner,* "is the image of a man vitally dedicated to life and to the art which has been such an inextricable part of that life; of an artist who is victim of no label, party to no 'school of thought' or endeavor except his own, alone somehow in wrestling with the matter of his art but wrestling from it creations that move other sensibilities in fresh and imaginative ways."

In the Fall, 1951, issue of *Vermont Life* there is an article about Carl Ruggles by Frances Reed. The article's opening paragraph states that "This 73-year-old Vermont composer, who has been placed among the musical immortals by critics in this country and abroad, is also a noted painter whose works have been exhibited with the Southern Vermont Artists, the Art Club of Chicago, the Addison, Brooklyn, and Whitney Museums, Bennington and Williams Colleges, and the Detroit Institute of Art." Mrs. Reed continues, "Two winters ago, Leopold Stokowski, standing on the hushed stage of Carnegie Hall, raised his hands and sent the New York Philharmonic sweeping through a warm and glowing work called *Organum*. The audience applauded with the excited fervor of having discovered a new and shining star; so long and heartily that Stokowski called the composer to the stage to acknowledge the tribute. Only this was more than a tribute. It was a triumph. Carl Ruggles, 73-year-old Vermont symphonic writer, had come into his own."

Leopold Stokowski performed Carl Ruggles' *Organum* again the following spring in London, Amsterdam, Paris, Munich, and Lucerne. His first composition to receive acclaim, in 1924, was titled *Marching Mountains*. I never drive up the valley from Bennington to Arlington, watching the glorious chain of mountains marching ahead of me, that I do not think of Carl's *Marching Mountains* symphony. He needs no recording of his symphony, in one sense, because centuries, millions of them, have already recorded it in the everlasting contours of Vermont's mountain beauty.

The deep spring of sustaining strength in Carl Ruggles' life was the profound understanding and devotion existing between him and his beautiful wife. Charlotte Ruggles was also an artist. She had had a professional career as a distinguished singer, appearing as soloist for many years with symphony orchestras in concerts. The gracious loveliness and wisdom she possessed, and the warmth of her friendship, are as alive today to those who knew her as though she and Carl and Micah, their son, might meet you at any moment on the street in Arlington.

Our own son was discharged from the Army when he returned from Italy in September of 1945. He began trying to find himself in a familiar world become strange and unfamiliar. He spent time in the bookshop. When he had dumped the contents of his duffel bag on the floor of his room the night he reached home, he pushed everything aside and seemed to value only one thing—his honorable discharge from the Army, after six years of service.

Now he picked up a copy of *Pickwick Papers* from a shelf of Dickens. "Remember, you sent me this when I was in Kiska? Before I went across? I think it was the most homesick-making, yet comforting thing you ever sent me." (At home he had six or seven different editions of it, having loved it from an early age when we used to read it aloud as a family during winter evenings. The edition I had sent to Kiska was a small Modern Library.) "I lay in my tent and read by the aid of a gasoline lantern one of the fellows loaned me. I think that book must have been the first that ever got to that desolate island. You'd even stuck a Johnny Appleseed label in it. I could see the exact spot on the shop desk where you kept the labels." He was silent for a long pause. Homesickness? How well he would have been prepared to understand that of his seven-year-old son fourteen years later! In each case, it was a book and the memories of home it brought that bridged the gulf of loneliness. Kiska and *Pickwick Papers*. Manchester and *The Wind in the Willows*.

Returned soldiers enjoyed Bill Mauldin, but they fought shy of war books that recounted the horrors of war. It was a certain group of women, not so many men, who seemed avid for the books of horror and agony. I tried to understand why they, perhaps, were the ones to whom the war had supplied excitement and activity and a sense of accomplishment, something which provided release from a sense of boredom and futility.

The women who drank in the horror accounts kept asking for the latest one out. The rental library held a sickening number.

"How can you stand them, one after another?" I asked.

"Oh, my dear! They're like a good, stiff drink!"

I tried to switch them to a different type of "war book"—stories of displaced persons who had achieved purpose and healing in a new environment, a new life. But such suggestions seldom appealed to them. Meanwhile, Walter carried piles of books left in the rental library from the "during-the-war" period outside the shop door and placed them on a bench. He made a reduced-sale sign and came inside with an expression of satisfaction. The sign read: "Sick-of-Seeing-'Em Sale."

Ralph Hill's book, *The Winooski*—the Onion River of Vermont, flowing into Lake Champlain and identified with Ethan and Ira Allen from the time when Vermont became an independent Republic because they created what they called the Onion River Land Company—was published in June of 1949 by Rinehart, and became the new volume in the Rivers of America series. This was an important and impressive book. Ralph Hill not only told the story of the Winooski, but by linking it to Ethan and Ira Allen and their Land Company, he had made it, in actuality, a fascinating history of Vermont in its early era, because wherever the Allens went they never lost sight of the possibilities of the Land Company, and they went everywhere—and Ralph Hill followed them with his river!

Rinehart and the Everyday Bookshop in Burlington combined to give Ralph Hill and the book a luncheon on the day the book came out. Walter was invited as a Rivers of America series author (*The Connecticut*) and I was invited as a bookshop owner. It was a delightful and moving occasion, for Ralph Hill was part of Burlington's finest traditions, and he was making a new one for himself and his family. Charlie Crane was master of ceremonies, and was at his very best. Since then, Ralph Hill has written many more valuable books and has become one of Vermont's distinguished writers.

Shortly after Walter, Jr., was discharged from the Army in September of 1945, he joined the Rutland *Herald* as a city reporter and feature writer. In August of 1946, he transferred to Montpelier to run the Morning Press Bureau, operated jointly by the Rutland *Herald* and the Burlington *Free Press*. He arrived in time to cover the 1946 special legislative session at which his father was a Senator from Bennington County.

He joined the State's Development Department in October, 1947, as publicity writer under H. H. Chadwick, and also became business manager of the one-year-old *Vermont Life* magazine under Earle Newton, then its editor. In 1949, he became public relations director in the Department, and in 1950 took over the editorship of *Vermont Life* after Earle Newton, who also had founded *American Heritage,* left for Sturbridge, Massachusetts. Walter, Jr., has been editor-in-chief of *Vermont Life* ever since, a period of sixteen years, which means he has been the editor for sixty-four issues of the magazine.

When I asked him to list these successive activities following his discharge from the Army so that they would be accurate, he wrote them out on a yellow sheet of pad paper, heading it: "W. H., Jr.—further adventures of."

CHAPTER SIXTEEN

The New Location—1949

*A*LREADY WE were outgrowing the space in our rented bookshop next to the drugstore and books were jammed so close together that both suffered. Twenty people would crowd it to its limit. Twenty people would, in fact, constitute a mob. We decided that we must do something about obtaining larger quarters.

Besides solving this problem we wanted to *own* our bookshop property. We had discovered the unsatisfactory features of renting. But renting or buying any business property in the village of Manchester presented almost insurmountable difficulties owing to the strict zoning laws surrounding business property. No new business structure might be built without special application and special hearing, and, invariably, the answer was "no." Even additions to already existing businesses had to run the gauntlet of Zoning Board requirements. No existing building might be rented or bought for business use unless it had a previous history of use for business. Thereby the cost of any property available, according to such zoning rules, became greatly increased. Values and taxes rose.

Then we learned that the old 1832 bank building next to the hotel on the north, a historic landmark, was for sale. We took the future in one stride. With all the available money and credit we could muster we bought the fine old brick building. That night, we sat at our dinner table almost in silence. We were realizing the leap and possible hazard we had taken.

Only thirteen years before, we had taken another leap entailing financial responsibility. We had bought the Old Square House out on the hill at the southern entrance to the village. It also was an historic landmark. We had restored it, and it had become our long-desired home. We had met the last necessary financial indebtedness and we were able to "look the whole world in the face, and owe not any man." And now we had done it again!

Finally, Walter looked across at me, as we sat in the candle-light, and smiled.

"I feel *young* again!" he said. "I have a challenge!"

"*We* have a challenge," I agreed, reaching across the table to take his hand.

Next morning people began to stop in to congratulate us.

"Now you'll have a *real* business," they said.

"This can really become *something*," they predicted.

Soon we were surrounded by carpenters, electricians, plumbers, furnace contractors, painters, and plasterers. Then came the people who wanted to plan the Johnny Appleseed's decor. Their suggestions fell under three heads: cute, comic, or quaint. At first we couldn't imagine why the rooms' fine proportions, the beautiful windows, their molding and paneling, could suggest such decorative schemes to them. Then we realized it was their conception of Johnny Appleseed as a novel, amusing, and pleasantly old-time character. But this did not agree with our ideas. We wanted a real bookshop. We wanted to use the simple beauty of the rooms, a large front room and a smaller, adjoining back one, in ways that would produce a sense of beauty and a dedicated interest in books.

As we finally arranged the shop, we eschewed all suggestions of those who wanted us to decorate the walls above the high and continuous bookshelf sections with a frieze of Johnny Appleseed episodes, in gay colors and slightly comic delineation, as well as to hang Johnny Appleseed "drapes" (!) at the windows. We would not profane the tall windows with their clear glass and beautiful facings of wood with any such anachronisms. We fought against the idea of any clever or cute innovations. Everyone gave us advice (they always have, in every field of life), and we stubbornly held to our own ideas (and always have)!

Above the bookshelves, on the south and north walls, we placed many of Clara Sipprell's beautiful photographs, which she allowed us to display and handle on consignment, the only such arrangement we knew of her having made. She was a photographer of international importance, having been invited to Sweden to make the portraits of the Nobel Prize winners and the royal family in 1938. To have such portraits on our walls gave not only distinction to the shop but an ennobling atmosphere. Years later, at the time of Dag Hammarskjöld's death, we were enabled, through these portraits, including his father's and his own and many related ones, to have our own memorial to him on the south wall of the shop. People came from miles around to see it.

On the north, and opposite wall, above the high bookshelves, later in the year we placed Harry Shokler's serigraphs. One of the most widely known artists in this field, and author of a book concerning it, he also had a studio over the mountain from Manchester. On the wall spaces between door and windows we hung etchings and paintings. The fireplace with its high mantel became the center for the shop. For years a reproduction of Rockwell Kent's painting of Mount Equinox hung above it. The original hangs in the Chicago Art Museum.

Sometimes our pictures and photographs led to disturbing outbursts on the part of customers, or even fellow artists. Observing the framed print of Rockwell Kent's Mount Equinox, Ella Fillmore Lillie told us heatedly that the craftsman who had framed our pictures for us for several years had assured her he would handle no more of our business and that she herself was removing all of her exquisite stone lithographs from our shop. Why? Because Rockwell Kent was a *Communist*. We looked at her in astonishment, thinking of the clean-cut, compelling beauty included in *Rockwell Kentiana*, the book-bound collection of his art. Then we replied that we doubted whether Mount Equinox was aware that Rockwell Kent was a Communist, but she was adamant.

One day Clara Sipprell came into the shop, carrying her portrait of Eleanor Roosevelt, which had been among a small group of portraits she had hung on display in the hotel. Mr. Ball, the hotel owner, had told her with sincere regret that he would have to ask her to remove it; it aroused too much furor among the guests.

We were delighted to have Eleanor Roosevelt's portrait on our bookshop wall. When it produced tirades, as it often did, we resorted to a statement made by Clare Boothe Luce regarding Mrs. Roosevelt. She said, "No woman of our era has lent so much comfort to the distressed, or distressed so many of the comfortable."

It was on Columbus Day, 1949, that we had moved across the street to our new location. Many guests from the hotel and nearby cottages helped us. By nightfall we were moved, but oh, what a sight!

Owning our building, with larger space, brought to us an immediate increase in business. This, in turn, meant strength-consuming and exacting problems. We were open from 9:00 A.M. until 10:00 P.M. without break, from June until October; from 9:00 A.M. until 6:00 P.M. in winter, except during certain days of the Christmas season when we went back to the summer schedule. These were hours which for many years meant lunch eaten off the edge of the desk in the office in the rear room, eaten during any pause when it could be squeezed in. Sunday afternoons and evenings became filled with efforts to do all the accumulated tasks of home. To me, an apron became the badge of a cherished life—the cherished badge of domesticity which I loved to practice in my Old Square House. And yet—I equally loved and gloried in the life of the bookshop, in the joy of creating and founding a concept of what a bookshop might become in its relationship to life. To share this with such a man as Walter Hard was a life complete in itself.

On a crisp October afternoon we had a housewarming for friends and customers in the new building. To serve cider and doughnuts seemed exactly right. I remember much interest and cordial friendliness. Especially I remember that Walter, Jr., came from Montpelier with his wife, Dorothea. Her charm and loveliness of mind and personality already were deeply rooted in our hearts.

We rented the upper floor of the building, once one huge room which had been used by the Orvis fishing tackle and sporting goods company for the hand manufacture of artificial fishing flies. All around the room were broad shelf worktable spaces where dozens of young women learned and worked upon this intricate craft, which demanded great dexterity and skill. We converted this big space into offices. There was a side entrance on the north side of the building which opened on stairs leading up to the offices.

They soon were rented by three young men who spoke of themselves to us beneath them as "the heavy-footed ones." They were Dick Ketchum, Aleck Brown, and Sydney Meachem. The first two were forming a business to be known as Vermonters, Limited, to sell through a mail-order system distinctive Vermont products. They were young men of ability and of unique ideas. Soon Dick Ketchum was involved in the Southern Vermont Artists, and in working to help them to obtain their present permanent Art Center, the Webster estate, which was bought in 1955. Shortly after, Dick became connected with *American Heritage* and embarked on a distinguished writing career. He and Aleck Brown, nephew of Horace Brown, the artist, gave up Vermonters, Limited, and left. Sydney Meachem, a young attorney recently graduated from Columbia Law School, remained. Besides his profession of law, he was—and is—a musician, playing the viola in the Vermont Symphony, and an amateur actor with professional skill. Above all, he became the respected and greatly loved friend and citizen of our Vermont valley and its many communities.

The vacated offices of the other "heavy-footed ones" were rented by another attorney, Charles Duke, and the Chamber of Commerce. One summer, Elizabeth Page occupied an office as a writing workroom while she was completing her life of Jefferson.

The space we thought we could never have enough books to

fill was already becoming crowded. We had thirty-nine categories, each with its own special section of shelves or tables, such as the table of New England and Vermont books, the table of non-fiction, and the one especially given to current affairs. There was a table of books on antiques and crafts, the novel table, and the table of beautiful art books. These tables always held the same book classifications although there was a constantly changing selection, week by week. And always there was certain standard and reordered stock. Over the years, our regular customers, and even those who returned from distant places, recalled these locations of different book categories and went at once to the different shelves or tables that particularly interested them. It seemed to give them a pleasant sense of familiarity and permanence.

We developed new music and ballet sections. The corner of children's books almost became a room by the position of shelves, tables, bookcases, and low benches. It was one of the most fully supplied and beautifully enticing portions of the shop. We welcomed browsers, but oh! those who just wanted to "poke around." And those who couldn't recall the name of the book they wanted, "but it was about a little girl."

In sections of more advanced reading there also were problems: those people who gather gratis information they have been wanting, from books on antiques and crafts, or recipes from expensive cookbooks, openly copying desired data onto small pads produced from handbags or pockets. If one lingered beside them, waiting, they would finally look up, finish copying the desired paragraph, thrust the pad into the handbag or pocket, and say stiffly, "I used to be a librarian." I suppose this alibi was intended to cover the right to use any book in the shop as a library reference book.

The chief troubles in the children's corner involved sticky lollipops, gooey ice-cream cones, and school reading lists. A school reading list naturally includes books of long past years, as well as the children's books which have won special prizes and awards over past years. It is almost impossible for a bookshop, even one that makes a special feature of children's books as ours did, to carry such a supply. The library should answer some of these needs, but what library can carry sufficient duplicate copies, especially if the books are to be carried away to summer camp?

Then there is the grandmother who had such a sweet book when she was a little girl. It had a yellow cover. At last, she succeeds in recalling the name. We look it up in *Books in Print,* and tell her regretfully it is no longer in print. "But *why* not? It was such a sweet story. Worth any number of the *silly* books they write for children today!"

The book-review-clipping parent is another nightmare. And then, there are the parents who boss their children; the mother who says, "No, I've no money to spend on a book for you," while her arms are full of packages from the gift shop across the street. There was the father who took a chair and sat in it, so placed as to close the opening into the children's corner, having first deposited his two-year-old inside it. He then sat with his back to this improvised baby-pen and thumbed through our precious replica of a Shakespeare folio while the baby crept, crawled, and grabbed all the books within reach.

Again, there were the father and mother who brought their baby stroller inside the shop and turned it and its contents over to a four-year-old child who ran up and down the aisles between tables, knocking books off, left and right, to the floor. They were angered when I explained that we couldn't have the stroller inside the shop, especially in action. They went out, but the father returned to read me a lecture. He said that I and my bookstore would never succeed.

And like a refrain from other parents came words addressed to their children, holding dripping ice-cream cones in their hands. "Just go over there into the children's part while we look at grown-up books."

Not only did the new bookshop contain the features of interest attached to the old building when founded in 1832, but also those added when it was owned later by the C. F. Orvis Company—"Fishing Tackle and Sporting Goods." From 1856 for one hundred and ten years, it bore an especial relationship to the entire Charles F. Orvis family. Charles Orvis and his sons' and daughter's gifts of ingenuity, inventiveness, vision, and writing ability have kept the name of Orvis alive, not only in Manchester and Vermont, but around the world where the lure of the angler is known.

Franklin Orvis, cousin of Charles Orvis, owned and developed the Equinox Hotel. He was a staunch Republican, and his initial success was carried on by his sons. Charles F. Orvis, his cousin, was an equally staunch Democrat, the only avowed one in Manchester at the time, or, as some would declare, in Vermont! He was a man of inventive genius applied to rods, reels, and artificial flies. His daughter, Mary Ellen Marbury, also possessed a strain of genius. She wrote a book about artificial flies and fly-tying that was a classic in its field, and now, in its original edition, is a collector's item. It won prizes at the 1939 World's Fair and became known for its writing, for its beautiful illustrations of the flies, and because of its veracity. She also wrote, years later, a book on the music and calls of the old square dances, and while the book was still only in manuscript, Henry Ford bought it for his private collection of rarities.

Mrs. Marbury early realized the charm and fascination of fine old pieces of furniture to be found in many of the houses up and down the valley, and in old farmhouses in the surrounding areas. Women bent on acquiring black walnut Victorian furniture, gladly parted with beautiful pieces, dating back to early cabinetmakers of the region. She eventually furnished the entire Orvis Inn with these fine pieces which made a unique and delightful impression. The guests also enjoyed her keen and stimulating mind. I recall hearing a distinguished New York newspaper editor, who customarily stayed at the Orvis Inn for fishing holidays, say that he knew of no one who had a finer grasp of United States political history than she did.

My first acquaintance with the Orvis Inn (then the Orvis Cottage) and the Orvis Company's business began when I was only six years old. My parents had come to Manchester from Philadelphia and had been guests at the Equinox Hotel in the early 1880's. They fell in love with the village and with Vermont, and my father bought land at the south entrance to the village, far back from the road. He built a house under the shadow of Mount Equinox. It was probably the first "summer people's house" in Manchester. Three of his children were born there, during later summers, and I was the last one.

When my mother would come on from Philadelphia in early June to "open the house," she brought me with her to my birth-place. We always stayed at the Orvis Cottage. After I had had my afternoon nap, she would allow me to go over to the Orvis Company building—where the post office was housed in the north portion of the big front room, Mr. Orvis then being post-master (it must have been during a rare Democratic administration)—to see whether a letter had come from my father.

I loved the journey along the marble-flagged sidewalk to the old building. Once there, I had some difficulty in getting myself up over the three big marble steps. This feat achieved, I would trot into the post office and wait for Mr. Orvis to come out from behind the letter boxes. He always came whether there was a letter or not, and held my hand while he burrowed with his other hand into his coat pocket. I waited, knowing perfectly what would follow—a white, transparent peppermint. This was journey's end, the goal of my expedition.

How many times in the years since 1949, when my husband and I bought the same building, I have walked up and down the same steps and looked at the old letter-slot beside the door. For an instant of memory I became six years old again.

During my first two or three years as a young wife in Man-chester I used to stop frequently at the Orvis Inn to see Mr. Orvis, especially during the year when he lay ill in a downstairs back bedroom. There was a window that gave a view of Mount Equinox reaching high above the roofs of houses and outbuildings. One November afternoon as I sat beside him in the autumn dusk, a sudden shaft of light from the setting sun pierced the clouds over Equinox and revealed how wasted and weary his body had become. I moved closer to him and laid my hand over his on the bed coverlet. He opened his eyes, eyes that still could hold a glance as penetrating as in his much younger years. But now, as he looked at me, his expression changed.

"Ellen," he said. "Little Ellen. My Ellen . . ."

I knew he was not speaking to me. I leaned over and drew the quilt more closely about his thin shoulders.

In 1920, five years later, *Harper's* published a poem I had written about him. It was called "A Village Portrait." It was a portrait of him as the village knew him, but I could have added something of tenderness with another brush, which perhaps they would not have recognized.

A VILLAGE PORTRAIT

They said he was a scoffer, had no faith—
His neighbors on the mountain-village street—
And added that he found his drink and meat
In argument; of course he shunned the church.
His passion was to urge some old-time score,
Do battle for some long-lost cause. He swore
And held one by the coat to gain a point.
When fired by talk he sang the "Marseillaise,"
His broken voice pitched high to catch the sway
And tumult that it stirred within his blood.
And then, without a word, perhaps, he'd slip away,
At eighty, on the mountain-side to stray
And fish the streams or hunt with his old hound.
When suddenly it came his time to die
He spoke without a quaver. His keen eye
With piercing glance searched every face near his;
And then he called his youngest son apart,
The son who was the kernel of his heart—
The hidden sweet of all his bitter years—
"I'm going across the river by and by.
When you come too, lad, bring your rod and fly."
They said he was a scoffer; had no faith.

CHAPTER SEVENTEEN

1953–1957

*I*T WAS the big front room in the bookshop that seemed to hold associations especially attached to the Orvis family. The smaller room adjoining the front room did have one interesting feature connected with their manufacture of fishing tackle and artificial flies. There was a large, cupboardlike closet reaching almost to ceiling height containing innumerable pigeonholes. On the edge of these pigeonholes were labels bearing the names of various artificial flies in the handwriting of some member of the Orvis family, with datings given as far back as 1863.

In this back room that had a wide double entrance from the front room was our bookshop office, with wide shelves and deep cupboards with sliding doors beneath. On the wide shelves stood racks of greeting cards (thus, unwittingly, did we enter upon a kind of enslavement!). In the cupboards were all the stock of stationery and business items connected with stationery supplies. We wanted to keep the big front room all bookshop and not have these other, more commercial supplies spoil its book atmosphere. Thus we attempted to keep the sheep separated from the goats.

The office was a small, compact space, yet it held Walter's large desk, steel files, typewriter and desk chair, large wrapping shelf, and counter, catalogue files, reference books, and telephone. It was amazing how we could maneuver to carry on the office business in this small space, a space in which we had to fit together almost like pieces of a jigsaw puzzle.

It was Ella Fillmore Lillie who first had introduced the ugly word "Communist" plus its attaching suspicion into our bookshop. Presently, we began to hear it constantly, but we resolved to keep level heads and not join the panic of suspicion. Shortly, however, we were annoyed by a woman who claimed to be a "secret informer." She buzzed about the shop, picking up and examining the titles of the books on current affairs on our nonfiction table. She even took books right out of our customers' hands and told them they were "dangerous" literature. We asked where she was staying, and found, to our surprise, that she was the new hostess at the hotel. Walter went over to talk to the manager about the situation, after which neither we nor the hotel saw her again.

This, however, was only the beginning of the wedge of suspicion seeking to pry us and the reading public apart. An aging former ambassador threatened to boycott us, and a local agitator put us on her private Pink List.

But we had no real trouble except that of keeping antagonistic customers apart. We were determined to maintain an openminded, traditionally independent, Vermont bookshop. Men like Senator Aiken and Senator Flanders congratulated us upon our stand.

Into all this atmosphere of dislike and fevered prejudice came the open and delightfully friendly approach of Phyllis Fenner, editor, reviewer of children's books, and compiler of children's stories. To our surprise and pleasure, we found she had dedicated her new book, *The Proof of the Pudding*—an invaluable book for any bookseller, teacher, or parent—to our Johnny Appleseed Bookshop.

Presently, we acquired three customers who ordered books almost weekly from London, and one who amazed us with lists of books she ordered in either French or Italian. We had a steady account with Foley's and the British Book Centre, and with French and European publishers. We began to feel we were acquiring an international flavor!

Dorothy Canfield's *Vermont Tradition,* which had been published in 1953, continued to be one of our steady best sellers, but she, herself, had become very frail and was having to curtail her public appearances as a speaker. One day she telephoned us that she was sending Elizabeth Yates, who had been commissioned by Dutton to write her biography, up to Manchester to talk to us about her life in Vermont, as we had known it. Increasingly, we felt alarmed by Dorothy's obviously reduced strength and ability to cope with her former schedules of activity. This showed in one small matter that involved the bookshop. Formerly, Dorothy was delighted to autograph her *Vermont Tradition* for us for customers at any time when Walter would send down copies to her. Now, realizing how frail she was, he questioned John about it one day when he came into the shop.

"No, it's too much for her to take on now," John answered.

Walter and I expressed loving concern about her.

"Besides," John said, shortly, "what earthly difference does an autograph make in a book?"

Walter looked astonished, and I answered, "Wouldn't you feel that a volume of Keats, containing his own signature, made a difference?"

"Not at all. The contents, the poems, would be just the same."

I didn't dare make the sentimental plea that the authentic autograph would prove that the book had once belonged to Keats, or had been touched by his hand. The shriveling breath of realism and sarcasm had too frequently blasted me.

But in the winter of 1955, Dorothy again seemed her old self when she espoused the cause of raising funds for the Arlington Historical Society, which was anxious to co-operate in making the small, fireproof addition to the Martha Canfield Library —it housed Dr. George Russell's rare and valuable collection of Vermontiana—both safe and available to the public. Her idea was that certain people in Arlington, Manchester, and Bennington should all co-operate in the effort. Dorothy would write and give a book of short stories about Arlington. The Canfield family (The Canfield Paper Company, New York City) would give the paper for the book. Robert Haas, of Random House, whose

Arlington home was close to Dorothy's, would arrange for the printing of the book. Lea Ehrich, an Arlington artist, would design the book cover. Jim McCabe, postmaster and devoted friend of all worthy projects, would deliver the books to the two bookshops which agreed to sell them without any profit— the Bennington Book Store and the Johnny Appleseed Bookshop. The book was called *Memories of My Home Town,* contained twenty stories, and cost $1.00.

The thousand copies, divided equally between the Bennington Book Store and ourselves, were all sold in less than a month, with overwhelming demands for more. It was a mad, joyous experience in community good will. Who else but Dorothy could have inaugurated it? Our last copy of the book went on Christmas Eve.

Of course, we ran into difficulties. This perfect story of interlocking, neighborly effort, especially as stamped by Dorothy's name, was supposed to be kept strictly unpublicized. But the New York and Boston newspapers learned about it in some roundabout way. It made too lovely and fitting a Christmas story not to be brought to the attention of the American public. Presently, the press burst forth with the captivating tale.

At once we were swamped with orders by mail and telephone and telegraph from all over the country. As it was, the gift wrapping and mailing of most of the five hundred copies we had sold had proved a big undertaking, linked with our usual Christmas rush of business. We worked long after our customary late hours getting the books all gift wrapped and ready to mail.

I recall one telegraphed order by day letter, giving separate addresses for twenty-five copies and asking that each copy be wrapped in a different kind of Christmas paper from the others. Twenty-five different designs? I was aghast until I, too, had an idea. That dear and valued friend of so many bookstore people, Fred Spooner, representative for the American Artist cards, had given me a huge box of sample Christmas cards he had salvaged from old albums. By using red, green, blue, or white tissue paper, and attaching a beautiful and suitable Christmas card to cover the major portion of the top of the package, and tying it with harmonizing ribbon, I achieved "all different" and lovely packages galore. But when Christmas came, my hands were so swollen that Walter had to untie my own Christmas gifts for me!

Long afterward, I asked Ron Sinclair of the Bennington Book Store how he ever managed such an amount of gift wrapping and mailing, along with his regular business, which was much larger than ours.

"Good Lord!" he exclaimed. "We never gift wrapped or mailed any of those books. I told people they must gift wrap and mail them themselves. *My* part was selling them without any profit."

It must have been about the next summer that we began to have a sudden raid upon our section of books that we listed under the category of general psychiatry and behaviorism. They ran all the way from a few new volumes on psychosomatic problems, treatment, and psychoanalysis, to books that attempted to divert one's thinking and approach to life along self-helpful channels. There were dozens of them, and new authors providing magic formulas for peace and quietude of mind.

I dipped into them and left them with a feeling that it was all to be had in *one* volume, if people would but read it.

Then a new phrase began to appear in conjunction with these same books—"the guilt complex."

I examined that, too, and wondered about it. But I was soon to receive elucidation. There appeared in our area a guide, a pseudo-analyzer and discerner of the root of all one's mental ills and frustrations. In an atmosphere tinged with frightening assurance, she could place her finger, or the penetrating glance of her brooding black eyes, upon the secret difficulty. It was explained to me that the root of trouble began in some hidden sense of guilt (that word again!) dating back to early childhood. My friends, who were surprisingly different in character, talked of "Fräulein" incessantly. I was finally urged to join the group who sought her ministrations.

"But why? I feel perfectly serene. I don't feel guilty about anything."

"Your conscience *must* be clouded," my friends insisted. "You should think back to your early childhood. Don't you remember feeling guilty about anything when you were a child?"

"Oh, gracious, yes—loads of things."

"No, not like that. One *particular* thing. Don't you remember one *especial* thing?"

"Well, yes," I said, after thinking back to my early frontier.

"There! That's what you should investigate."

"Investigate?"

"Yes. Fräulein has us write out, in our own words, our memory of the happening that caused our first deep sense of guilt. Sometimes it is rather embarrassing and painful, but it is necessary."

I was silent.

"Do do it, Margaret," urged my friends. "You can just send it to Fräulein on trial. She won't charge you for reading it. It will tell her whether she wants you for a patient or not."

"Patient?"

"Yes."

"But I'm not sick," I answered stoutly.

"Oh, but yes you *are,* only you don't know it."

"Then ignorance is bliss."

"Don't be flippant. Fräulein is a wonderful woman. She can look right through you. It almost makes you shiver when you hear what she has discovered in you."

"No," I said, decidedly, "it sounds like bunkum to me."

"You've no right to say that until you've at least given it a trial."

"A trial?"

"Yes. At least, you can write out the facts of that one especial experience of feeling guilt when you were a little girl. You needn't even use your own name in it. You can use a fictitious name and only put your real name on the envelope. You see, she uses these confessions of guilt that we write for her as 'case histories.' They may prove very valuable to her. She may make a book of them, someday, even—of course, using the fictitious names. Ever so many psychoanalysts and marriage counselors do it."

"Marriage counselors!" I cried hotly.

"Now, dearie, don't get excited. You're stubborn and self-willed."

"Maybe I am," I agreed.

"Now, won't you write out your story of that incident of guilt, using a fictitious name? Just for us—just to please us?"

Suddenly, a way of escape seemed to open to me. Instead of anger, I began to feel a wave of inward amusement, even anticipatory pleasure, sweep over me.

"Yes," I said sweetly, "I'll write my story of it, using a fictitious name, just for you. When *you* read it, you'll know whether my story of guilt would prove a good 'case history.' "

Astonished and delighted by my capitulation, my friends almost hugged me.

The next night, I had a wonderful time writing the story of my secret guilt. Seldom had I enjoyed anything more thoroughly. I even gave it a provocative title and wrote in pencil above the typed sheets—"A Case History." I invented a delightful pseudonym for myself—Mary Grenolda. When I read it aloud to Walter, he enjoyed it; and when I told him why I was sending it to my friends in lieu of a proper case history, he shouted with laughter. "They won't like it—or understand," he said.

He was right. They never even mentioned receiving it, and I didn't become Fräulein's patient.

Always in Bed

"Listen, Mary Grenolda! Don't you know what a Pin Fair is?"

Mary Grenolda shook her head so vigorously that the hair of her carefully brushed bang fell into her eyes.

"Well, it's a fair where you pay for things with pins—common pins."

"Oh."

It was so surprising a revelation that it took her a moment to absorb it. Pins! The processes of barter and trade, as she had observed them during her six years, had always involved hard cash. Something she had never possessed. Grownups always paid for things with money. But pins! The possibilities were limitless.

"You get them from your mother or anyone who'll spare you four or five from her pincushion. Then you use them to buy something at the fair."

"Dolls? Baby carriages?"

"Oh, not big things. Just things we older girls have made. Sachets and needle books. Things like that. Maybe there'll be some *little* dolls. You know, those penny china ones that we've dressed in pieces of ribbon and lace."

Mary Grenolda nodded but her interest wasn't as keen as it had been. After all, there still was economic balance in the matter. Even at a pin fair there was a parallel between goods offered on the market and the price required from the consumer to pay for them. "I wanted a baby carriage," she explained.

Greta Holden spoke with impatience, "But, Mary, how could you think a big thing like a baby carriage could be bought with pins?"

"I didn't think. I hoped."

Suddenly Greta's face brightened. "I'll tell you, Mary. Grace Blanchard has one of those little, painted wire baby carriages. It's a tiny one that came from Huyler's with bonbons in it. She got it in her stocking at Christmas. We're having the fair at her house, and she's getting it up. I'll ask her to put the baby carriage in the fair. One of the china dolls will just fit into it."

"Oh, Greta, will you? Really?"

"Yes, I will, but it'll take loads of pins, Mary Grenolda."

"How many?"

"Oh, I don't know. All you'd have. Fifty, maybe. You wouldn't be able to get anything else, probably."

Mary Grenolda climbed the stairs to her mother's room. Mrs. Ferris was writing letters at her black walnut desk, with its blotter mounted in robin's-egg-blue plush, the corners of which had been hand-painted by her sister, Gladys.

"What is it, dearie?"

"Mama, have you some pins?"

"Pins? Common pins or hair pins?"

"Common pins."

"Of course I have. Just take one from my pincushion."

Mary Grenolda hung over the pincushion fashioned like a fat tomato. She counted. "There're only fourteen pins."

"Well, how many do you want?"

"All of them."

"Oh, I couldn't let you take them *all*, Mary Grenolda. Why do you want so many pins?"

"I want them for a Pin Fair Greta and the big girls are having tomorrow."

"Oh, I see. Well, you may take half of them. Then, maybe, Aunt Gladys will give you some."

But Aunt Gladys took only three out of the embroidered cushion on her bureau. "Now you'll have ten, Mary Grenolda. When I was a little girl, ten pins would buy ever so many things at a pin fair."

"It's different now, Aunt Gladys. You have to have fifty."

"Fifty? Nonsense!"

So Mary Grenolda went down the stairs again. Delia, in the kitchen, and Maggie, the second girl, gave her eight pins between them. But that didn't make even half of fifty. All afternoon she wondered how to increase her fund. At supper time, when Papa came home from his office in Philadelphia, on the train that left Broad Street Station at 5:14, she confided her problem to him.

"Have you asked your mother and aunt for pins?"

"Oh, yes, Papa. And even Delia and Maggie."

He turned over the lapel of his Prince Albert coat and removed two plain pins that were hidden there.

"Why, Papa, I didn't know you carried pins!"

"Just for a possible emergency. My cravat or a loose loop, you know."

Now she had twenty, but the situation still was bad. She dreamed of arriving at the Pin Fair, and of seeing the baby carriage grown to amazing proportions. It even boasted a shirred hood of pink silk edged with ball-fringe of velvet, like the ball-fringe on the green plush seat of her tricycle.

When she awoke, it was a clear day. Just right for the Pin Fair. She could fancy Greta and the older girls setting tables out on the big side porch of the Blanchard house, and arranging another table under the horse chestnut trees on the lawn. The latter would hold a large pitcher of lemonade, glasses, and plates of cookies. Probably all she could buy would be lemonade and some of those fig cookies that the Blanchards' cook always made for Grace's parties. But on the center table on the side porch would stand the baby carriage! Mary Grenolda felt she couldn't bear it. There must be some way to get thirty more pins.

She took out her tricycle and pedaled slowly up the street, looking speculatively at the houses which she passed. Old Mr. and Mrs. Lane lived in the yellow house that stood far back from the street on a wide lawn. Its porch was covered with wisteria vines. But Mr. and Mrs. Lane didn't like children. She couldn't think of approaching them. She propelled herself to the corner and turned into a tree-shaded avenue. Mama and Aunt Gladys called on the people who lived in these houses, but they were too elegant for her to consider a foray upon their inmates. She drew up beside the stone gates of one of them and sat thinking.

Presently, she saw a lady coming down the avenue under a purple and white parasol. It was Mrs. Bishop who lived in the brick house with the porte-cochere. "Good morning, Mary Grenolda. And how do you find yourself this morning?"

"I'm trying to find pins, thank you, Mrs. Bishop."

"Pins?" Mrs. Bishop looked puzzled. Mary Grenolda explained. "Oh, I see." Mrs. Bishop opened the chatelaine bag that hung at her belt. She took out a small pincushion made of two cardboard circles covered with figured silk. Around the edge of the circles, which were sewed together, pins had been inserted at intervals. Mrs. Bishop drew out five and gave them to Mary Grenolda with a smile. But although she reconnoitered along the avenue for most of the morning, Mary Grenolda had only thirty-two pins when she went home toward noon time.

Aunt Gladys was out in the back garden telling William how to trim the trumpet vine that grew all over the trellis on the carriage house. Miss Murray, who had come for two weeks of dressmaking, was looking over Butterick pattern books with Mama. "Mama, haven't you some more pins?" She could see a whole row of them stuck into the folds of cloth that covered Miss Murray's fat bosom. "No, dearie. Don't bother us now. Besides, we'll need every pin we have for the sewing Miss Murray's going to do."

Mary Grenolda went down the hall wondering what to do next. She glanced into her aunt's empty room. Aunt Gladys must have gone out in a hurry. Probably Maggie had come running upstairs to say, "Miss Gladys, William's here to see about that trumpet vine." She'd left the top drawer of her bureau open. Mary Grenolda walked over and looked into it. She saw neat piles of handkerchiefs and ruchings, a satin glove case, hairpins and crimpers carefully sorted, and a row of small jewel boxes—BAILEY, BANKS AND BIDDLE, CALDWELL AND COMPANY. Further back she could see the Liberty silk scarf and the white lace shawl that Aunt Gladys had brought back from abroad.

Suddenly Mary Grenolda's glance became fixed upon something lying at the front of the drawer. She hadn't noticed it at first because it was partially hidden by little bolts of pink ribbon. It was a brand new paper of pins. All of its folds were set with rows of gleaming points and heads!

When she reached the Pin Fair there was a swarm of girls on the porch. They were arranging and rearranging the articles for sale, and discussing the number of pins which should be charged for each thing. At the center of the middle table, well toward the front, stood the baby carriage. It was still of its original size, despite Mary Grenolda's dream, but it was lovely! It had a woven wire hood and wheels that actually turned. Its handle bent outward in a delicate curve. It was marked "100 pins."

Mary Grenolda was the only customer, as yet, but she was filled with anxiety that someone else might arrive and procure the baby carriage before she could do so. However, she sauntered down the length of the porch looking at all the things on the tables. There were seven or eight china dolls, dressed in bits of bright silk. The ones with bonnets made from tiny pieces of lace cost more pins than the plain ones. Fifteen pins for the bonneted ones, and ten for the others. There were sachets and needle books, chamois pen wipers, decorated blotters, button bags, and handkerchief and glove cases.

Keeping one eye on the porch, Mary Grenolda went down the steps toward the lemonade and cookie table.

"I'm awfully sorry the baby carriage is so much, Mary Grenolda," Greta said, as she followed her, "but Grace said it ought to be lots more than fifty pins, and all the other girls thought so, too. But there're ever so many other things that are nice."

"Oh, that's all right, Greta. I can buy the baby carriage."

"You can?"

"Yes. I've got that many pins."

"Oh, good! I'll go tell the girls to save it for you."

In the seclusion of a syringa bush near the refreshment table, Mary Grenolda tore off four rows of pins, twenty-five in each row, and carefully refolded the paper. She pulled the pins out, one by one, and held them in her hot, moist palm. They pricked and she was afraid she'd drop them. She carried them to the porch and handed them to Grace who counted them over twice while Greta wrapped up the baby carriage in a piece of tissue paper reclaimed from some previous use.

After that, Mary Grenolda swept into an orgy of buying. Presently, the older girls as well as the customers who had begun to arrive in numbers commenced to murmur and grumble. Mary Grenolda Ferris had bought practically every good thing on the tables! Now she was down at the refreshment stand, having her fifth glass of lemonade and her sixth cookie.

When she went home with her parcels the girls barely replied to her goodbye. "How on earth did she get so many pins?" asked Greta indignantly. "Why, she had a *whole* paper of them!" exclaimed Grace, hotly. "I saw it when she pulled it out of her dress pocket. It was a brand new paper. *Full!* She must have had hundreds of pins. It wasn't fair!"

The next day being Saturday, Papa came out from Philadelphia on the 12:20 and had luncheon at home. He'd sat beside Mr. Holden on the train, and Mr. Holden had told him something amusing. He'd said that his daughter, Greta, and some of her friends had had a pin fair the day before. One of the children had come with a whole paper of pins and bought practically everything. The fair had been almost sold out before anyone else could buy. "That must have been the bazaar for which I gave you the two pins from under my coat lapel, Mary Grenolda. I hope you weren't too late to make some sort of a purchase."

"No," said Mary Grenolda in a small voice, "I got a baby carriage."

"A baby carriage!"

"Oh, it was just one of those little favors from Huyler's," explained Mrs. Ferris. But Mary Grenolda felt sick.

In the afternoon her mother called her. "Mary Grenolda, run and ask Aunt Gladys to give you the new paper of pins she has saved for Miss Murray. We need them now to pin this Spanish flounce on the yellow dimity."

Mary Grenolda didn't move.

"Hurry, dearie—Miss Murray's waiting."

"I can't."

"Can't? What do you mean?"

"Aunt Gladys hasn't got the pins." Mrs. Ferris and Miss Murray both stopped sewing and looked at her. "I . . . I took them for the Pin Fair."

Mama had been surprised and pained. Aunt Gladys had been horrified and shocked. Put to bed, Mary Grenolda listened, miserable and overwhelmed, to Mama's troubled voice, and to Aunt Gladys' accusing one. "I can't see, Mary Grenolda, how my little girl could have done such a thing! It makes me feel dreadfully." "Don't you know that you *stole,* Mary Grenolda? To go into my room and take something out of my bureau drawer! And, then, never to tell me! It was *stealing.* It was *deceitful.* No mother will want her little girl to play with you. She won't want her little girl to be friends with a *thief!*"

Papa came into her room after supper. He sat down by her bed and took her hand, but all he said was, "It was selfish, Mary Grenolda. Selfish toward the other children, and selfish toward Mama and Aunt Gladys."

Next morning, Mary Grenolda stole across the back lawns to the Blanchards' house. She asked the maid for Grace.

"I think she's upstairs getting ready for Sunday School, but I'll call her."

Mary Grenolda spoke in a gulping tone. "Grace, have you still got all those pins I gave you at the Pin Fair?"

"Yes, they're upstairs in a box. Why?"

"Grace, I . . . I want them." Mary Grenolda pulled forward a toy satchel she'd been holding behind her. "The baby carriage, and all the other things I bought, are in here. I haven't hurt them a bit. So, will you let me have the pins?"

"But what do I want with all those things?"

"You can have another Pin Fair."

"I don't want another fair."

"But I want the pins *awfully*, Grace."

Grace stared at her. "Oh, well, I don't need them. Besides, you took everything else at the fair. You might as well have the pins, too."

"Only you *must* take back the baby carriage and all the other things, Grace."

"I tell you, I don't want them!"

But when Grace returned and handed her a large box filled with pins, Mary Grenolda grasped it in her hand, shoved the satchel toward her, and ran.

Maggie and Delia saw her hurrying across the back garden with the box clutched under her arm.

"Wonder what she's been up to now," said Delia. "Hope it's nothing to get her put to bed again."

"Poor kid," answered Maggie, "she's always in bed!"

CHAPTER EIGHTEEN

1957–1962

Over the eight years since we had moved our bookshop to its third and final location we had become a kind of nonecclesiastical parish. The people who came regularly, often daily, to the shop and to whom we became closely attached, or who had previously been long-time friends, were the members of this parish.

I fell to thinking of them in this way, or of feeling toward them in this fashion, because it is impossible to come in contact almost daily with people without sensing something of their moods, their joys and sorrows. Both Walter and I responded with concern for them. It was a human relation equation. It was an indispensable attitude we automatically maintained in the shop. Here was something we could *give,* not sell—something entirely different from books. So many people need someone they can trust and confide in. It was amazing how books, and discussion of them, often released thoughtful revelations of belief in ultimate goodness, of acceptance of situations almost intolerable.

We are sure that realistic, competent people, impersonally geared to business life would estimate our attitude as sentimental and demented—one that would eventually ruin our business. We never found that it did. In fact, it provided income that never was rung up on the cash register, assets that never appeared on the income tax sheet.

This was the period when the word *appointment* was the

necessary password to reaching all specialized professional services. Walter and I were not specialists, nor were we of professional caliber. No one had to have an appointment—we were
always there.

Often I thought about this feature of the matter. I admit
that many times it proved exhausting, but then I was ashamed
of myself. What business was worth the having unless one could
render unto Caesar the things which are Caesar's; but also, unto
God the things that are God's.

Long ago, a lovely French-Canadian girl, Jeanne, had made
her home with us while she attended Burr and Burton Seminary.
In return for the home we extended to her she helped with household tasks, just as Ruth did. They were about the same age,
both attending Burr and Burton, and they became devoted friends.
Jeanne had been reared by gentle nuns, and she bestowed many
lovely habits she had acquired from them on us. I recall in particular that at this time either Ruth or I made our own homemade bread. Jeanne never took up a fresh, warm loaf to cut it
without first making the sign of the cross upon its brown top
crust. Literally, she was reminding herself of that other bread, the
Bread of Life, and of the symbolism thereby attached to
all bread, the food most common to human need chosen sym-
bolically to satisfy the spiritual hunger of mankind as well.

Sometimes, at the beginning of a day in the bookshop that
I knew would hold troubling situations and hectic, disturbing
hours, I would quietly, unobserved by anyone, make the sign of
the cross on the top of the counter which lay between me and
all those who would come my way. A reminder for me.

People came with their griefs. They came with their personal joys that they longed to tell about, loving, prideful joy
brought by the success of some son or daughter, or that of a
faraway member of their family. But often these joys were told
almost with fear. This sharing of such wonderful news was so
often met by bored response, reluctant enthusiasm. Suddenly
they realized they were being considered too prideful, too happy,
guilty of the poor taste of boasting. Yet, how achingly necessary

it became to share such joy! There are always those who will weep with one. It is harder to find those who will rejoice with one. Knowing this from personal experience, I gladly lent a willing ear to rehearsals of achievement and success. I asked for them, not as a planned approach, but with the sincere feeling of sharing a kindred happiness. Their good news was good news for me, too. A kind of reverse application of "and therefore never send to know for whom the bell tolls; it tolls for thee." So do the bells of joy!

Often I watched Walter writing a letter at the bookshop typewriter. As I glanced at the opening sentence, I saw that it was not a business letter but one in answer to someone who had sent him a distressed note about a bill they could not immediately pay because of unexpected loss of occupation or the adversity of a snowless ski season. He was replying in reassuring and understanding terms. I realized that he was also writing something else, besides this letter. He was writing his own translation of the Gospel in our bookshop.

So they came, bringing their griefs and joys, problems involving family relationships, financial burdens, and need for jobs. And among the anxiety and weariness there often were indications of inward terror and secret anguish. I have listened as my husband explored these situations almost with a surgeon's skillful and searching technique and tried to bring hope and healing to those concerned. Sometimes, when I commented on his generous responsiveness, he looked genuinely surprised. "It's just sharing," he'd say. "Sharing all you've found out about life."

In October, 1963, Walter had a friendly letter from Witter Bynner, who had been living in Arizona for several years. He spoke of the time when he had lived in Cornish, New Hampshire, with his friends Homer and Carlotta Saint-Gaudens, and often had driven through the covered bridge to Windsor, Vermont, across the river. He said how sorry he was that he had never met Walter and added that he knew how much Robert Frost had liked his poems.

The purpose of Witter Bynner's letter was to tell Walter

this and to say that when he read Walter's poetry he felt that he was back in the old region he had known and among its people.

The old courthouse which stands at the corner of the street across from the bookshop holds a session of court each June because Manchester is a shire, courthouse town. The winter session of court is held in Bennington. During the summer court session, if there were spectacular trials, as occasionally would happen, people crowded the street in front of the courthouse when the presiding judge may have called a brief recess, and always when the jury was out making its verdict in a case.

During many years' passage, I recall two or three murder trials when excitement ran high. Guests at the hotel would often go over and sit in the courtroom, following the course of each day's developments. Or, if they learned a case was being heard which involved some amusing "character" (in their eyes), man or woman, they would flock across the street to listen to testimony or replies to cross-examination which produced laughter and amused, muttered comments until the judge would rap his gavel smartly for silence.

During court session, Walter was often called on the jury, and when women were legally qualified for jury service, I was called also. Walter and I often realized, from reading the lists in the county and town newspapers, that the number of separation and divorce pleas and cases involving non-support and assistance to elderly dependents constantly increased. It was after discussion of such cases that Walter wrote "Matt Meets His Mate" and "At the Court House."

MATT MEETS HIS MATE

Few of the neighbors blamed Nettie Cornwall
For wanting to die.
She had married Matt when she was sixteen.
Within a year everybody knew that the shabby house by the tracks
Was anything but a happy home for Nettie.
When Matt was drinking he was cruel.
When he was sober he was far from pleasant.

"It was just dusk when I see a figger wrapped in a shawl
A-walkin' down th' track."
A neighbor was telling about it the next day.
"She kep' a-turnin' 'round's though she was expectin' somebody.
The next I heard was them brakes screechin'
And I see folks runnin'."
She stopped to put wood into the stove.
"I ain't one to blame Nettie, not one mite,
Knowin' as I do what she put up with with that man."
Two months later a new Mrs. Matt
Was sitting by the same neighbor's kitchen stove.
Matt had brought her from over the mountain.
The neighbor had been making some delicate attempts
To warn her about her new husband.
The new wife shrugged her shoulders.
"There ain't no need fer nobody t'worry 'bout me an' Matt.
I've buried two husbands already and I tell you—"
She leaned forward in her chair—
"If you ever see a figger in a shawl
A-walkin' down th' track 'bout train time some evenin'
It'll be Matt."
She settled back in her chair and rocked.

AT THE COURT HOUSE

Down the rough mountain road
The man, silent, drove the rattling Ford,
Seeing only the road ahead.

The mother sat on the back seat.
She kept saying over and over:
"He never done it. . . . He never done it."
All the familiar beauty of the cool June morning,
The perfume of the mountain woods,
But added to her woe.
"He never done it. . . . He never done it."

A crowd stood about the Court House door,
Laughing, talking.
"Nope. Been out all night.

No verdict yet.
Tough case."

The bell had rung.
Slowly the careworn jurors,
Unshaven, tired eyed, serious,
Filed into the courtroom.
The Sheriff brought in the prisoner—
Her boy.
"O God, he never done it!"
"Deserved all he got."
"Shh. That's his folks."

Slowly the creaking car
Crept back up the mountain.
At the clearing on the summit
They could see the broad valley,
The mountains to the east
A peaceful green in the light of the setting sun.
But in their valley the sun had set.

Looking back over the years, especially the years between 1949 and 1965, in our bookshop's final location, I realize how strong and sincere became our attachment to the men who came to us, year after year, representing the many publishers with whom we dealt. Their names, and they, compose a long-time list I never shall forget, or fail to appreciate. My mind and heart respond with gratitude and affection that spells close friendship in many cases. In many instances, these fine representatives were publishers themselves, or became so. I will name them alphabetically:

Robert Dike Blair, Fred Blau, Joe Consolino, John Dixon, James Downs, Thomas Gogarty, Stephen Greene, Tom Hurley, William K. Lane, Mr. Malloy, William Palmatier, Bradley Parliman, Sid Phelps, Al Pierson, John Scott, Peter Sykas, Walter Walsh, Robert White, and Marion Wyeth.

Now as I read this list I can think of so many friendly, heartwarming things these men did for us in times of stress, anxiety, and sorrow. They form one of my fondest recollections. To look

up on a busy day in the shop and meet the friendly glance of one
of them was so often the presage of delightful discussion of books
—ones that had "gone" especially well with us; ones for which
we and the publisher's representative in question felt particular
enthusiasm.

Bob White of Harper and Row and Walter Walsh of Harcourt,
Brace seemed to acquire a seventh sense regarding our private
enjoyment of certain types of books. Again and again, special
copies—"readers' copies"—of biographies, like *Mrs. G.B.S.* and
The Worlds of Robert E. Sherwood, came addressed to us at the
shop, and children's books of enchanting character, like *The
Quarreling Book* by Charlotte Zolotow and the exquisite edition
of *The Nightingale,* as told by Eva Le Gallienne. All of these we
dutifully "reported" upon to Harper and Row, but we were
boundlessly grateful to Robert White for his friendly and sympathetic understanding of our private tastes and enjoyments.

It was a similar situation with Walter Walsh, of Harcourt,
Brace, who with his kindred love of symphonic music and opera
introduced us to Samuel Chotzinoff. He sent us not only *Day's
at the Morn* and *Lost Paradise,* but his own copy of *A Little
Nightmusic.* And always in his hand he carried Joan Walsh
Anglund's latest little book to give to me. Truly, A Friend Is
Someone Who Likes You, and how wonderfully Walter Walsh
proved it for us.

Our list of important Vermont books was now increased by
a long-desired history of Manchester, *Manchester, Vermont:
A Pleasant Land Among the Mountains, 1761–1961,* written
by Edwin Bigelow, our former school superintendent, geologist
and historian of Stowe, Vermont, and a native of that place, and
by Nancy Otis, whose husband is one of the most valued members of the Burr and Burton faculty. Nancy is a graduate journalist
and has made a recognized name for herself. She is a member of
the editorial staff of the Bennington *Banner.*

The Manchester history contained, besides its 289 pages, a
reproduction of Manchester's original charter as granted by Benning Wentworth in 1761, a fine map of Manchester from the
Atlas of Bennington County, Vermont, by F. W. Beers, 1869,

numerous photographs and a fine index, an indispensable feature of any book, and was published by the town of Manchester in 1961.

Manchester and its history were of sufficient interest even to tourists that the Information Booth personnel in the park at Manchester Center often found themselves confronted with questions not commonly asked town information centers, more used, perhaps, to furnishing information as to state routes and lodging possibilities. Therefore, we frequently found ourselves as a kind of second information bureau, supplying historical facts about the town and village. My husband often said that this must be because we were looked upon as Manchester's oldest inhabitants. That could only have been considered true for *him,* in consideration of the fact that his family had lived in the Batten Kill Valley since 1764, and he himself was a sixth-generation Vermonter.

Questioning people most frequently stopped in to identify the location of a house or farm long since owned by some past-generation family connection. Walter would try to trace the Manchester names or boundary lines, and eventually resort to other authorities than himself. In this connection, the history of Manchester when it appeared upon the scene proved of great interest. But it sometimes aroused so much discussion and conversation that we were even driven to call Mr. Bigelow on the phone and draw him into a kind of three-cornered conference. Listening to all of this, we decided that Manchester history was a knotty assignment at best.

I recall an occasion when my son was about twelve, when I was regretting that although I happened to be born in Vermont I possessed no actual Vermont inheritance or background. He had looked at me speculatively for a few moments, and then he said, "I don't see why you worry about Vermont *background,* Mother. Just think of all the Vermont *foreground* you're getting."

I smile now as I think of how much of that foreground he and his father and sister have provided for me through their own devotion to Vermont and their writing concerning it.

Into the shop, day by day, came people who enriched our life: Tom FitzSimons, wood carver and artist whose display room was next door to us, whose delightful vein of humor and deep well of quiet understanding often refreshed us in times of stress and strain. Pearl Buck came frequently, bringing some of her Amerasian children with her. She was prodigal in her sympathetic understanding of their delight in books, and they would leave with arms literally filled with them. Clara Sipprell brought Elizabeth Vining to the shop. She had made a portrait of Mrs. Vining that later appeared upon the jacket of her book *Friend of Life,* a life of Rufus Jones, the great Quaker mystic. Miriam Van Waters, world-known penologist, became our devoted friend through Helen Bryan, author of the heart-searching book *Inside,* that book which told the story of her imprisonment, caused by her refusal to give the Dies Committee the names of certain Spanish refugees, known to her, because members of their families, left in Spain, might thereby become known to Franco and be "liquidated." Thus, rather than betray them, she risked a Federal prison sentence (which she received) and "swore to her own hurt but changed not."

It was Helen Bryan who as long ago as 1929, when we occupied the orchard bookshop, called Walter and me one day and invited us to her home to meet James Welden Johnson and his wife, who were visiting her. "Do you by any chance have a copy of his *God's Trombones* in the shop?"

"Yes, indeed," we answered.

"Oh, do bring it when you come. Just bill me for it. I know he will read from it for us."

I went to take it from the shelf, and then an idea came to me. I'd take my own copy from home. It would add so much to my joy of its possession to have him read from it. The afternoon was a never-to-be-forgotten one. He and his beautiful wife had all the graciousness and warmth of kindness that can belong to the Negro race, and in the moving poems he read, great spirituals minus music, he spoke the language of unequaled faith of Negro tradition and of the old-time Negro pastor speaking to his trusting congregation.

Later, Lillian Gilkes was in Manchester for a long winter, completing her work of editing Stephen Crane's letters with Robert Stallman, and beginning her life of Cora Crane. Soon she was a daily visitor at the shop, stopping in on her way to or from the post office. Later she became a friend of such delightful and endearing character that we rejoiced when she would come out to the house in the evenings bringing her book, chapter by chapter, to read to us. At first she had thought of writing it as a novel, but it was material and research too valuable to be preserved only in that form, so finally she wrote it as a biography that held all the fascination of a novel's best features. The University of Indiana Press published it in 1960 with a jacket drawing of Cora Crane by Lynd Ward.

It often seemed that each bookshop year brought us the unexpected discovery of some rare and gifted personality. Such a man was Edward Brundage, naturalist and artist and soldier of fortune. Edward Brundage was a graduate of the University of Wisconsin with a degree in botanical science. When World War II came, he found himself giving valuable service in the French underground. His father, then dead, had been an American and his mother, who maintained the French Château at Russell Sage College, was French.

One day he walked into the bookshop, carrying the beautiful page of a rare, leather-bound herbal manual, published in the late 1500's.

"This comes," he explained to us, "from the type of book which Shakespeare may often have held in his hands. As you look through its pages, which I have, though they are discolored and so loosened from the binding that they almost fall apart, you find all the herbs mentioned in Shakespeare's sonnets and plays. I've made many of the old woodcuts into cards, and some of the larger ones I've framed."

He showed them to me: *Original Woodcuts From the Herbal of Matthiolus, printed in 1598.* Along with the woodcuts, he handed me a bunch of herbs he'd grown. "I thought you might like them," he said.

Thus began the experience of friendship with a man so gifted and so erudite in the field of natural science that each time (which often was several times a week) he came to the book-shop people gathered around him to ask him some question related to botany or ornithology. He confessed he had finally broken loose from a desk job which he hated.

"I have to be in the woods—outdoors."

He came, tattered and torn by brambles, but his manner and bearing held all the marks of distinction and cultivation. Presently, he was bringing us exquisite water colors and pen-and-ink drawings of his own of birds and wild flowers.

"Since I'm so wilful as to relinquish all the high-paying indoor jobs I can have, I must keep myself by this sort of thing." He marked his work at outrageously low prices. We bought them outright, not taking them on commission. "I do have to eat," he said ruefully. It was like being visited by a young Audubon. The pictures sold almost as soon as they were hung on the broad space below the fireplace mantel. How many years this continued I do not accurately recall—perhaps four or five. We had only one doubting Thomas as to their veracity, only in this case it was a doubting Martha, not a Thomas. She looked upon the pictures and declared them of no worth at all.

Suddenly, tragedy swooped down upon Edward Brundage. He became a victim of lymphatic cancer. During the early months of his seizure, he came in and out of the shop, still painting with a heroic intent. The work he was doing held all of the art he possessed. When he finally said good-bye to us, saying simply that he was going into the Veterans' Hospital in Albany "for a time," we knew there would be no more pictures. We took those last ones he had brought, about eight or ten, and made a special arrangement of them with a sign: "Exhibition of Edward Brundage's work. Not for sale."

A few weeks later, a gentleman came in from the hotel. He came several times and always walked directly to Edward Brundage's water colors of birds. He studied them. He even took out a magnifying glass to study the treatment of some ornithological detail.

"I must have all of these," he said.

"Oh," I exclaimed, "they are only on exhibition. It is true that the bookshop owns them, but I could not think of selling them just now, all to one person. . . ."
I then explained the situation.
He introduced himself. He was the director of the oceanographic museum at Woods Hole. He told me that the museum possessed his private collection of bird paintings from all over the world, several Audubons among them. He said that he was always on the lookout for any original bird paintings he felt were worthy of hanging in his collection which, he added, was to be left by him to hang there in perpetuity.
"Then you must surely have them," I said.
As I wrapped them for him, he asked for Edward Brundage's address.
"I will give you a letter to send to him," he said. "That will be the best way. I will tell him all about the collection where his bird paintings will hang, and tell him what I feel about them."
The next day he brought me the letter and I at once sent it to Edward Brundage's sister to give him. I was fearful he might not live to hear its contents. But later she wrote to me that the letter had come a week or so before he died and that he had been able to hear it and grasp its significance. I wrote the director at the oceanographic museum and ended it by saying, "You gave Edward Brundage his final accolade."
How Edward Brundage came by the 1598 *Herbal of Matthiolus* is another story. He had been stationed in London during the terrible nights of Hitler's bombing blitz. It was one of his duties to search the ruins of bombed buildings for bodies or possible survivors. On one such occasion, near a ruined private home, he had come upon the blasted remains of the old herbal. I have often thought by what unusual chance it was found by a soldier who realized what it was, or felt any interest in it.

The death of Dorothy Canfield, which came in November, still seems unbelievable to me. Perhaps this is the surest proof of the immortality of her vital and enduring personality. When, within a year's passage, her husband, John, and her beloved brother,

Jim, both died, I felt strangely eased of grief. They had been inseparable in their mutual devotion; now they were together once more in the world which awaited their spirits.

Today, Sarah Cleghorn's poem about Dorothy, called "Dorothea," holds new significance and attachment for me because of our own Dorothea, our son's wife. I never read it without feeling a fulfilled stirring of my heart. She is all we could have longed for, for our son and for ourselves. But it is those lovely lines "And I saw bright phantoms race,/Thousand phantoms fleet and rally/ All across her lighted face" that hold especial meaning for me. For Dorothea has beauty of expression, her own "lighted face." "With that look I would not part." She has passed it on to her second son, our grandson Stephen.

Writing of daughters-in-law makes me think of a description of Walter's grandmother which was contained in a story I wrote for Frank Doubleday when he was living here in the summers. He had asked me to write an article about the valley farm which was Walter's family's homestead. I did so with joy, realizing only later that what he had wanted was the factual data regarding the old farm which now had become a model dairy with a prize Jersey herd. He sent the story back to me with a couple of lines: "What I want is something about the butter-fat content of the milk that farm produces. Not something that belongs in the *Atlantic* Contributor's Club."

Now, since I came across it the other day, I include it because it belongs here as the actual portrait of a daughter-in-law of more than a century ago.

The children have gone down to the valley for the day. Aunt Mary sent for them early this morning when Ernest brought the milk up to the creamery. Down the elm-lined street I watched them drive away— Ruth with an arm about Walter and Walter with radiant face looking over her shoulder. Their cries of farewell were drowned by the rattle of milk cans.

It seemed impossible to go back into the house and set to work methodically, after a taste of the morning's radiance. I made excuses for delay. There were some withered petals on the roses that ought to be pulled off—I must look to see whether the puppy had dug up the phlox

I set out the night before—I wondered if the vireo was still on the nest in the lilac bush. After all, I wouldn't go in just yet!

Sitting on the doorstep, looking across the valley, I realized that the full tide of the year had come. Everywhere I saw green—green—but of such varying tones! Now that summer was here, I loved it; yet when I thought of it, at other times, it was the season which meant least to me. Why was it? Perhaps, because its beauty was too obvious. Its loveliness lacked the subtlety of spring and autumn. Winter was different. It even transcended subtlety. It needed a profounder characterization. The ultimate mystery—the border of revelation. Was that what winter meant?

Yet, for my neighbors with farms on the mountainside and in the valley, I knew that summer must be the desired season. Then planting was finished, harvesting was not yet begun, and the difficulties of winter and its storms were for the time being thrust into the background. At the Valley Farm I was certain that this must be the case, although I remembered days spent there, at all times of year, when everything had seemed touched with peculiar beauty.

Now in imagination I followed the children around the bend in the road that swings east to the river. Down the hill I went, past the spot where the grist mill used to stand, along the roadside where hepatica and bloodroot grow thick in spring. There was the one-room school house, where Walter Jr.'s and Ruth's grandfather and great-grandfather learned their three R's and romped at recess. On past meadows and stone walls I traveled, while between maple trees I caught glimpses of the river and the mountains across a narrow valley. Beside hedges of elderberry and thickets of alder and osier, I journeyed until, in the bend of the river's arm, I came to the farm.

I like to think that when my husband's great-grandfather bought its three hundred and sixty acres, he had an eye for beauty as well as for material return. The white house, with its graceful fluted columns, would confirm the supposition.

Such a satisfying picture I have of the life of the farm in those early days! Stories and anecdotes of the family who have lived there for six generations—old daguerreotypes—brief but illuminating entries in the family Bible—all these have helped to fill in the background, trace the outlines of that picture and touch it with shadows and highlights.

Great-Grandfather Jesse raised sheep upon the farm, and his wife, Ruth, spun the wool and wove it into blankets—blankets oddly long and narrow to our modern eyes. Added to this I have a story from the old doctor who recollects, when a small boy, seeing Great-Grandmother ride to church in the family sleigh. She had rosy cheeks, he says, although she was over eighty at that time, and she wore a wadded hood and cloak. Something which he did not observe in her apparel, or in its decoration, I can fancy as being part of it that day. I wonder whether she did not wear the rose-topaz brooch which is now so cherished a possession of our Ruth.

The old doctor says that Great-Grandmother and her husband were genial and pleasure-loving, and gentle-tempered.¯ Gentle-tempered even when their son fell in love with Mary Jennings, the adopted niece of Squire Cyrus Munson who lived in the only brick house in the village. Not that they had anything but admiration for Mary Jennings but the Squire made stern demands of her suitors.

He ruled his household with authority equal to that of the patriarchs, and his women folk would have been the last to gainsay him. Tradition says that Mary had had at least one lover when Grandfather came to seek her hand. The Squire, however, had been adamant regarding that young lawyer from Boston. He did not wish his niece to marry a lawyer, or to live in Massachusetts. He was determined that she should be established as the wife of a well-to-do Vermont farmer! Therefore when Grandfather came courting her, there was but one objection to his suit. The Squire would not hear of Mary marrying outside his own denomination, and Grandfather had a long line of Episcopalian forebears. Again the Squire was adamant. He said, with finality, that unless Grandfather became a reliable Congregationalist, and pledged himself to the life of a farmer, he could not be considered as a possible husband for Mary Jennings. And Grandfather, caring for nothing so much as Mary, acceded to both requirements.

And Grandmother? Of what did she think, in these days before her wedding? Was it of her former lover, or did Grandfather succeed in entirely erasing the mark which he had made upon her heart? Was she docile and self-contained to the last?

Long ago, an old lady who lived in the North Village told me an amusing, though pathetic, incident which belonged to this period of Grandmother's story. It fitted into the pattern of the tale as neatly as the square of dotted muslin which the old lady was setting into a quilt, fitted into the patchwork.

"I was just a child then," she said, "but I often heard my mother tell of the day she went over to the brick house to help when Mary Jennings was married. It seems that old Cyrus Munson who was her guardian and uncle by marriage was terrible stern and particular. He wasn't exactly

close, as you might say, but he had queer notions about things." She
paused and bit off a thread, then continued, "One of the notions he had
was that it was a wicked waste to put frosting on a cake. He'd never allow
it in his house.

"Well, it seems that when Miss Mary was planning to get married the
old man made most of the plans. He wouldn't have thought of letting
her get married in the church, I guess—that would have been too much
like the Episcopalian way of doing things! He hated anyone who wasn't
a member of his denomination, and especially the Episcopalians, whom
he always called 'those Church of England Tories'—though I don't think
he had it just right, at that. Well, anyway, Miss Mary was to be married
in the brick house, and my mother and some of the neighbor women went
over to help her get the house ready and some things made for her
wedding supper.

"Miss Mary was kind of doubtful about having a frosted cake, and she
didn't dare ask old man Munson if she might. Mother was real firm
about it and told her that it was every girl's right to have a wedding
cake—and she was going to make her one!" There was quite a pause
before the old lady went on with the story. I fancied that she rather
relished creating a sense of suspense.

"Everything went on well enough, and the day of the wedding came.
There weren't many folks asked to it, but Mother was there, of course,
helping. She said that it had got to be about four o'clock and folks were
beginning to arrive when old Mr. Munson came out through the kitchen
to hitch the minister's horse by the carriage shed. He'd let the hired man
help the other folks, but the parson was different.

"When he went past the pantry, he looked in. He wanted to see just
how everything was, I guess, and make sure that there wasn't anything
going on that he didn't know about. Well! He found out that there was!
The cake sat right there on the shelf in front of him! It was all covered—
top and sides—with a white frosting an inch thick!

"Mother said she shook in her shoes when she saw him look at it, but
he didn't look at it long, I can tell you! He grabbed it up, quick as lightning, and carried it out to the pig pen and dumped it in!"

I have often thought of this tragedy of Mary's wedding cake, for it
must have been the culminating disappointment in a series of depriva-
tions. I hope that when Grandfather drove away with his bride he told
her that she should have all the frosted cake she could eat for the rest
of her life.

Grandmother was a devoted daughter-in-law. Her husband's parents,

ter brought the book back to me, Mr. Frost had
Margaret Hard from her friend, Robert Frost,
gard. Ripton, Vermont. Sept. 23, 1962."

ographed one of Karsh's photographs of himself
haracteristic study which shows him sitting infor-
over the arm of his chair, his dog beside him, as
to students and friends. It is the wonderful bits
as carried on between Mr. Frost and Karsh, as he
ait, that add such tremendous interest to a portrait
hold all the facets of Robert Frost's personality as

lete Poems, a first printing (1949), he had written:
and Walter Hard who don't have to be shown
rmont poetically—Robert Frost. Ripton, Vermont,
ter talking to Walter about his own poetry, he
opy of *In the Clearing,* in which he had written:
rd from Robert Frost, with admiration and more
rmont, Sept. 23, 1962."

Walter's writing, Mr. Frost had said, "It exas-
ave people or publishers promote you as a humor-
mphasize the humor inherent in the nature of
, dry and pungent, without which your portraits
't be what they are—true; and filled with philo-
nding of their quirks and moods. But there is
en, lyricism in them, too.

d Harcourt published your *Mountain Township
alley,* he understood you for the poet that you
st book Dike Blair brought out, *Vermont Neigh-*
esn't need to be stressed in it, but those fine
s you've written for the beginning of each of
are the story-setting, the long-time heritage of
involved in the poem."

his coveted understanding from such a poet as
d stayed in Walter's mind with such richness
of appreciation, that it was tremendous comfort
low his reporting and write it down as he talked.
added that Walter must frequently feel the
on that he did when people took it upon them-

whatever they may have felt regarding the Squire's denominational demands, loved her dearly. Her gentle spirit and charming ways spread up
and down the valley.

When the Sewing Circle met, it was Grandmother's deft fingers that
cut and planned the work. Her kindly welcome made newcomers feel
that they were strangers no longer; and if the voice of scandal was raised
in that group, it was her grave and candid glance that hushed it.

Dozens of stories of her still linger in the recollection of old people who
live in surrounding villages. It was she, they tell me, who carried apples
and taffy to the old men at the Poor Farm at Christmastime, and who
cut over her sprigged muslin to make Nellie Sawyer a wedding gown. Do
I not know it for a certainty? Nellie's own grandchild has told me of it!
Also, that Grandmother brought the bride a four-leaf clover to wear
inside her shoe for good luck.

It was not only in such happy occurrences that Grandmother had a
part. Often her presence brought courage into a room where despair and
hope struggled. When a new grave was opened in the hillside cemetery,
it was she who stood close to the bereaved. Such memories of her her
children and friends carried through life.

CHAPTER NINETEEN

1962–1964

IN 1962, our bookshop seemed to come of age, not in the actual matter of years (because it was thirty-two by then), but its mature services in response to the book-reading public had now established it as grown to full maturity since its early days in the apple orchard.

It was in late September, 1962, that Robert Frost, just home from his visit to Russia, told Ál Henry, headmaster of Burr and Burton, "Come up and spend a day with me at my cabin" (in Ripton) "and bring Walter Hard along with you." He added that if Ruth (Mrs. Henry) and I would put up a lunch for them, they could eat it by his open fire. "I like Ruth's fried chicken. We'll throw the bones into the fire, and talk."

September 23rd was a perfect autumn day, and Al and Walter set out early with enough lunch to feed an army. They returned along about six o'clock, and as Walter talked to me about the day and Mr. Frost's conversation, I sat writing down what he was saying.

It was like stopping in to see a close friend who'd just come home from a long visit with people in whom you, too, were interested. He had not only given news about them, but now he was eager to talk about things at home since he was back again. He had been particularly interested in Yevtushenko, and he had had conversation with him through the aid of an interpreter. He had had no feeling of guarded and uneasy statements and replies

to his own comments a
the natural difficulties
an intermediary. There
part of a misstep fror
This was all the more
big work had been on
because he had also kr
shchev had gone well
and Robert Frost had
almost teasing, contair

"But, of course, I
was no possibility of
sense that he was b
abuse of my govern
rudeness.

"When I had a
physician come to se
sat down on the ed
left he had me giv
safely out of the cou

It had been an i
tired and glad to be

When Walter
given him our copy
to me the afternoc
fore. With it, I sen

Dear Mr. Frost:

You came to our
had spoken at the
me in our study a
book. "Come, I'll
you.

I know each po
since your own re
so much more. W
the book for me?

When Wa
written: "To
with the old r

He had au
for us, that c
mally, one le
he would talk
of conversatio
made the port
that seems to
we knew him.

In his *Comp*
"To Margaret
how to take Ve
1949." And a
handed him a c
"To Walter H
too. Ripton, Ve

Talking of
perates me to h
ist. They over
real Vermonters
of them wouldr
sophic understa
tragedy, and, oft

"When Alfre
and *Vermont V*
are. Now this la
bors—humor do
creative build-u
the poems—the
all the characters

These words,
Robert Frost, ha
of comfort, born
for me, too, to fo

Mr. Frost had
kind of exasperat

selves to write articles *explaining* what he really meant in some
of his poems, or a collection of them.

"Oh, well," he finished, "I'm too old now to get exasperated.
Too old . . . especially when it's just that they're too young!"

He then had branched off upon a less personal annoyance. "All
this nonsense about New England having become decadent. Well,
I can tell them that if it has, it's the richest compost heap in the
United States!"

He had walked around outside his cabin with them; sent
messages to Ruth Henry and to me; and bade them a feeling
and affectionate farewell. It was the last time they were to see him.
A day or so afterward, he had left for New York and Boston,
where he was seized by his fatal illness.

When news of his death came on January 29, 1963, memories
of the day in Ripton with him became touched with especial
meaning for Al Henry and Walter. They received the in-
vitations to the memorial service for Robert Frost on Sunday, the
17th of February, in Johnson Chapel, Amherst College. Walter,
who had had an attack of pneumonia, was not well enough to
go, but we sat in our study and heard it clearly, from beginning
to end, over the radio.

The poem Walter wrote in his Rutland *Herald* column on
February 7, 1963, "Robert Frost—1874-1963," was the one which
Senator Ralph Flanders told the *Herald* satisfied him most among
all of the poems and tributes he had read to Robert Frost following his death.

At the request of Dr. Davis, the librarian of the Abernethy
Library at Middlebury College at that time, an autographed copy
of the poem was framed and hung in the Library's Robert Frost
Room.

ROBERT FROST
1874-1963

"I shall be telling this with a sigh
Somewhere ages and ages hence:
Two roads diverged in a wood, and I—
I took the one less traveled by,
And that has made all the difference."

When dawn was nearing,
On Tuesday, January twenty-ninth,
Robert Frost began those "ages hence."
Shortly before, he had said to his doctors,
"I have a long poem in my head."
The world will never cease to wonder
What it was about.
Would it have told the "difference"—
The differences made by the road he chose?

The DIFFERENCE in life after his father's death,
When the ten-year-old boy
Moved East with his mother and sister
To Lawrence, Massachusetts.

The DIFFERENCE, five years later,
When the Lawrence High School
Published his first poem,
"LA NOCHE TRISTE" in its Bulletin.

The DIFFERENCE, when after graduating from High School
With honor, he suddenly left Dartmouth College.
His only known reason for this retreat
His overwhelming need to avoid the beaten path.

"Wall within wall to shut fear out.
But Thought has need of no such things,
For Thought has a pair of dauntless wings."
The DIFFERENCE in 1894 when he sold his first poem
To THE INDEPENDENT, and after a year married Elinor White,
Who had been his brilliant classmate in High School—
Always companionable, always understanding.

The DIFFERENCE when he rejected his Grandfather's
Practical plans for him and his bride;
He preferred mill-work to such plans
And occasional elementary teaching.

The DIFFERENCE, when after two undergraduate years at Harvard
He and his wife moved onto an unfertile New Hampshire farm;
Struggling with farming and teaching in the village school,
Once and for all he gave himself forever to writing.

"I'm going out to clear the pasture spring;
I'll only stop to rake the leaves away
(And wait to watch the water clear, I may);
I shan't be gone long—You come too."

The DIFFERENCE during this decade made by the loss
Of their first child,
A four-year-old son; and the subsequent birth
Of their four other children—three daughters and a son.

"The little graveyard where my people are!
So small the window frames the whole of it. . . .
There are three stones of slate and one of marble.
. . . We haven't to mind those.
But I understand: it is not the stones,
But the child's mound—"

The DIFFERENCE when they mortgaged the rocky farm
And he and his family went to England.
Brought about by the insistent courage of his wife
In a final desperate hope for recognition.

The DIFFERENCE three years later when he had been acclaimed
By England upon the publication of A BOY'S WILL and NORTH OF BOSTON.
Then his return to America to find himself recognized at last
By his own country.

The DIFFERENCE over the years:
    A dozen volumes, adding to his fame;
Innumerable scholastic honors and awards here and abroad;
Named as Consultant in Poetry for the Library of Congress;
Government recognition, and Ambassador of Goodwill
    Extraordinary. . . .

"I HAVE A LONG POEM IN MY HEAD."
Is this road he chose ended?
"I do not see why I should ever turn back,
Or those should not set forth upon my track
To overtake me, who should miss me here
And long to know if still I hold them dear.
They would not find me changed from him they knew—
Only more sure of all I thought was true."

In 1963, Al Pierson joined Dike Blair for a short time in his publishing firm, Vermont Books, in Middlebury, Vermont. He suggested bringing out a limited edition of Walter's poems: *A Vermont Sampler,* poems contained in *A Matter of Fifty Houses, Vermont Valley* (reprinted by Vermont Books when it had long been out of print as originally published by Harcourt, Brace), and *Vermont Neighbors.*

So it was that *Vermont Sampler, Limited Edition* came out with a handsome format, hard-covered, and limited to a printing of 500 copies. These were exhausted within a few weeks, and Vermont Books followed it with a paperback edition which has sold in the thousands.

One of the editors of *Life* saw a copy of the limited edition and the paperback in Brentano's window, went in and bought them. Presently he wrote to Walter, saying that *Life* would like to have an article about him and would he work with one of their staff writers and one of their photographers. Of course Walter would!

Constance Tubbs, of the writing staff, and Hanson Carroll, the photographer, arrived with notebooks and cameras and their cordial personalities in early September. Walter and the bookshop spent two of the most strenuous days they had ever experienced. Walter said he had climbed over more stone walls and crawled under more barbed wire fences in an effort to pose for photographs of himself that had "local color" than since his boyhood. As it was, the article was a success when it came out in *Life*'s October 11th issue. *Life* sent him a large, handsome book containing a dozen or more of the different photographs taken, as well as the complete article, mounted in the book. Best of all was the pleasant friendship made with Constance Tubbs and Hanson Carroll, who was also doing photography for *Vermont Life,* we later discovered.

The Mad Tom Book Store, as carried on and developed by Carl and Harriet Parsons, was opened on Route 7, just north of Manchester Center. It was unique in that it carried paperbacks exclusively, but ones selected with rare ability and knowledge, enticingly and cleverly arranged in different rooms, so as to give instant pleasure and convenience to the customer.

Mr. and Mrs. Parsons not only had their bookshop, but in the northern portion of their building beside the road they sold the apples and other apple products from their Mad Tom Orchards. But the books remained the most important part of their shop with its charming bow window and the sign: "Mad Tom Books."

We welcomed this bookstore with delight, not only because of our friendship with the Parsons, but because it relieved us from the overwhelming problem of handling paperbacks. Today no shop can carry the huge quantity of paperback books necessary for adequate coverage without space for an entirely separate department, or specialize, as the Parsons are doing, in paperbacks only.

Frequently people asked us, "Mad Tom? Why?" when we directed them to the Parsons' Mad Tom Book Store if they asked us for paperbacks.

"Because," we would explain, "their bookstore is associated with the Mad Tom Brook that comes down the mountains not far distant. The Parsons' apple orchards follow along the beginning of the trail and the brook's overflow. If you were here in the spring when the ice and snow are melting and flooding into the brook you would hear it rushing down the mountain—a mountain torrent become a cataract gone mad. Mad Tom is a brook, not a man!"

One day a customer said to me, "This is the craziest bookshop I ever got into."

"Why?" I asked.

"I've stood here and heard you send at least four different people to some bookstore up the road. Sending business away from your own door!"

I explained the situation.

"Well, just the same—*giving business to another fellow!*"

"We're their business neighbors. We believe in helping each other when we can. Why, they have a card up in their bookstore that says: 'Have you visited the Johnny Appleseed Bookshop lately?' That's the way we do things in our part of Vermont."

He just snorted with disgust.

I tried to tell him the story of Dorothy Canfield and the co-operative effort she had enlisted among Manchester, Arlington, and Bennington for the sale of *Memories of My Home Town* in behalf of Arlington's Historical Society and Dr. George Russell's rare collection of Vermontiana housed in Arlington's Martha Canfield Library.

I branched into other incidents I recalled where Manchester and Dorset, Arlington and Bennington had all combined in efforts to promote programs and causes, where profits were sacrificed, and the villages up and down the valley joined hands with good will and pleasure.

The man still looked at me askance.

"Lady, you're daffy! Business is business." He stood looking around the shop. People began coming in. The telephone began to ring. He must have heard orders being repeated to customers over the phone. The expressman came in with a big case of books and thumped it down by the door as he drew out his slip for me to sign. "Six you've had this week," he said. The man still stood looking on. Then he heaved a sigh, but suddenly he admitted defeat. "I don't understand it," he said.

MAD TOM ROAD

They want to close the Mad Tom Road
That climbs the gorge to 'Derry,
And ruts that knew the logging-load
Will soon grow up to berry.

"A hundred water-bars," they say,
"To keep repaired each melting spring,
With scarce a team from day to day,
Would surely be a foolish thing."
Oh, they will not remember long,
When once the road grows lost and blind,
The haunting spell its mad brook's song
Could cast upon an errant mind.

Those amber pools, as deep as doubt,
Foam-flecked and russet in the shade,
Where once they cast for lurking trout,
From rural memories will fade.
And when they hear the storm at night,
As by the fire they dream and doze,
They'll stir and think again, how right,
How fortunate the road is closed.

When apple trees are sweet with bloom
The wives will talk of "bleaching days,"
And stay indoors with mop and broom
And never see the white birch haze
That stirs against the cloudless sky,
Or pause to hear the distant sound
Of Mad Tom's laugh, as he leaps high
Upon the rocks, with mirth unbound.

But I will idle in the sun,
And turn the thought that pleases me,
That constant in my head must run:
Is Mad Tom mad . . . or is it we?

M. H.

Years ago, it was usual to see the stages, drawn by two horses and equipped with heavy brakes, coming down into East Dorset over the road, the ironshod wheels cutting deep into leaf mold or scraping across rock ledge until grooves were cut into stone. Every summer this was one of the outstanding trips for summer guests at hotels and inns. Mad Tom, hurling its torrents in a continuous cascade beside the road, was declared as spectacular as mountain scenery in the Swiss Alps.

When my husband and I returned from a Vermont honeymoon that had included much camping, walking, and climbing, we eventually returned to Manchester on foot, down the Mad Tom Road through the gorge which led from Londonderry, beyond Bromley Mountain and Peru. It was a twelve-mile trip from mountain top to the valley below. Thick foliage and masses of wild flowers surrounded us, and bird notes followed us. The wood thrush and the white-throated sparrow are an inseparable part of that memory. Walter took sandwiches from the pack-basket and climbed down the rocks for water from the brook. As we came to the end of the trail that entered the village, he stopped. "Listen!" he said. "How Mad Tom is shouting!" "He's shouting for joy," I answered. "Because of our joy."

When the hotel closed for the season, only slight change came over the bookshop clientele. Fall activities were in the air. Apple orchard owners advertised for apple pickers and packers. All the way from Pownal through the Dorsets, there were stands and open sheds offering many varieties of apples and gallon jugs of cider. Cars bounced over the dirt road to Dufresne's Cider Mill. Cider appeared in pitchers at church suppers with hot doughnuts and big wedges of cheese. The air became crisp and cold, and a gorgeous tapestry of color was flung upon the mountains. By and by, the Vermont Development Department inaugurated the idea of Color Season Tours. The bookshop was filled with rapturous visitors to Vermont, experiencing such beauty as they had never seen.

The questions, "When will be the best time to see it?" "When will it be at its peak?" rang continually in our ears, or came to us with self-addressed postcards enclosed. It was dreadful to commit ourselves! Suppose a sudden driving rain or a high wind came a week or two too early; or the change of color arrived, for some mysterious reason, a week or two behind schedule. The joy of scuffing through fallen leaves, of garnering especially beautiful and brilliant ones, was subject to all these troubling questions and possibilities. But as late as the first November days, the mountainsides were touched with burnished gold and occasional trees stood out like bonfires or tongues of flame. We hung ears of deep red and orange Indian corn on the hook over the shop's entrance door, where, in a few weeks, a Christmas wreath would hang.

But with November a certain touch of melancholy seemed to seep into the village, along with the coming of dusk. Lamps had not yet been lit along the street, and people hurried past with their faces turned sidewise against the rising wind.

These were the times when all the strange and new innovations of a Democratic administration were turning our bookshop into a battleground between warring factions. All the ferocity of a Presidential campaign was suddenly upon us. We could not comprehend the thinking of the extremists, their tactics, and their supporters. Those who had bought the documented *What We Must Know About Communism* by the Overstreets were now branding *The Strange Tactics of Extremism,* written by the same authors, as dangerous Communist propaganda!

This was also coupled with all the outcry against Government assistance to the aged, the ill-housed, the sick, and the impoverished.

"What's all this rubbish about Social Security? And something they call Medicare? All these grants and loans for education? In our day, people had to work or starve or go to the poorhouse!"

It set me to thinking about an incident Miss Hermie Canfield had told me of—the actual case of what had happened when a broken, old woman had been faced with the possibility of the poorhouse. If there then had been old-age assistance, there would have been no death notice in the Manchester *Journal* about this case near Glastonbury. With educational grants and loans, some of the ill-mated marriages might have been delayed, or the sharp and suspicious encounters between complaining wives and husbands, worn thin by nagging, might have had some other sequel than the divorce court. As I walked along the darkened street of my village, I suddenly sensed drama in each house I passed.

USELESS

She stops to rest although it's hardly noon,
Easing her weight into a kitchen chair,
Then struggles to her feet and takes a spoon
(At sound of her son's wife upon the stair)
To stir the apples stewing on the fire.

She does not raise her weary eyes to see
The sharp ones watching her. Will Fate conspire
To place her out at village charity?
She overhears the words her son attends:
"You'd ought to hire me help that's young and strong.
She don't pay for her house-room! All my friends . . ."
He shuffles out. She knows it won't be long
Before such ceaseless nagging finds a way.
With trembling knees and sweating back she stands,
Not sitting once, through all the endless day.
At last he tells her that the extra hands
At haying time mean hardship for his wife:
"We need some girl whose back and legs are tough."
(She waits without a sound to feel the knife)
"Poormaster says that they've got room enough."
Next day, work stopped, they're searching far and wide.
"That place below the millrace . . . on her side."

TOO FREE

They stare at her with eyes of covert doubt.
She steps too carelessly and whirls about
To laugh. A blue jay's saucy note, the play
Of squirrels upon a bough, a windy day
With racing clouds and intermittent sun
Weave the strange spell that bid her feet to run.
Hatless and clad in clothes no women folk
They know would wear (unless it was in joke)
She roams the hills. They watch her pass at dusk
(And Gossip scatters seed from her dry husk.)
Then skipping through the autumn gloom she calls
A greeting to a farmer at his stalls.
His stern, young housewife, at her righteous task,
Stares from her kitchen window, turns to ask,
As he comes humming in to get his tea:
"I'd like to know what anyone can see
In such a girl? Her house from all I hear—
Oh, don't step there! I've mopped—is mighty queer."
And when he idles, singing, with a frown
She marks the clock and quickly turns around:

"It's time for chores. Whatever crazy thing
Possesses you to act as though 'twas spring!"

GENTLEWOMAN

She bids the homesick youth to drink her tea
And eat her pound cake, gold as flowering broom,
With Homer's Iliad upon his knee
His shyness lessens in the firelit room.
And then she tells, with reminiscent looks,
How her dead husband loved the classic page,
And gestures, sighing, to his shelves of books,
To well-worn tomes of THE HELLENIC AGE.
Then, as he questions her, she drops a word
Regarding their disparity in years—
(It wings as gently to him as a bird)—
She was an old man's fancy, so he hears.
And then she says that to his day of death
Her husband played she was his stolen prize
And called her his "Greek Helen." Catching breath
He notices the beauty of her eyes.
He listens strangely stirred to the low speech
With which she paints, as though with thoughtless art,
The portrait of a woman one might teach
The birth of passion in an untried heart.
Troubled, he stammers, blurts his private news:
". . . a girl at home . . . who's promised that someday . . ."
As though, so doing, all this talk shall lose
The agitation it has set at play.
But when he passes through the village street,
And climbs the lonely Seminary hill,
He thinks to kiss her would be wildly sweet,
And then his racing thoughts will not be still. . . .
He urges pledges broken for her sake,
And pleads with her to say she'll be his wife.
She laughs and calls it "all a boy's mistake";
But finally her mirth becomes a knife.
And all the time she offers him her love
In fashion that he never guesses of.

When I wrote the above poems, as "Portraits of Three Women" for a session of the League of Vermont Writers, Mrs. Flanders wrote me, "How terribly grim these are! Do you really see Vermont this way? Especially that first one about the suicide." Yes, I did—for I knew how frequently tragedy became a terrible link with comedy and well-being.

And in the years of 1963 and 1964 we ourselves became acquainted with disaster, tragedy, and grief.

Our daughter, Ruth, and her husband lost their home by fire in the middle of a winter night when the temperature was four below zero. They were saved only by the devoted intelligence of Sheba, their beautiful Labrador retriever. She slept with her puppies in a kennel on the porch near the kitchen door. When the fire started at the back of the house, she managed with her paw to turn the knob of the kitchen door. Bursting indoors, she ran up the stairs to the side of Janey's bed—Janey, who was her constant companion. Dragging Janey by the arm, she awakened her. Instantly, Janey smelled smoke. She woke the family and dashed down the stairway to try to rescue the puppies. It was too late. The back of the house was already a sheet of flames, and soon the stairway was enveloped. Philip escaped through a window down a rope he kept knotted about the foot of his bed, a Boy Scout habit that he still respected. Finally, they all stood outside in drifts of snow, wrapped in blankets they had caught up as they fled, watching every material thing they owned go up in flames. Norman was a chemical engineer, and the company to which he was attached found lodging for them until they could manage to get themselves established in some fashion in a home of their own.

Ruth's first newspaper column (for the Brattleboro *Reformer*) was given entirely to thankfulness for their lives saved by Sheba, and for the North Country neighbors and people afar who had rallied to their assistance. Eventually Sheba received a medal for heroic life-saving. She refused to wear it around her neck so it lay in its velvet box on the living-room table in the new home they eventually bought—"The Upper Forty," which was an old farmhouse belonging to the upper forty acres of a tract of land lying along the road about five miles beyond Natural Bridge, New York, and slightly farther from Watertown. All of them, including parents, two sons and two daughters, were delighted with their forty acres which were "like a little piece of Vermont set down in New York State," they insisted. There was a winding road up the hillside upon which the house stood, old maples, lilac bushes, an apple orchard, and a pond where the hill dropped away at the back of their hillside. They all worked like beavers, after carpenters, electricians, and plumbers had finished, refinishing floors, papering and painting. It was the loss of their library and pictures that made them feel more stricken than that of china and silver and glass.

I wrote Ruth that with the aid of the bookshop facilities we would do all we could to help. It had been only three days after the fire that she had written us an unforgettable note. Her rapidly increasing deafness made it impossible, even with a hearing aid, to talk to us satisfactorily on a telephone.

Darlings:

Don't worry about us. We have each other, safe and unhurt. Nothing else matters. But there are three or four books I must have. The King James version of the Bible, *The Joy of Cooking,* a good dictionary, and any books by Walter Hard you may have lying around.

It was in 1964, less than two years after this event, that real tragedy came. Ruth's and Norman's eldest son, Daniel Hard Bonner, just twenty-one and in his junior year at St. Lawrence University, was killed in an automobile accident.

It was not what the dean of the University said to Ruth and Norman of their son's brilliance as a student and their admiration for him, but his statement that Danny was loved and respected by faculty and students alike, that sank deepest in their hearts. The memorial service which the University held for him had been crowded. Then, within two months' time, Ruth went upstairs to call her husband to the phone and found him dead upon the floor. He had suffered a heart attack. "He really died when his son died," the doctor said. "His heart could not sustain the shock."

Is there any excuse, any allowable reason, for telling of these intimate, personal tragedies? Yes. Without knowing them, one cannot evaluate Ruth today, and the healing and triumphant quality of the personality she has acquired and which she passes on to others. From her overwhelming experiences she has achieved an attitude that has enabled her to demonstrate the promise of Isaiah to give unto them that mourn "beauty for ashes, the oil of joy for mourning, the garment of praise for the spirit of heaviness."

In those first weeks of her trouble, she said, "At first I thought I could not live. Then I thought: What was it that I had before I had marriage and motherhood that made life seem so good and wonderful? It was my parents, my brother, devoted friends; my *faith,* my *work,* and the *future.* Today I still have my parents, my brother and his wife, who is truly a sister to me. I have devoted friends. I have the imperishable memories of my husband and my eldest son.

"I still have three fine, devoted children, and a little grandson whose charms I cannot describe. I have my *faith,* my *work,* and the *future.* If, with all these, I cannot now go forward, accepting life as it is given to me, I am a weak and selfish woman."

And so it is that she has gone forward.

Her first step was to carry out an appointment, already made, to have an ear operation that would restore her hearing; for by now she had had to resort almost entirely to lip reading. Dr. Bradley, of the Syracuse Clinic, performed the operation. A few moments before it was completed, she suddenly heard Dr. Bradley and the nurses talking. And then, another sound.

"Dr. Bradley, is it possible I hear rain falling?"

"Yes. It's raining. You are hearing it against the operating room window."

"I haven't heard the sound of rain in twenty-four years!"

She went home in a couple of days to hear the sound of birds singing all around her Forty Acres. And ever since the operation on her second ear, in 1965, she has had completely normal hearing.

With this handicap removed, she applied for admission to the

Syracuse University Graduate School of Library Science in the fall of '65. As this is written, she has just graduated (August, 1966) and received her advanced degree in Library Science, and has been elected to membership in the international honor society of librarians, Beta Phi Mu. She will begin work on August 22nd at the headquarters of the North Country Library System, Watertown, New York, as reference librarian. Now she has her work and faith; and her future awaits her.

Also, to be fitted into her new schedule, which will include broadcasting her own book reviews from the headquarters library in Watertown to those of the North Country Library System, and inaugurating a Department of Young Adult Reading for the System, will be the writing of a book for Alfred A. Knopf, Inc.

This seems to have become "Ruth's chapter," but it seems rightfully so. The Johnny Appleseed Bookshop was her idea originally, and it was her first undertaking in the world of books. Now her life has seemed to come full circle and brought her back to a world fuller than ever with books and their meaning.

CHAPTER TWENTY

1964–1965

THE YEAR from 1964 to 1965 might be called the harvest year of our bookshop. It had held its place in the community for thirty-five years. The original personnel were still extant, although Ruth's and Walter, Jr.'s positions upon its staff were, in a sense, somewhat analogous to those who are known as "contributing editors" upon a magazine.

Ruth's book-review columns had become a useful part of our rental library and book recommendations. People often came in with them in their hands and asked for the books she had discussed and spoken of as especially suited to readers of different tastes.

Mr. Knopf had told her that she had supplied herself with two reading audiences for her column in a manner he thought unique. "You begin your column with an entertaining, readable account of some incident in your home or in the community in which you live. It becomes a cross-section of small human happenings that are universal to all sorts and conditions of people. At once you have supplied yourself with a reading public. They instantly see themselves, their relatives and neighbors in what you tell; and by making it involve your own family, they learn to know you all, you and your husband, your children, their names and ages, and they feel acquainted with you. Then you go on to a really fine book review. But it's the unique way in which you connect the human incident story and your book review that is so unusual. I've never seen it done before. After reading the two parts of the column your reader suddenly realizes that your personal incident story holds, in miniature, exactly the same problem that forms the major situation or crux of the subject matter of the book you are reviewing. It's an original and interesting approach, and you have thereby created *two* audiences for your column; the ones who read it for its human, 'everybody's experience' sort of an angle, and those who read it for a fine book review, for you write extremely well."

It was this feeling upon Mr. Knopf's part which caused him later to ask Ruth to come to New York to see him and to discuss writing a book for them. Since this followed her son's and husband's deaths, she explained that she would have to ask for an extended time period since she must first gain her training as a librarian. Perhaps Knopf would not be interested to wait so long. "It's all right," she was told. "All we want to be sure of is that Knopf will publish your first book."

When it came to Walter, Jr.—the "whenever-in-trouble-or-desperation" member of the original personnel, his connection with *Vermont Life* magazine, as its editor-in-chief since 1950, held a distinct relationship with the life of our bookshop. During the past fifteen years, *Vermont Life*'s circulation had increased until it was sold nationally, and internationally by subscription. Over thirty-nine foreign countries had subscriptions for it; and an interesting item was that both Buckingham Palace and the Soviet Union Library were on the regular subscription list.

Walter and I were at the shop every day for a full day of work. Walter was regularly writing his columns which appeared each Thursday in the Manchester *Journal* and the Rutland *Herald,* and writing articles for other papers and magazines, as well.

It was also during this year that Walter, stirred by the success of Ruth's ear operation, decided to see whether he too could have such an operation. His rapidly increasing deafness had become more and more distressing to him, especially as it created continual nervous strain and difficulties for him as the most sought-after member of the bookshop personnel. His patience, humor, and gentleness under these trying circumstances were remarkable.

We made the trip to Burlington to consult an ear surgeon by appointment made by Walter, Jr. It is because that day and its incident give me the opportunity to tell something about our grandson, Stephen, then ten years old, and his relation with his grandfather, that I am including it here.

After all the doctor's tests and examinations were concluded, he told us regretfully that nothing could be done. Not because of Walter's age, because he had frequently performed the operation successfully for people older than he, but because the nerves in the ears had atrophied.

When we returned to Walter, Jr.'s home, Stephen and his mother were waiting for us as we stepped out of the car. They realized immediately that the result of the examination had been unfavorable, not from any downcast expression on Walter's face, because he was simply his usual smiling and gentle self as he shook his head. We went indoors to the big room with its superb view across the lake to Colchester Point, and Walter sat down on the long couch beside one of the windows. Stephen followed, watching his grandfather in silence. Then he sat beside him and, putting an arm around his shoulders, he drew Walter's head down to his own shoulder and gently stroked his hand. It made me think of Walter's own words, a few years before, about Crosby, Stephen's brother, who had been staying with us. "There can be much in common between seven and seventy." Also between ten and eighty.

These grandsons of ours, including Ruth's son, Philip, who was then eighteen, have the same quality of sensitive insight. They each possess it, yet each of them is rugged, self-reliant, and thoroughly masculine.

I think that Walter had not built upon possible success of the ear operation as I had. To have had his hearing restored would have saved him from all the countless difficulties which deafness occasions. But when we reached home he was as busy and cheerful as ever. He began planning a prose collection of his articles which had appeared in *Vermont Life* under the heading "Only Yesterday"—nostalgic yet amusing stories of incidents and seasons of his own boyhood. These, with appropriate woodcuts, would make a delightful book. There were, also, an accumulated number of new poems which had never appeared in book form.

The June days lengthened into approaching autumn. People returned who had not visited the bookshop in a couple of years or more. They still longed for the sight of Vermont and a call at the Johnny Appleseed. This was always one of our especial pleasures of the season. There was good talk; catching up on book or family news; or Walter was endlessly being asked to stand on the bookshop steps to have a snapshot made by someone's camera.

It was not only the shop and Walter and his talk that people remembered, but the devoted and able assistants we had had over the fifteen years we had occupied the old bank building, that first location large enough to require a full-time summer and winter assistant.

Of these there were three: Addie Roberts, who left us when she became the wife of Dr. Richard Overton; Eleanor Souville, who left us when she and her sister moved to Maryland; and Millicent (Mrs. Albert) Lawrence, whose presence is still of inestimable assistance and congeniality to the bookshop and all the customers who recognize her charm and ability.

Addie Roberts possessed a personality as filled with versatility and understanding as the skilled and lovely touch with which she played the piano. Eleanor Souville bestowed warmth of friendship and capability upon us. She became a part of our lives as well as of the bookshop. In fact, this became true for us with each one of these three women who gave the bookshop and us continual devoted service. The things they did for us far exceeded "the call of duty." They were innumerable and will be remembered forever.

Often I felt that before they left us we should in some way bestow a diploma, or certificate of merit, upon them. Each one of them had learned all the detailed steps of managing the shop. Each one of them would have been valuable to any bookshop and capable of carrying its responsibilities.

No good bookshop assistant or owner should ever appear to manage his or her customers, despite the often irritating moments when this seems to work in reverse—the customer who at once informs one that "I once worked in a bookstore" or "I've had a bookshop of my own." The reply should be a cordial inquiry as to where and when. But frequently the questions begin from the other side.

"Have you ever thought of arranging your stock differently? Your shop seems dreadfully cramped and crowded. Especially through this space between your rental library and your office. Let me draw a little plan of rearrangement for you." Or, "I'm sure I could help you in simplifying your rental library system. I'll just take out the cards and demonstrate how the bookshop I worked in managed their rental shelves. Much better than this confusing way you have." Soon it became confusion worse confounded. Or, "Have you never carried the Dottie Dimple cards? Everyone in the store where I was in charge of the card section was crazy about them. I'll give you the firm's address. You'll find they'll sell like hot cakes!" Or, "My dear, you shouldn't talk so much—so long to one customer. All that going-on about Eugene O'Neill and *Anna Christie* and *Mourning Becomes Electra,* and the fact that he and his family lived up beyond here, in Pawlet, for a while when he was a boy. It's interesting, perhaps, but all the time you were talking you had a customer over by the cookbooks, trying to find a good recipe for beet soup. You get so interested in your own talk, in telling a story about something, that you neglect other customers. You really *neglect business.*"

Yes, I know it. It is my besetting sin. I've often thought how efficient I would prove on one of those guided bus tours. As to the bookshop, I began to develop a guilt complex at last. (How pleased my friends and "Fräulein" would be!) I started out each morning resolved to be a silent, efficient, and satisfactory Business Woman. I won't say, Executive. I'm not cut out to be an executive. But it's really alarming how every other woman who crosses my path *is*. All of this produced bad results. I began to feel a sense of inferiority as well as guilt when certain people entered the bookshop door. I felt their eyes upon me and I swallowed my words quickly and tried to appear efficient and business-minded.

Walter talked, too. But that was different. Walter was an author. People came miles just to talk to him or hear him talk to them. When I told him my troubles, confessed my inadequacies, and warned him to nudge me and shut me up when I got going, he laughed and comforted me. "I guess it's true we aren't a streamlined business, but, after all, people seem to like the shop, and us."

After all, how could we help getting involved in conversation when one considers the people who came into our shop. Not only strangers, but long-established friends. I will never forget the stormy winter afternoon when Ola (Mrs. James) Glenn first came into the shop. Soon we were talking, not about her violinist daughter, Carol Glenn, and her pianist son-in-law, Eugene List, who had just returned from a foreign concert tour, but about something that is inherent and deep-rooted in her nature: her concern for people, people in general as well as people in particular. Creatively and unobtrusively, she goes about helping to solve difficulties for them and to heal their sorrows without any intrusive or confusing advice. When I look at her, one phrase occurs again and again to me, "When saw we thee, sick and in prison, and came unto thee?" Day by day, she became one of the enriching factors in our bookshop life, so often extending her warmth of spirit to other people. I remember someone saying of another woman: "She kindled a fire on so many cold and lonely hearths." That, too, is Ola Glenn.

Leonebel Jacobs bought a home in Manchester Village and turned one of its upper rooms that faced the north into her studio. The bookshop acquired an internationally recognized portrait painter as one who almost daily frequented it, and we acquired a dear and valued friend.

The Southern Vermont Art Center had had a showing of

prints made from her portraits of men and women, contained in her beautiful book published by Scribner's.

One of her great fascinations for people who had the opportunity to talk with her was her amazing knowledge of "old" China, and, also, of "new" China. She had spent years there, prior to World War I, and afterward. Her house was filled with rare Chinese furnishings, many of them obtained from "the Forbidden City," after the death of the Dowager Empress. Often her home, filled with these beautiful Chinese objects and furniture, becomes the background for her generosity, sharing her friends—writers, painters, and sculptors—with new Vermont friends.

And there was Paul Stephenson, who also enriched our bookshop contacts. In 1958, the Southern Vermont Art Center presented his *Vermontiana—the Telling of the Story of a State,* adapted from Vermont history and staged by him. Not only is Paul Stephenson a skilled stage producer, a teacher of dramatic art, but a writer of lyric prose that perfectly fits his purpose.

This production of *Vermontiana* was so truthfully and beautifully executed that it was repeated. It not only awakened interest and enthusiasm among people who were just becoming acquainted with Vermont's history, but it moved Vermonters, themselves, with deep pride in their birthright. In the bookshop, people who had seen it poured in and out, day after day, talking about it, saying it should become a Vermont tradition and be produced every year, not only because of its own value and beauty, but for the sake of all new generations of Vermonters.

A further enrichment from people who came in and out of the shop were Carl Ramsey's exquisite paintings (ready for book reproduction) of orchids, studies as detailed and rare as the orchids themselves. Constantly, there were new avenues of interest. Heman Chase brought his delightful humor and insight, often contained in his conversation. Then, in 1963, he brought us his book, *American Ideals: Their Economic and Social Basis.* It has since gone into three printings. We were delighted to have it in the shop. Heman Chase is a civil engineer, surveyor, and meticulous craftsman. But he is far more than that. He is a student and thinker and a rare friend. The inscription he wrote in his book for us tells it better than I can: "Here are the efforts of my mind for the past several years; good or bad, they have depended upon help from many sources, old, new, here and there. Anyhow, it was the stories of Walter's that first impelled me to write on such subjects in my life as he wrote on, or on the great problems of humanity. I owe him a great debt of thankfulness."

Finally, I would speak of Ormsby Hill as one of the influences which we felt bestowed an enriching atmosphere to the bookshop, especially as it involved young people. "What is Ormsby Hill? How do you explain its place in the welfare and education and happiness of young people?" I asked Mr. and Mrs. William Martin, who are its dedicated guiding spirits. They brought me an article by Mary Dillmann which had appeared in the August 23, 1963, issue of the Bennington *Banner*—a fine article containing all the requisite information, but with so much more: a comprehension of the spirit and purpose behind Ormsby Hill that enlists responding interest, admiration, and joyfulness that such an adventure in growth and development for young people exists in our midst.

In 1944, Susan Isham Hardyman and her late husband, Hugh Hardyman, decided to turn the family estate into a summer recreation center for underprivileged boys. . . . The Hardyman Foundation provides their estate and money to be used in perpetuity to care for underprivileged city youngsters. It is a haven for boys of all races whose urban environment has given them little chance to flourish, and offers them no opportunity to stretch their minds and bodies in small-town surroundings.

The old house with its rolling acres, its expansive lawns and lovely gardens overlooking the beautiful Batten Kill Valley is "the place that becomes home to these boys," said Mr. Martin to me. "Not home spelled in capitals as a HOME, but home as the place where one lives with his family. A place of surrounding affection, understanding, and spiritual security, of education in all the Christian virtues of self-discipline, honor, thoughtfulness, and respect for others.

"The ten or twelve boys who are year-round residents go to

the schools and churches in Manchester and participate widely in community activities. The summer group numbers twice as many. They have responsibilities attached to all the indoor and outdoor tasks at Ormsby Hill. They graduate with fine records from Burr and Burton, and go on to college and into the professions. One of Ormsby Hill's young men has just received appointment to West Point. The spirit present among these young people, many of them gifted in certain special fields, permeates the town and its institutions."

One day, when Manchester's former School Superintendent, Edwin Bigelow, was in the shop, I heard him say to my husband, "If I could feel that all the young people here in town who go to our schools were as fine as the boys from Ormsby Hill, I would have no worries. I would be entirely satisfied." This surely is a fine influence and contribution to *all* the young people of our community.

Ormsby Hill also becomes a focal point for gatherings of significance and importance to the entire community. Such are the times when Pearl Buck has appeared there to speak to people from all over the area on the subject dearest to her heart—children, and their needs.

It was in the early spring of 1965 that we were asked, "Have you ever thought of selling your bookshop?" Once we had, several years before. And when the deal had fallen through, we had been so happy and relieved that we felt like frauds when people came in to sympathize with us. We couldn't imagine ourselves without its life. But now, we would have been utterly unrealistic had we not faced the fact that even with our wonderful assistant, it was becoming more and more a situation beyond our strength. We made the decision to sell. Business had increased to the point where we had to devote ourselves more and more to the larger administrative features which it entailed. We were constantly aware of potentialities which we were unable to develop. The pleasant relationships of a smaller business must gradually lessen. Not only renewed strength was needed, but youth. We were painfully conscious that no matter how great our spirit of enthusiasm and eagerness, strength and youth were diminishing quantities.

The experiences of our first venture in offering the bookshop for sale still haunted us. We had attempted to do it "on our own." It had been like attempting a juggler's feat, trying to keep five or six oranges in the air at the same time without letting any of them fall. When we entered upon our second undertaking to sell, we were wiser. We engaged experienced real-estate brokers.

After one or two initial "on location" experiences that were disheartening, our realtors advertised the shop in the New York *Times,* the *Herald Tribune,* the *Wall Street Journal,* and the *Saturday Review.* Meanwhile, we were constantly filling out questionnaires and assuring people who kept coming into the shop, "No, we can't deal with you *directly*. You must see the real-estate brokers who are handling this for us. No, it would not do for *us* to talk to you. We would only confuse things. They will confer with us, if necessary, but it is unwise for us to take any part in conversations with you."

So many people came. So many people we sent on to Mr. Markey and Mr. Glenn! Often, the results were fantastic.

"No, they weren't interested in *books*. They don't know anything about a book business. They might keep a newsstand, but they want to buy the building and make it into bunk rooms for skiers. They said they'd meet your price because it would be the first ski lodge right in the most desirable part of the village." Or, "They have no knowledge of books, but they would make it into a dress shop, with fitting rooms upstairs. We told them we knew you would not consider selling it for such a business." Or, "They'd use upstairs for a kind of editorial office for the books the man who would go in with them writes. Books on highly controversial subjects. They wouldn't think of having it a bookstore in the accepted sense of the word. It would be a bookstore acting as an outlet to sell only this type of books." Or, "Their real idea would be to sell chiefly antiques and *objets d'art*."

We were horrified by some of these proposals and determined not to capitulate from our intention that when we eventually sold it should be to someone who would maintain a true bookshop, and who would be welcomed as an asset to the community. The name and character of the bookshop had earned a reputation that gave us an obligation to our village, to a wider community, and even to an extended public, interested in books and in Vermont. The obligation involved not only finding a buyer who would maintain what we had tried to achieve, but who would develop new avenues of worth and promise.

When people of the community learned that we were serious in our intention to sell, there were divided reactions, but I feel sure that most of them agreed that the burden of hours and work, plus the heavy winters, were too much for us. "You're getting older, you know." We did. And one amusing incident emphasized it, at least for me.

Two young girls entered the shop, up for the Columbus Day holiday. They explained that somehow or other they must manage to write papers to present in class when they returned to school after the holiday.

I surmised that the subject involved dealt with woman's position in this country in the mid-1800's. They asked me whether I had ever heard of anyone named Lucretia Mott. Oh, yes, I had. They looked surprised and doubtful. Would I have any *book* about her? Something to give them some inkling about her? I thought of our village library, and realized that it was closed over the holiday. I could give them a small story of her but it would chiefly involve her childhood, not her life as a humanitarian and reformer. They then asked whether I had ever heard of someone named Dr. Anna Howard Shaw. "Oh, yes, indeed." She also had been a humanitarian and reformer, but chiefly, she had won the battle of gaining a medical degree when women were almost outcasts if they attempted medical careers. Did I have a book about her, too? No, but I had one at home I would lend them for the next couple of days. They looked at me in relief and astonishment. I then explained the situation.

My father was forty-six when he married my mother, who was twenty-four. This meant that his mother, my grandmother, had lived as an active, outstanding woman during the Civil War. Lucretia Mott had been one of her closest friends. As to Dr. Anna

Howard Shaw, I explained that I myself had met and talked with her at the time of the great Women's Suffrage Rally, held in Carnegie Hall. I was in my beginning twenties, and was a delegate from my New York City Assembly District to the meeting.

The young girls looked at me almost with awe. Then one of them said in a hushed voice, "Why, you've really been a *part of history!*"

"Well—yes," I agreed, after a moment.

I then decided that probably I did seem older than I felt; that very likely it was time that I should retire.

After all the thwarting and difficult experiences of trying to find the right owner for the shop, the miracle suddenly happened almost overnight. We sold to a young man with every type of experience, education, and background that we could most have craved, and who had an established Vermont connection. But perhaps the nicest part of it was that Frederic Taylor was a constant reader of the *Saturday Review* and had seen the advertisement concerning the sale of the Johnny Appleseed Bookshop. The shop had had its first thirty-five years and was, we hoped, to begin another thirty-five years.

Before the actual "day of signing," we worked like beavers. I had never done such amounts of clearing and regulating. When November 29th came, Walter and I were so tired that it was hard to feel any emotion except relief.

Next morning dawned: one of the final burnished-gold days of the year. We sat late at breakfast, without any need to hurry, any long lists of last things to see to that must be checked off one by one.

"How's it feel?"

"Don't you feel lost?"

"What are you going to do?"

People kept asking us.

"It will be *awful just to stay at home.*"

"Oh, no, *home,* as we understand it, has no boundaries of the heart and mind. We'll just go on to a further adventure."

O SINGING GREENNESS

The silence of the winter wood
Lay deep around us as we stood
Upon the drifted hemlock crest
Where Equinox holds back the west.

The distant glen—half ice, half cloud—
Was where we read Masefield aloud,
The verses leaping with the brook
While June leaf-shadows touched our book.

Beyond the frozen marsh and brush
White throats once sang at evening's hush;
Above the quarry wrapped in snow
Wild yellow orchids used to grow.

And from those cliffs one twilight night
We breathless watched the hermit's flight
And heard those notes more crystal far
Than winter evening's single star.

O singing greenness for a space,
And then the snow that leaves no trace;
O Life and Love—green hills I know—
How shall I find you lost in snow?

M. H.